"As Maxwell takes readers on a humorous safari to observe Jews in their natural habitat, even Jews who have never set foot in a synagogue or JCC will recognize themselves with wondrous insight. And Jews who love learning—in other words, all of us—will delight in learning a lot from *Typically Jewish*. I definitely did."

—MAGGIE ANTON, author of *Rashi's Daughters* and *Fifty Shades of Talmud*

"As a pulpit rabbi I'm often asked, 'What does it mean to be Jewish? Is it a religion? A race? A nationality? Speaking a certain language? A faith? A way of life?' *Typically Jewish* answers these questions—and, like any other great Jewish book, raises many others. Complete with a superb, extremely user-friendly study guide, it's a fantastic source for adult education study sessions. I also plan to make it required reading for my Introduction to Judaism students."

—RABBI JACQUES CUKIERKORN, Temple Israel of Greater Kansas City

"I loved this book and look forward to sharing it with my book groups. There are many 'Aha' moments when you'll find yourself shaking your head in agreement and laughing."

—SHARON CURTIS, coordinator of Lunch 'N' Lit and Ladies of the Night, Hadassah book groups

"Maxwell took me on a fascinating whirlwind discovery tour of the top historical and modern insights into my Jewish identity, concluding with the Typically Jewish, Atypically Fun Discussion Guide. I highly recommend this book for Jewish book clubs, JCCs, organizations, federations, and home conversations where you too, may laugh, nosh, and kvell together over your Jewish identities."

—GAIL K. HARRIS, coauthor of *Journey from Invisibility to Visibility: A Guide for Women Sixty and Beyond*

"When you are about to enter Jewish life, wouldn't it be great to have a friendly, knowledgeable, and down-to-earth tour guide? *Typically Jewish* is just that: a witty, unpretentious, and comprehensive explanation of the complexities and conundrums in the twenty-first-century mostly Ashkenazic American Jewish experience."

—RABBI PERETZ WOLF-PRUSAN, chief program officer and senior educator, Lehrhaus Judaica

"Ever wish you could chat with a warm, funny, smart, and candid person about being a Jew or becoming a Jew? Meet Nancy Kalikow Maxwell, whose delightfully breezy and erudite *Typically Jewish* takes a refreshingly honest and comically affirming look at the Jewish past, present and future."

—RABBI BOB ALPER, stand-up comedian and author of *Thanks, I Needed That*

Typically Jewish

UNIVERSITY OF NEBRASKA PRESS

LINCOLN

Typically Jewish

Nancy Kalikow Maxwell

THE JEWISH PUBLICATION SOCIETY

PHILADELPHIA

All rights reserved. Published by the University of
Nebraska Press as a Jewish Publication Society book.
Manufactured in the United States of America. ♾

Library of Congress Cataloging-in-Publication Data
Names: Maxwell, Nancy Kalikow, author.
Title: Typically Jewish / Nancy Kalikow Maxwell.
Description: Lincoln: University of Nebraska Press;
Philadelphia: The Jewish Publication Society, [2018]
Identifiers: LCCN 2018040711
ISBN 9780827613027 (cloth: alk. paper)
ISBN 9780827617926 (epub)
ISBN 9780827617933 (mobi)
ISBN 9780827617940 (pdf)
Subjects: LCSH: Jews—United States—Identity.
| Judaism—United States.
Classification: LCC E184.36.E84 M38 2018
| DDC 305.892407—dc23
LC record available at
https://lccn.loc.gov/2018040711

Set in ITC New Baskerville by E. Cuddy.

Rodney J. Maxwell, 1942–2009
Your memory is a blessing.

Contents

Acknowledgments

Right at the beginning, here we are at the section of the book that supposedly no one ever reads. You're reading it, though, so that's obviously not true. Most of you turning to this section know me and are looking for your name. Please, please forgive me. I forgot to mention you. The minute I submitted the final manuscript it dawned on me that *you* were the one I meant to include. I'm so sorry. As for everybody else, read on to find your name—which, thank goodness, I remembered.

First and foremost, to my dear friends who agreed to—okay, were coerced into—serving as my Jewish Jury. Without your insights, jokes, flowing coffee pots, and uncorked wine bottles, this book would not be. Thank you, alphabetically: Sandy Babchick, Gale Baker, Ruth Baruch, Maya Bat-Ami, Elisa Cohen Becher, Donna Chase, Bev Farron, Jo Fisher Felman, Roz Fishman, Ellen Forman, Linda Gaibel, Micheline Haas-Hanser, Judy Lodish, Erica Manfred, Ilana Miller, Laura Miller, Judith Pertnoy, Anita Platt, Lea Rasabi, Susan Robbins, Susan Rose, Ellen Sabety, Ronni Sandroff, Sharon Stillson, Susan Stark, Ellen Turko, Miriam Weiss, Carol Weissman, and Anita Werner.

Dawn Kepler and Danielle Gold also took the time to share their unique perspectives on Jewish identity. Many thanks.

Many thanks to the staff of the West Regional and Interlibrary Loan Departments of the Broward County Library, Reference Department of the Alvin Sherman Library, Research and Information Technology Center at Nova Southeastern University, and Ruth Haber of the Judaic, Yiddish and Israel Studies Collection at the University of California, Berkeley. When a librarian appreciates a librarian's work, you know you are doing something right. Bradette Michel and the Broward County Dan Pearl Library Writer's Group helped transform my ideas into a successful book proposal.

Thank you, Cami Hofstadter, PhD, without whom this book would not have been conceived, approved, or written. Yes, the PhD should be included.

Julie McGinty has not only been my Catholic go-to gal and study guide guru, but my dear friend. Judy Mesch, of blessed memory, would be thrilled with the result of having introduced us.

Stephen King's wife supposedly rescued an early draft of the novel *Carrie* from the wastebasket. Linda Iacovini was my own manuscript savior. Without you this book would remain forever in my computer's trash bucket. Thanks for resuscitating it and furnishing encouragement along the way.

To the rabbis in my life: Rabbi Andrew Jacobs and Rabbi Cheryl Jacobs. Ramat Shalom is lucky to have both of you. Thanks for your support of this project from preapproval to publication. Rabbi Neal Gold: no words could convey my deep gratitude for providing just the right amount of meat (kosher and *treif*) to flesh out this work. Many, many thanks. Rabbi Barry Schwartz, thanks for turning down my offer to write an academic tome for JPS and, instead, submit another idea. I am grateful you recognized the potential in this work and, more important, were willing to give it a chance. It was a pleasure working with you and everyone at The Jewish Publication Society (JPS), as well as Ann Baker, Debra Hirsch Corman, and everyone at the University of Nebraska Press, which produced this book.

And, finally, to Joy Weinberg, the JPS managing editor. Every word, sentence, paragraph, and page of this book (including this one) is better because of you. In my twenty years of professional writing I have never worked with an editor as skillful, warm, and wise as you. It has been a blessing to work with you.

To the family of my beloved husband, Rod Maxwell: Scott and Eva Maxwell, Elaine and Richard Miller, and their children and grandchildren. Though Rod's gone, you remain vital to my life.

And, most important, to all my *mishpachah* (family), especially my mother, Betty Kalikow; my sister, Barb Kalikow-Schwartz; my brother, Harvey Kalikow; and their spouses and kids. And to my beloved daughter, Amanda S. Kalikow Maxwell, who turned out so good. Love you all.

Introduction

Why Is This Book Different from All Other Books?

The idea for this book grew out of a comment made at one of my book club meetings. All of the members are Jewish, which is interesting because the sponsoring organization is a professional women's club without a religious affiliation.

Still, this overrepresentation of Jews at a book-related event is not surprising. As publishers are well aware, Jewish women over fifty are considered one of the largest book-buying demographics in the country, a fact that helped me land this book contract. (Thanks, ladies.) And gathering to discuss books is a time-honored tradition for Jews. Torah study has been called the longest continuous book club in the world. Of course, that activity, unlike my book club, is rarely conducted in a delicatessen restaurant.

We had just been seated and were waiting to order when the woman next to me made her book-inspiring remark. "I'm glad I made it in time," she said. "I was at my mah jongg game."

"I don't play," I responded. "I never really got into the game."

The server appeared, and we placed our order.

"I'll have corned beef with mayonnaise," I said.

"What?" said my seatmate in disbelief. "You don't play mah jongg, and you put mayonnaise on your sandwich. Are you sure you're really Jewish?"

"At least I asked for rye, not white bread," I said. "Maybe that makes me half Jewish."

We laughed, but on the way home her comment made me think. Can pastime preferences and condiment choices define one's Jewish identity? Do they—and thousands of other inconsequential, trivial selections—form the essence of contemporary Judaism? To paraphrase Hillel's famous quote:

> If so, why?
> If not, why not?
> If not now, when?

If that ancient Jewish sage were still around, he'd have these answers. But since he lives on only through his name emblazoned on campus buildings, we are left to figure all this out for ourselves.

And so, I get to write a book about what I think binds all of us Jewish coreligionists together. The word "religion," by the way, derives from the root word *ligare*, meaning "to tie or fasten together." Jews, however, are such a diverse, disparate people, sometimes it's difficult to find anything we all share.

Except, perhaps, that we are Jews and "they" are not, which as a youngster I emphatically pointed out to Chloe Ann, my non-Jewish next-door playmate, when she announced, "My older brother just told us he's getting married to a Jewish girl."

"He can't," I corrected her. "Jews can't marry people who aren't Jewish." My proclamation wasn't grounded in any existing societal norms or halakhic (Jewish law) restrictions. I simply thought that we were separate species—like a bird and a fish, as Tevye described it in *Fiddler on the Roof.* It's not that I considered this physical union impossible. Rather, in my child-mind, the union of Jews and non-Jews was simply unimaginable.

As I grew, I realized that Jews and non-Jews of the opposite sex fit together just fine—which is the reason most of my Jewish girlfriends and I were forbidden to date non-Jewish boys. Even having non-Jewish girlfriends was frowned upon, because they would have non-Jewish brothers and friends, all of whom would prove too great a temptation for us. After becoming a parent myself, I realized just how counterproductive such dating prohibitions are. Our own Bible starts with a tale of how enticing forbidden fruit can be. Somewhere deep in my *kishkas* (guts), though, something remains of that naïve belief in our innate difference.

Of course, discussing an ethnic, racial, or linguistic minority's distinctiveness is unfashionable these days. To contend that your group shares unique characteristics contradicts the notion of the unity of humankind. Some people are insulted by what they perceive as offensive self-promotion generated by blind ethnocentrism. Others fear that pronouncements about ethnic differences portend trouble; don't even go there. But "there" is exactly where I'm headed.

Before you slam the book shut, denouncing me as a pro-Jewish bigot, allow me to explain. No, I no longer believe Jews are a separate species. Most Jewish distinctiveness can be explained through history, income, culture, class, education, or other factors. That's assuming such differences even exist. Maybe they do, maybe they don't.

That's what this book sets out to explore: to investigate if Jews are essentially different and what it means for us to say we are Jewish.

From kindergarten to my sixties, I have been thinking about this issue for (gulp) half a century. It all came to a head three years ago when I saw a tiny, gold crucifix gleaming from the neck of my girlfriend's granddaughter. Yes, the five-year-old grandchild has intermarried parents. Yes, the girl's Christian mother is religious. Even so, that little cross stabbed directly into my heart.

My daughter is not yet married. But someday, God willing, she will be married with children. Is it possible that *my* future grandchildren will wear Christian jewelry? Before they are conceived, I've determined I have to do my darndest to "make them Jewish."

But what exactly will that mean? Should I force-feed them lox and bagels? Encourage them to go to law school? Make sure they vote Democratic? What makes someone Jewish?

You can see I'm a cultural Jew, ethnically Jewish, secular humanist, spiritual-but-not-religious Jew. Whatever you want to call me—bottom line, I'm "more deli than deity." Like the majority of Jews in America, I rarely go to shul, guiltlessly use butter at meat meals, and frequently food shop on *Shabbos*. Yet, studies show that Jews like me have an "unshakable loyalty" to our Jewish identity. What, then, inspires such devotion within us—and can it be transferred to future generations?

Many religious leaders question whether the ethnicity, culture, food, and politics that constitute the foundation of someone who is "typically Jewish" like me can sustain the Jewish religion. I worry about that, too. (For what else I worry about, see chapter 1.)

But my concern has not gotten me into keeping kosher or dragging myself to synagogue every Friday night. I'm not a "religious Jew" or an "observant Jew" and don't think I will ever be one. But I do think, act, eat, laugh, kvell, and kvetch as a Jew, and I hope that is good enough.

This book is not intended to be the deli Jew's self-help guide to living a meaningful Jewish life. (Actually the term "self-help" is a misnomer because—unless you wrote the book—you are not self-helping.) Nor is it an academic treatise on the historical foundations of Jewish identity, beliefs, and rituals.

This book, rather, is about what it *feels like* to be Jewish. Or, maybe better said, it's about the core elements emanating from the *kishkas* of us cultural Jews over fifty—who, regardless of what very traditional Jews might say, will sing (even with bad voices), "You can't take that [Jewishness] away from me."

Which parts of this Jewishness, though, are essential to Jewish identity? That is the question—or, at least, the question posed in these pages. In the chapters to follow, I ponder: Does Jewdar— our often inexplicable ability to detect fellow Jews we've never met—somehow define Jewish identity? Might this identity be inextricably interwoven with the sense of ease and comfort many of us experience in the presence of other Jews—or its mirrored opposite: that rarely recognized, but real underlying apprehension upon discovering we're the only Jew in the place? Or could the connection many of us feel when lighting Shabbat candles with Bubbe's candlesticks be what's crucial? Is plopping a coin into a *pushke* pivotal? What about my (and, perhaps, your?) obsessive identifying of and kvelling over Jews who've won a you-fill-in-the-blank-of-the-feat? In short: could worrying, kvelling, dying, noshing, laughing, detecting, dwelling, or joining be foundational to being Jewish?

I arrived at this conjecture through not one, but three sources on Jewish identity: my Catholic education, my gentile husband, and my Jewish friends. Have I confused you yet? Stay with me.

No, I'm not Catholic and never considered becoming one. I did, however, rather enjoy being called "Sister Nancy," which happened frequently during the years I was employed as a librarian at a Catholic college. Taking advantage of the school's free tuition for employees, I enrolled in the graduate religion program. However, when the chairperson of the school's theology department, who was also a priest, received my application with "Jewish" written as my religion, I was summoned for an interview.

As I recounted in a *National Catholic Reporter* article (which they endearingly entitled "A Nice Jewish Girl Studying Catholicism?"), Father Chairperson began the meeting by asking about my motivation. "I've always been interested in religions," I began, "and I'm hoping that by studying here I'll come to understand more about my own Judaism."

He leaned back in his swivel chair, stared at the ceiling, stroked his chin, and said nothing. We sat in silence for what felt like an eternity, while I thought, "This must be what confession is like." After enduring another eternity (I know—you can't have two eternities, but that's how it felt), he leaned forward and said, "I want you to understand something. What we teach here is not comparative religions, it is *Catholic* theology" (he nearly spitted out that word). "You are welcome to join us, but you will be studying Catholicism."

So that's what I did. Since the classes were free, I freely struggled through classes on the Eucharist (what they call Communion), ecumenism (or how Christians didn't get along so great throughout history), and, of course, the Bible, both "ours/theirs" and "theirs." At one point in my academic career, I probably knew more about Catholicism than many born into the faith.

Now in my sixties, though, I have forgotten most of my Bible studies. That said, I can still recite the sentence "General Electric lightbulbs never die," the mnemonic device to recall the Five Books of Moses: Genesis, Exodus, Leviticus, Numbers, Deuteronomy. And I can recall the Christian Bible sections by singing the childhood ditty "Matthew, Mark, Luke, and John. Hold my horse till I leap on."

I persevered and ultimately obtained a master's degree in Catholic theology, which had the additional distinction of allowing me to become the first Jew to get this degree at the school. Despite the chairperson-priest's warning, my education did turn out to be in comparative religions. It provided me with insights about my own Judaism.

It is often said that the best way to learn something is to be forced to teach it. Likewise, one of the best methods to truly understand your own religion is to explain it to others. As the only Jewish student, I stuck out like a dandelion in a newly mowed lawn. Regardless of the topic being discussed—life after death, salvation, euthanasia—my fellow students would ask me for the Jewish take on it. I always began my answer with "Some Jews . . ." and then I'd add, "But other Jews . . . ," and say the opposite. They soon quit asking.

Still, my non-answers allowed me to glimpse what I came to see as a fundamental difference between Catholics and Jews. "Two Jews, three opinions" is heard so often it has become a cliché. But not once during my time at the Catholic college did I hear "Two Catholics, three opinions." Nor was this a core element in the psyche of many other Christians I knew, including the man I married.

Like one-third of Jews of my baby boomer generation, I "married out." Despite (or perhaps subconsciously because of) my family's prohibition, I chose Rod Maxwell, a nominally raised Christian whose professed religion at the time we met was "a nothing." Though counterintuitive, marriage to this *shaygetz* (a somewhat derogatory term for an attractive non-Jewish person of the opposite sex) made me more Jewish.

Casting aside all previous reservations, my family fell for Rod as much as I did. My father, especially enamored, dubbed Rod "a prince."

Rod and I established a Jewish home (or my version of same) and raised our daughter Amanda as a Jew. We sent her to Hebrew school and "Jew camp" (her term). Now in her twenties, she proclaims her current religion as Jewish. "I guess all that 'Jewish stuff' paid off," she assures me.

In conjunction with Amanda's bat mitzvah, Rod converted to Judaism. This decision was largely motivated by his desire to participate in all aspects of her coming-of-age ceremony. At the time our synagogue required anyone touching the Torah to be Jewish, and he wanted to avoid embarrassment from being shunted aside during that portion of the service. Besides, in many ways he was already "one of us," accompanying my daughter and me to High Holiday and Friday night services on those occasions when we did attend. He even briefly served on the synagogue's board of directors, accepting that thankless job of building chairperson. He also enjoyed the Shabbat dinners we hosted, reciting the wine and challah blessings like a born Jew. Dear Rod didn't even mind getting stuck scrubbing the brisket pan long after the guests had left. As I said, he was a prince. Tragically, he died of cancer six years after officially becoming Jewish, and his conversion enabled his Jewish burial. He now lies in a Jewish cemetery, resting eternally next to my adoring father.

During the thirty years Rod and I were together, I plumbed our union for differences between Jews and gentiles. From the mundane to the everlasting, I kept trying to discern which of my attitudes were Jewish. I needed to know if our personalities, actions, beliefs, worldviews were divergent because of my Jewish and his Christian background. His conversion further complicated the situation.

Rod, all the while, was oblivious to this quest—which became one of my first insights: asking what is typically Jewish *is* typically Jewish. Or, as playwright Daniel Goldfarb puts it, "If you are in the process of trying to figure out what it means that you're Jewish, then you're Jewish."

Over the course of our married life, I began to assemble more insights about essential Jewishness. Combining these revelations with the religious dissimilarities I discovered studying Catholicism, I began constructing my own hypothesis about what constitutes a Jewish identity.

To test my initial inklings, I buried myself in the library, reading everything I could find about Jewish identity. I am a librarian, after all, so immersing myself in bookstacks is like a fish swimming in the ocean. Diving into works on sociology, social psychology, comparative religions, ethnic studies, and Judaism, I read anything that could help explain what makes us Jewish and them not. Over time I began to discover what seemed to be some quintessential Jewish qualities—questioning, arguing, laughing, caring, and worrying—while still enjoying life to its fullest.

But sometimes—many times, actually—I found myself drowning in seas of unintelligible academic tomes beyond my comprehension. When that happened, I had the good fortune of being able to consult Rabbi Neal Gold. A personal fount of knowledge on all things Jewish, he helped me make sense of what I was discovering. With his patient, measured explanations, I could comprehend what I was finding. With his help, I began devising my own theory about what it means to be Jewish.

But to know if any of my conclusions made sense, I needed one more reference source. I needed to ask some lay Jews.

That's when I assembled my "Jury on Jewishness," a handful of friends I considered to be "typical Jews" (as if such a thing could exist). The idea came to me from comedian Baratunde Thurston's book *How to Be Black.* (There's the librarian in me, suggesting good books.) Thurston admits that covering such a topic is preposterous, "but I'm doing it anyway." To back up his ridiculous statements about authentic blackness in millions of black people, he formed the Black Panel, seven people who he thought "did blackness well."

For my Jury on Jewishness, I couldn't find any people who "did Jewishness well," because I wasn't sure what that meant. So, instead, I asked some of my Jewish friends to serve as consultants for my "typically Jewish" conclusions. I use the word "consultants" loosely, since their only payment was having their names included in this book. Some didn't even want that; or, I should say, they refused to be publicly associated with this project. Those brave enough to expose themselves are listed in the acknowledgments.

As expected from such a two-Jews, three-opinions crowd, they rarely agreed on anything. But that was fine, because when they didn't agree, I just used my own opinion, which *someone* will surely think is correct, right? These jurors give me cover when you question my conclusions, which, naturally, you will do, especially if you're Jewish.

But why accept what my jurors or I have decided is typically Jewish? Wouldn't it be better to decide for yourself?

Toward that end, at the back of this book you will find the Typically Jewish, Atypically Fun Discussion Guide. This text will provide the structure for Jews to come together and talk about what makes them Jewish—how they live, love, work, eat, and even plan to die as Jews. Among the pressing questions you will discuss through the discussion guide are the following:

Do Jews worry more than other people? Who among you is the
   biggest worrier?

What does it mean to "sound Jewish"? Have you ever been told
   you do or don't?

How can you tell when you are in a Jewish person's home?
   (Spotting a mezuzah on the door doesn't count.)

Who makes the best and the worst bagels in town? Feel free to
   bring in samples to support your answer, but be prepared
   for arguments anyway. This is serious stuff among Jews.

Such fun—and still meaningful—conversations can be held
in synagogues, Jewish Community Centers, even your own living
room. Simply gather together some Jews, have everyone buy
the book (yes, we'll give you a group discount), put out some
rugelach, and start talking. I guarantee you'll have a lively, enjoy-
able discussion about what everyone thinks is typically Jewish,
spiced with typically Jewish disagreement.

So, are you wondering what conclusions I reached about what
it means to be Jewish? Grab a nosh (snack, but more delicious
in Yiddish), sit back, and read on.

Typically Jewish

1

Worrying

You don't need to be Jewish to be a worrier, but it helps. As Dan Greenburg notes in that classic joke book *How to Be a Jewish Mother*, an Irish waitress or an Italian barber could qualify. Worry is the definition of what a Jewish mother is not doing when she hears you will be driving home from the airport at midnight and says, "Don't give it a thought. I'm not worried or anything." It takes just three minutes for her to shout "Are you okay?" at an occupied bathroom door. Joyce Antler titled her book on the history of the Jewish mother, *You Never Call! You Never Write!* and an Elaine May and Mike Nichols skit (both Jews) features a telephone exchange with a mother calling her son.

"It's your mother. Remember me?"

"I feel awful for not calling," says the sheepish son.

"If only I could believe that, I'd be the happiest woman in the world."

It's not just the females among us who worry. In a *Forward* essay, Moshe Schulman attributes his ever-present state of apprehension to his Orthodox upbringing. Someday he expects his epitaph will read, "Dead. But still worried."

Jews, of course, are not the only ethnic/religious group whose members suffer from what could gently be called a tendency to fret. Several of my non-Jewish friends can match me dread for dread. I took a road trip with one who became uncharacteristically quiet whenever we approached a bridge. After traversing our third concrete span, I asked her about it. "Yeah," she admitted. "I can't talk when I pass over water. I have to concentrate on staying upright."

The Impending Catastrophe

The average adult spends 12 percent of the day thinking about the future, but I'll bet my average is twice that. I'm especially adept at envisioning disasters involving my daughter. Whenever she travels, I tell her, "Don't forget to send me your flight schedule; I need to know what time I can stop worrying." Like a Charlie Brown comic, I picture a rain cloud above her, filled with disasters that make the Ten Plagues look like minor annoyances. Like my friend, I'm obligated to concentrate on these calamities to prevent them from happening.

Not all Jews are so obsessed. Gloria Steinem wrote in her autobiography that her Jewish father had a carefree, laid-back approach to life. Her non-Jewish mother was attracted by this attitude, though later came to regret being tethered to someone who refused to worry. "It left my mother to worry alone."

According to the Talmud, Jews should be more like Steinem's dad. We're advised, "Do not worry about tomorrow's trouble, for you do not know what the day may bring." Maimonides expanded on the futility of future-angst: "Whatever a man fears may happen to him is only a matter of probability—either it will happen or it will not happen." And here's my personal rabbinic favorite, courtesy of Rabbi Mordechai of Lechovitz: "All worrying is forbidden, except to worry that one is worried."

Despite these rabbinic exhortations, the majority of Jews I know—and probably the majority of Jews everywhere—are big worriers like me. The song "Don't Worry, Be Happy" is definitely not a Jewish tune. Quite the contrary, the song's composer Bobby McFerrin credits Indian guru Meher Baba with inspiring his lyrics. If a Jew had written it, the song would have been lamented in a minor key: "Do Worry, You're Jewish." Or, as Albert Vorspan wrote in his book thus titled: *Start Worrying: Details to Follow.*

As evidence, I submit for consideration some of our Jewish superstitions to supposedly ward off evil. There is our all-purpose Yiddish term *kine-ahora*, a contraction of the Yiddish words *kayn* (not), *ha-ra* (evil), and *ayin* (eye), in essence an incantation to fend off possible misfortune when speaking about something positive that has or will occur. Some liken it to the English equivalent of "knock on wood," but with more of a *Yiddishe* punch. Telling someone that my mother turns ninety this year or hearing that a new baby was nine pounds requires the exclamation of *kine-ahora* within seconds. When I rode in a car with my father, my saying "Looks like we're making good time" led to his invariable rejoinder: "Please. Don't give me any *kine-ahoras.*" Even Clint Eastwood knew enough to borrow the word from us. When asked about his chances of being awarded an Oscar, he said, "*Kine-ahora!* I'll win." (As far as I know, Eastwood didn't employ my mother's favorite bad-luck prevention tactic: repeating "pooh, pooh, pooh," which her mother's mother would probably have augmented by spitting on her fingers.)

Stuffy Nose? I Must Be Dying

Jews are not the only people who attempt to derail dire events from happening. And yet, there is something typically Jewish about being apprehensive, especially where our health is concerned. Comic Howie Mandel has noted that even if things are good, Jews will question it: "'Fabulous' is not in the Jewish lexicon. No Jew ever answers, 'How are you?' using that word. The correct response is 'How should I be?'" As a Jewish therapist blogged in the *Huffington Post*: "I'm Not a Hypochondriac, I'm Just a Jew."

I can think of three reasons Jews are particularly prone to excessive health concerns. The first can be explained through theology—or doubt thereof. Author and self-proclaimed Jewish hypochondriac Jennifer Traig explains it this way: "You can make yourself safe and you can make yourself financially secure, but health, God decides that one." The problem is, how can you calmly accept that God will decree whether or not you are inscribed in the Book of Life this year—if you don't believe in the Almighty? Here, Jews have it tough. As the Pew Research Center's 2014 Religious Landscape Study reveals, a smaller percentage of Jews—37 percent—report they believe in God, as compared to 88 percent of evangelical Protestants, 76 percent of Christians, 64 percent of Catholics, 86 percent of Mormons, and 84 percent of Muslims.

Second, a Jew feeling ill is unsurprising because Jews always expect the worst. As the Yiddish proverb puts it, "Your health comes first—you can always hang yourself later." Some academics posit that hypochondriacs view good health as a neutral void, a hole waiting to be filled with disease. Likewise, many Jews see good times as precarious and fleeting—any moment might be supplanted by *tsuris* (strife).

The third explanation could be that Jewish *sekhel* (intelligence) fosters inventive imaginations (something else to kvell about in chapter 2). For instance, the tiny nation of Israel has produced more start-up companies per capita than any other country and is number three globally in patents per person. Approximately 25 percent of Nobel Prize winners have been Jewish, which demonstrates creative minds—as does interpreting an outbreak of chapped lips as a possible brain tumor, which Woody Allen did in the *New York Times*.

My Bags Are Packed

Speaking of Jewish comics, I proudly share one of my worries about the future security of Jews in America with none other than Jon Stewart. On the Larry King show he admitted, "I'm a Jew. I always have my bags packed. . . . I never know when they're going to knock on my door and [tell me to leave]. There are very few countries that don't have at least one museum going, 'And this is when we chased you out.'"

I, too, have made preparations to flee. My nightgown and toothbrush aren't tucked into a suitcase—yet—but I like knowing my exit visa is in order. I insisted that my family's passports be renewed far in advance of their expiration dates. My husband countered that this service was costly and we had no imminent travel plans. When I wouldn't back down, he acquiesced, chalking up my obstinacy to my "nervous disposition." I know what he was really thinking: *You're nuts.* Nope, I'm just Jewish.

Even Jews who never attended Hebrew school and have zero Jewish education know this history of Jewish persecution on a gut level. There is a reason why Jews joke that nine words describe all Jewish holidays: "They tried to kill us. We won. Let's eat." Starting with the original Exodus story ("Every boy that is born to the Hebrews, you shall throw into the Nile"), to the royal vizier Haman's edict ("Let an order be made in writing for them to be exterminated"), to the Final Solution, Jews have known massacres. That knowledge, I contend, predisposes Jews to Mount Sinai–size states of anxiety.

The comedian Judy Gold tells the childhood story of having brought a new non-Jewish friend to her home for the first time. "Ma, I want you to meet my new friend, Beth." Her mother's immediate response: "What? Do you think she would hide you?"

I don't actually believe I will be awakened by a knock on the door in the middle of the night and told, "Get out." On the other hand, I sort of think I might. I can experience feeling "I'm perfectly safe" simultaneously with "Well, maybe not." Jews may be uniquely adept at keeping two contradictory thoughts in mind at once (see chapter 5, "Laughing").

If I Don't Fast, I Won't Last

When enacting religious rituals, many of us "wink at ourselves," knowing the action is baseless, yet doing it anyway. I admit that much of my religious observance is largely based in what could be called magical thinking. In theology school we would often repeat the joke "What's the difference between a religion and a superstition? Mine is a religion, yours is a superstition." For instance, I know intellectually that fasting on Yom Kippur will not guarantee me a good year. I am also well aware that touching the Torah paraded around the room during services is irrational, in the sense that it won't keep my daughter or me from getting cancer—but at the same time, you had better get out of my way when that Torah comes down the aisle. I always give my chest solid thumps while reciting the High Holiday *Ashamnu* prayer confessing the sins we committed and quiver as I contemplate the haunting words of the *U-netaneh Tokef:* "Who shall live and who shall die? Who by sword and who by wild beast?" As for the "who by famine" part, I do make a valiant effort to refrain from eating on Yom Kippur until somewhere around dinnertime (though I usually only make it to lunchtime, if you must know).

You don't have to be Jewish to both believe and not believe religious rituals simultaneously. Many non-Jews perform their own mental gymnastics. I remember during a course I took on the Eucharist (Last Supper), one of our assignments was to compose and present to the class a version of the prayer traditionally said during Mass to bless the bread and wine. The day of our presentations, most of us just stood and recited our prayers. One student, hoping to add dramatic flair to his prayer, brought in a loaf of Publix whole wheat bread. He unwrapped the bread, held it aloft, and intoned his version of a Eucharistic prayer. Jokingly, he half-bowed when finished, gathered up the bread and wrapper and tossed them into the trash can. The woman next to me immediately burst into tears. Several students rushed to comfort her as the professor dismissed the class. I shook my head in bafflement as I left the classroom.

A fellow student caught up to me in the hallway. "You have no idea what just happened, do you?"

"You got that right," I admitted.

"She was upset because once those words were said over the bread, it became sanctified," my classmate explained. Evidently, though it was simply a class exercise, the bread had been made holy. My crying classmate knew intellectually that at the bottom of the wastebasket lay an ordinary loaf of bread. But then again, it wasn't.

Public Displays of Judaism

When I recounted this incident to my Catholic friend Julie, she understood the emotions that had evoked the student's sobs. She, too, knew that the bread could be holy and not holy simultaneously. But she did not comprehend how I could feel both safe and not safe as a Jew in this country. She was astounded to learn that I kept my passport up to date, so I refrained from commenting that I won't take Jewish-related reading material on a plane, and I never leave anything with Hebrew or the word "Jew" or "Jewish" visible in my car.

Like me, many Jews feel squeamish about public displays of Judaism. One of this book's Jewish jurors (see the introduction) admitted she was reluctant to hang her mezuzah on the door-frame of her new home in rural Florida. "I had no problem with it being outside when I lived in South Florida," she said, "but now that I live out here in the boonies, well . . ."

Rich Enough Today, But What about Tomorrow?

Typically Jewish fretting also extends to that tricky topic of Jews and money. I admit I worry a lot about that one. *Kine-ahora*, I have enough to cover the necessities—mortgage, car payments, and the like—with enough left over to spring for the expensive brand of coffee and an occasional theater ticket. But I take to heart the Talmudic wisdom "He who is rich today may not be so tomorrow." I never have enough money to cover all of the "what-ifs": the encyclopedic volumes-full of wretched situations that would require me to have more money than I do. I can't be more specific; if I said them, they could actually happen.

Many people, Jewish or otherwise, have money anxieties. But if there is such a thing as a money-worry gene, I contend it is predominantly found among my coreligionists. From our long history of persecution, Jews have learned the valuable lesson that all immigrants come to know: money equals survival. Some people believe the truth will set you free. Others claim Jesus saves. But Jews know that when forced to escape in the middle of the night, cold hard cash paves the way to freedom. One of the Jewish jurors told me that jewels sewn into her grandmother's coat lining saved the family. It's a potent and common Jewish story.

Shanda for the *Goyim*

The Yiddish phrase *shanda far di goyim* translates literally as "a scandal performed before non-Jews," but it embodies a deep, intense sense of embarrassment and shame. As one Jewish pundit explained, it's how you feel when a fellow Jew does something REALLY BAD in front of non-Jews. Far more intense than simply "washing dirty linen," this kind of *shanda* makes you cringe and want to crawl under a table out of the worry that this disaster will confirm what antisemites think about Jews and wreak havoc upon us all.

For instance, there is a name, Bernie Madoff, whose utterance makes 100 percent of my Jewish jurors wince. It doesn't matter that many of his victims were Jewish. As one juror noted, the "money-relatedness" of Madoff's crime worried her. It hits a nerve.

Notably, the revelation that the mass murderer Son of Sam, a.k.a. David Berkowitz, was Jewish didn't have the same effect. One juror reminded me of the joke "No one locks their doors when they drive through a Jewish neighborhood." "That's funny," she said, "because Jews aren't associated with violent crime."

The association of Jews and money has a long history. In the Middle Ages Jews were allowed to lend money, while Christians were not. This allowed Jews to prosper, though they were seen to benefit at the borrower's expense. Because of prohibitions against owning land, Jews were forced to pursue opportunities in commodities and retailing, the modern-day equivalents of being forced to go into computers. The result, according to Catholic University economic history professor Jerry Muller, was that Jews "did well disproportionately" in almost every society in which they lived. In many times and places, enraged non-Jewish neighbors made undeserved accusations against the Jews, inciting dire consequences. Money maligning, including myths of Jewish bankers running the world, became perhaps the most ubiquitous antisemitic trope in modern times.

So, here's the truth: yes, many Jews are rich. Some are *really* rich. But many Jews are poor. According to a 2013 Pew Research Center survey, one in five Jewish households earn less than $30,000; for Jews under thirty that number grows to nearly 40 percent. The *New York Times* reported that the poorest place in the United States is "not a dusty Texas border town, or a hollow in Appalachia," but the *haredi* Orthodox community Kiryas Joel in Monroe, New York, where 70 percent of residents live below the poverty level and the median family income is less than $18,000.

Still, money and Jews is a taboo subject for many of us, including yours truly. Can't we talk about something else, like *shtupping* (fornicating)?

Three sex scandals involving prominent Jewish men provoked plenty of worrying. Former New York congressman Anthony Weiner was caught texting photos of his eponymous body part to various women around the same time that former International Monetary Fund chief Dominique Strauss-Kahn was accused of sexually assaulting a hotel maid. Then Harvey Weinstein confirmed that the Hollywood casting couch continues to this day. While the list of bawdy men behaving badly has included those of all faiths, we Jews do tend to flinch over our own, overly conscious that such perpetrators represent "all of us" to the outside world when their offending part has been ritually circumcised by a *mohel*.

I am well aware—and extremely proud—that Jews have been accepted into almost all aspects of American life. Jews hold high-level positions in business, education, medical, scientific, and nonprofit organizations. And when in 2014 surveyors asked Americans to rank religious groups on a "feeling thermometer," respondents reported feeling warmer toward Jews than any other group, including Catholics and evangelical Christians.

Yet, history has taught that our acceptance is precarious and we need to constantly be on our best behavior. All it takes is one too many public scandals involving prominent Jews and sooner or later, I worry, we could all be facing expulsion, or worse.

The Only Jew

Subliminally expecting to be kicked out might also explain why Jews live where we do—or, to be more accurate, why we don't live where we don't. If Jews are "clannish," a well-known antisemitic accusation, it might be because we believe there is strength in numbers. Distinctively Jewish neighborhoods often exist in metropolitan areas. Growing up as a Jew in greater Kansas City, Missouri, I could tell you if someone was Jewish from the address.

Many Jews harbor unspoken trepidations about being isolated from other "landsmen." Comic Mark Breslin admits that he sometimes grows apprehensive when he realizes he's the only Jew in a room. He may have inherited this concern from his dad, who told him, "In the 1930s if I was the only Jew in the room, I'd be looking for the exit." Writer Michael Wex notes that historically "when one Jew saw three gentiles, he automatically assumed they're going to beat the hell out of him." Just a few generations ago, that Jew was often right. *The Big Book of Jewish Humor* relates the old joke: "Two Jews are walking down a dark street, and two large figures are walking their way. One says to his friend, 'Let's get out of here. There's two of them, and we're all alone.'"

I, too, frequently take inventory of other Jews in a room—a process that isn't even on the radar for non-Jews. Given the wrong economic, political, and social factors, the twenty-first-century acceptance of Jews could evaporate. Even if things are fine right now, at any moment I could become the one despised, running for my life. No wonder I'm worried.

The Jews Are Dying Out

As if worrying about others annihilating us isn't enough. Jews also worry that we will kill Judaism off ourselves. In a 1976 essay sociologist Marshall Sklare claimed that American Jews are "an ever-dying people." Generation after generation we have worried that we will be the last Jews on earth and it will all be our fault. As Joanne Greenberg, author of *I Never Promised You a Rose Garden*, put it, "The gentiles have stopped trying to tear down Judaism and left the job to Jews, who do it better."

Ironically, the typically Jewish constant worrying that Judaism has no future has probably contributed to Judaism's future. I grew up in the 1960s and '70s, a period when American Jews were obsessed about their apparently dwindling numbers. Like everything else, Jews hotly debated the data-gathering techniques, but according to several studies of the time, American Jewry was sliding from fewer than 4 percent of the U.S. population in 1937 to fewer than 3 percent in the 1980s. A *Look* magazine cover story, "The Vanishing American Jew," zeroed in on our declining birthrate. According to one estimate, by the year 2076, only ten thousand Jews would be left in the country.

By the late 1980s many of these dire predictions were called into question, doubt having been cast upon those studies' assumptions, outlook, and methodology. As the joke goes, we're still here; *Look* magazine is not.

Nonetheless, troubling trends are still with us. According to Jewish history professor Jack Wertheimer, the most recent survey of American Jews reveals "a very grim portrait of the health of the American Jewish population." Especially worrisome is the increasing percentage of "Jews of no religion," which is not an oxymoron, but a description of those among us who identify as Jews solely because "they have a Jewish parent or were raised

Jewish, and feel Jewish by culture and ethnicity." Twenty-two percent of Jews fall into this category, according to the 2013 Pew study, and this figure rises to 32 percent of those born after 1980.

That said, discussing the exact numbers of Jews or interpreting the data can be controversial—or, as the Pew 2013 survey politely puts it, "has been a matter of lively debate among academic experts." Professors Ira M. Sheskin and Arnold Dashefsky, for example, offer a different demographic scenario. According to their "United States Jewish Population, 2016" report, the American Jewish community is estimated at 6.856 million, an increase of about 26,000 from the 2015 estimate. As they see it, "overall, the data reveal an increase of 770,200 (13.1%) Jews from 1971–2016."

Before I could get too excited, the professors continued by noting the internal changes within these numbers. "The share of the American Jewish community represented by the Orthodox, especially the Haredi community (fervently Orthodox), is growing; and the non-Orthodox is shrinking. At the same time, 'Jews, no religion' or secular Jews are also a growing group."

A vision of a growing chasm akin to our polarized political landscape suddenly seized hold of me: ardent Orthodox Jews on one side and "whatever" Jews on the other. No wonder I'm worried.

Intermarriage Will Doom Us All

As if our divided numbers aren't enough, I'm also worried because the intermarriage rate has grown to 58 percent from a mere 17 percent in 1970. Of those Jews "marrying out," only one in five are raising their children as Jews. Two-thirds of Jews do not belong to a synagogue—though as I discuss throughout this book, shul affiliation may not be an accurate measure of a person's Jewish identity.

And, of course, I feel like it's all my fault. *I* betrayed the Jewish people by marrying a non-Jew. In *The Modern Jewish Girl's Guide to Guilt,* Ruth Andrew Ellenson captures my internal reprimand perfectly: "Jews have barely managed to survive for thousands of years, and you, you little *pisher,* are going to make one bad decision and screw it up for everybody."

My internal angst, however, didn't keep me from my "exogamous marriage" (as sociologists call it). Nor did it stop a minority and eventually a majority of Jews from marrying out either. Indeed, intermarriages have been rising steadily in America for the past forty years. In 1970 the percentage of Jews marrying out was 17 percent; by 1995 more Jews were choosing non-Jewish spouses than Jewish ones. For marriages since 2005, the 2013 Pew survey shows the overall Jewish intermarriage percentage increasing to 58 percent for Jews overall and to 71 percent for non-Orthodox Jews (approximately 27 percent of Conservative Jews and 50 percent of Reform Jews). What is more, for those in the aforementioned "Jews of no religion" category, the intermarriage rate increases to a whopping 79 percent.

That leads me to ponder: how can we encourage more Jews to marry in while still sanctioning their right to eat bacon cheeseburgers?

Perhaps the Jewish community should try discouraging divorce. Second marriages are often likely to be between Jews and non-Jews. As far back as 1989 demographers identified the pattern of Jews divorcing a Jewish spouse and remarrying a non-Jew, leading some to joke that divorce was a leading cause of intermarriage.

For females like me who intermarry and reproduce, the worry magnifies out of our fear that the Jewish people's future is up to us. It's always the mother's fault, right? The problem is, when it comes to passing on religion, it really is. As

Keren McGinity, a Jewish history professor and intermarriage expert, notes, most children inherit their faith—Judaism or another religion—from the mother. Half of religious adherents in America take their mother's religion, she says, compared to just over one-fourth following dad's and the other one-fourth doing neither. Likewise, journalist Naomi Schaefer Riley includes different statistics that make the same point in her 2013 book *'Til Faith Do Us Part:* about 33 percent of children in American interfaith families are being reared in their mother's religion, compared to approximately 20 percent who follow the father's religion.

Unfortunately, it also doesn't look like we intermarried Jewish mommies are doing such a great job passing on the faith. The 2013 Pew survey reveals vast differences in the child-rearing practices of Jews married to Jews compared to those married to non-Jews. Among Jews married to Jews, "96% say they are raising their children Jewish by religion, and just 1% say they are not raising their children Jewish. But among Jews married to non-Jews, just 20% say they are raising their children Jewish by religion, and 37% say their children are not being raised Jewish."

I Don't Do Enough Like a Jew

As if worrying about our declining numbers isn't enough to keep me up at night, I also worry that I haven't been a good enough Jewish model to pass on Judaism to my daughter.

As an intermarried Jew, I tried to give my daughter a double dose of Judaism to counter her non-Jewishly-born father, regardless of the fact that there was nothing to "counter," because he had zero interest in any religion. My reaction was far from unusual. Many intermarried Jews who never gave a thought to their religion prior to marriage suddenly discover an overwhelming need to teach Judaism to their children. The problem is, many Jews don't exactly know what Judaism is, so how can we possibly transmit it?

According to scholars, religions can be boiled down to the three *B*s, "behaving," "believing," and "belonging," but I, like many American Jews, don't do so good on these. Several generations ago Jews "behaved" more like Jews, or at least they would perform or refrain from certain behaviors because they were Jews. Today, though, most American Jews don't observe the majority of the 613 biblically commanded mitzvot—heck, I can't even name a tiny portion of them. I'm also right there with the three-fourths of Jews who don't keep kosher. I don't light Sabbath candles, though I did when my daughter was young, to "give her" some Judaism. Though I used to observe a self-imposed day of rest on Saturday, I'm now one of the nine in ten Jews who will gladly dash to the mall.

Nor do I engage in that other behavior that has sustained the Jewish people for a thousand years: Torah study. Non-Jews call us the People of the Book, which is apt if we're talking about the *New York Times* bestseller list, but not so much the holy books. While thousands of Jews are in fact actively involved in Torah study, as a librarian I can also attest that Jewish religious volumes remain untouched in public libraries for weeks—unlike the constantly used Christian Bible shelf, which requires reshelving several times a day.

When I began my theology studies, my Catholic classmates assumed that as a Jew I would know my Torah backward and forward. Boy, were they wrong. I did attempt to learn Hebrew several times, motivated by a half-hearted desire to join one of the cohorts of women studying to have the bat mitzvah they never experienced as youngsters. But I abandoned the effort when I kept mixing up the letter *dalet* with the *resh*.

Fortunately for the Jewish people, other Jews are more dedicated than I am. "Adult Jewish learning is a flourishing part of the contemporary American Jewish landscape," one 2008 survey concluded. The Melton School of Adult Jewish Learning, a pluralistic adult Jewish education network with nearly fifty locations worldwide, is just one example of many intellectually stimulating Jewish educational programs throughout the globe. However, the same survey admitted that "enrollments remain relatively low and the same people 'come over and over again.'"

I admit that I'm one of those who don't show up for many Jewish learning programs. Even worse, sometimes it's the before-and-after-class shmoozing that gets me there. Is that any kind of example to set for my daughter? This leads to another worry.

Where's the Creed?

Since I can't pass on to my daughter a model for "behaving" religiously, another potential source of my Judaism could be my beliefs. But here, too, I come up short. I agree with many of the Jewish jurors who explained that being Jewish is "what you are, not what you believe." But how can I pass on "what I am" to my daughter?

Beyond a belief in the saving power of chicken soup, I can't say I believe in an underlying Jewish dogma. Looking for a Jewish creed, I feel like that little old lady in the old Wendy's commercial, asking, "Where's the beef?"

Ours is far from the first generation to search in vain for central Jewish beliefs. In medieval times, the distinguished Jewish philosopher Moses Maimonides promulgated his Thirteen Principles of Faith to quiet complaints from his contemporaries that, unlike Christianity, Judaism had no creed. Despite this valiant attempt by the towering intellectual figure of the time,

Maimonides's Principles never caught on; few Jews are even aware they exist.

Other attempts to summarize Jewish beliefs have included the medieval trinity: Israel (the people, not the country), Torah, and God. Other commentators cite the concept of chosenness and/or *tikkun olam* (repairing the world) as essential Judaism. But as Rabbi Milton Steinberg explained in *Basic Judaism*, every principle "has been challenged by someone or another."

Once again, the typically Jewish behavior is not to adhere to—but to argue about—Jewish beliefs. Which leads me to an ancillary worry: no matter what I say in these pages, someone—most likely lots of someones—will disagree. And because they are Jews, their objections will be expressed loudly and emphatically, because Jews, if nothing else, don't believe in staying silent (see chapter 6, "Detecting").

If I'd Only . . .

When Amanda was old enough for Hebrew school, I did attempt the "belonging" part by joining one of the liberal congregations in our area. Known for welcoming intermarried families, the Reconstructionist synagogue I chose offered an extensive early childhood and Torah school program, but what really sold me was the education director's offhand comment while giving me a tour of the building. Just outside the sanctuary she spotted a frilly white children's sock lying on the carpet. Shaking her head, she picked it up and said, "Oh, please excuse this. As you can see, our kids treat this place like home." This was exactly my kind of place. I joined that day.

Attempting to set an example, I began attending Shabbat services (okay, sporadically), encouraging (okay, dragging) Rod and Amanda along when I could. Even our intermittent synagogue attendance was more than that of three-fourths of other Jews, who admit to survey takers that they seldom or never show up for services. Unlike Christians who see worshiping as redemptive, writer Lisa Schiffman notes, many Jews have the attitude "Today I'll be Jewish. Tomorrow I'll play tennis."

I also tried to give Amanda a sense of Jewish belonging by sending her to Jewish camp every year. In addition, many years later, I noodged her to sign up for Taglit-Birthright Israel, the free ten-day trip to Israel for Jewish young adults sponsored by the Israeli government and Jewish philanthropic groups. At twenty-six—the last year she was eligible—she finally went.

But despite all these efforts, I, like many other Jewish parents, worry that I didn't do enough. Rabbi Neal Gold eases my anxiety a little by assuring me that there is no magic bullet that will ensure Jewish identity. Rather, studies conclude it is the collective result of Jewish education, programs, and activities that "makes children Jewish." As Gold explains, "When kids go to Hebrew school through high school, attend summer camps, have an Israel experience, and participate in youth group, the cumulative effect works more often than we care to admit."

Even so, I'm still worried that I didn't send Amanda to more Jewish programs. I'm worried because I'm too fuzzy about certain components of my Judaism to pass them on to my daughter. I don't want to end up like Franz Kafka's father, who, according to the famous author, tried to instill in Kafka some sort of Jewish identity primarily through impressions and memories, "but it was too little . . . , it all dribbled away." I'm worried because as the Hanukkah song "Light One Candle" implores, I can't "let the light go out, it's lasted for so many years"—but I'm not sure what "it" is.

And, worst of all, I'm worried because my daughter is not a worrier. This is especially worrying, because worrying is definitely typically Jewish.

2

Kvelling

I'm sitting at the kitchen table, coffee cup in hand, perusing the grocery ads in the newspaper. Boneless chicken breasts are buy one, get one free. *Sounds good*, I think, as I turn the page. Putting my cup down, I lean forward and spot, atop the page, this semester's high school honor roll. *Forget the chickens*, I tell myself as I prepare to indulge in one of my favorite guilty pleasures. Positioning my finger on the top of the list, I slowly drag it down the column as I search for Jewish names.

Yay, I think, there's a Goldberg, a Levine, and a Silverman. And a Block and a Gordon. You can never tell with those names, so I'll just assume they're part of the tribe. I see a couple of color names too—Brown and Green—which likewise can be confusing; some are and some aren't. I count them in. When I finish my review, I sit back and smile, relishing that moment of kvelling at all the Jews on the list.

As checklists go, I know my indulgence is inaccurate. With half of Jews intermarrying, the old-fashioned name-sounds-Jewish technique is obsolete. My own daughter, with her "*goyish*" (non-Jewish) moniker Amanda Maxwell, would be missed. And a man I know named Jeffrey Cohen is Catholic.

And even if my kvell list was accurate, it's stupid. What possible difference does it make how many achievers belong to one ethnic/religious group or another? Intellectually, I know it's inconsequential . . . and yet, somehow, I like seeing Jews excelling. High school honor rolls are just the beginning of places where I succumb to this list looking. Spelling bees, Nobel Prize winners, influential comedians, artists, scientists, even librarians (yes, there is such a list) inspire similar episodes of "good-Jew" hunting in me. Like an addict, I need that momentary high I get from a good kvell.

Kvelling is taking pride. One attempted translation of the Yiddish term into English calls it "excessive pride," but that sounds like Gaston's bellicose boasting in *Beauty and the Beast*. Kvelling is not the same as strutting or swaggering one's superiority. Rather, it is an experience of absolute delight in the accomplishment of others. Many Yiddish dictionaries explain it as "bursting with pride," harkening back to the word's water-associated meaning "to gush," which perfectly describes how I feel. I'm bursting over when I discover examples of the outsized accomplishments of my people, such as Jews making up 7 percent of history's most influential people listed in the book *The 100*. Or that the great writer Mark Twain (not Jewish) wrote in 1896, "The Jews constitute but one percent of the human race. Properly the Jew ought hardly to be heard of; but he is heard of, has always been heard of. He is as prominent on the planet as any other people in literature, science art, music, finance, medicine." Or that approximately one-quarter of Nobel Prize winners have been one of us—think Saul Bellow, Isaac Bashevis Singer, Nadine Gordimer, and Harold Pinter for literature; Paul Samuelson, Joseph Stiglitz, and Milton Friedman for economics; Henry Kissinger, Elie Wiesel, and Yitzhak Rabin for world peace; and Richard Feynman and Albert Einstein for physics.

Speaking of the latter, some historians credit three Jews—Einstein, Sigmund Freud, and Karl Marx—as being the most influential thinkers in modern history. To be fair, Marx's Jewish parents converted to Christianity and became Lutherans the year before he was born, but I still include him for kvelling purposes.

Nachas (Not Nachos)

Kvelling is closely associated with, but not exactly the same as, what I feel when I *shep nachas. Nachas,* like kvelling, refers to the pleasure elicited by public accolades attained by others. Historian Paula Hyman defines it as "a unique mix of pride, joy, and gratification." For me, and I am not alone here, the term is most often associated with my family's accomplishments rather than those of our group as a whole. *Nachas* is what I felt sitting in the first row of the synagogue watching my daughter chant from the Torah at her bat mitzvah. *Nachas* extends to non-Jewish-related activities too. When my daughter was eight years old, she uttered her first of three lines in the children's musical *Honk!* Walking on stage, she announced, "Here's your present," plunked a wrapped gift down on a table, turned, and exited the stage. "That was my daughter!" I wanted to trumpet to the audience. "Did you see how perfectly she put that present down?"

The term *shep,* which means "to derive," is often combined with *nachas.* For instance, one would say I was *shepping nachas* listening to my cousin deliver the commencement address at the Columbia University Law School graduation. (Was I ever!) Be careful, though: the word *shep* is often mistaken for *shlep,* which means "to haul." *Nachas* doesn't require any heavy lifting, except for the lifting of one's heartstrings.

Sometimes the word is erroneously substituted for *shtup,* which means "to fornicate." I know this for a fact because, watching my mother beam over a book of my cousin's bat mitzvah photos, I said to her, "It's great to see you *shtupping nachas* like this." In two seconds she was laughing so hard the book fell to the floor. "I did enjoy the bat mitzvah," she said, "but don't remember any *shtupping* happening there."

Shtupping nachas, however, would be appropriate if referring to the sexual prowess of one's Jewish family "member" (pardon the pun). This expression, for example, would be fitting for the parents of "Seymore Butts," a.k.a. Adam Glasser, a Jew who, according to historian Nathan Abrams, is one of the most famous porn stars today.

But I digress. *Nachas* is what you get when your kid is accepted to Harvard, but kvelling is what you do when you realize that almost one-quarter of that esteemed student body is Jewish. And perhaps it's not surprising that many of us kvell at such stats, given college admissions history. In the 1920s, after participating in some list making of his own, Harvard University president Lawrence Lowell suggested implementing a quota system to limit the admittance of Jews.

And Harvard was far from the only esteemed institution to employ list making to discriminate against Jews. Many colleges engaged in what legal experts call "numerus clauses" (closed number), restricting the number of certain groups of people. During the first half of the twentieth century, numerous American colleges and universities participated in the practice specifically to reduce the number of Jews. Studies conducted by B'nai B'rith and the City of New York City in 1946 found "inescapable evidence" that some of the best schools had been restricting Jewish admissions. Several medical schools had been methodically limiting admissions not only of Jews, but also of African Americans and Italians.

According to historian Arthur Hertzberg, the turning point for ending these practices came in 1946, when Rabbi Steven S. Wise threatened to sue Columbia University on account of its tax-exempt status, arguing that the university's admission and hiring practices meant they were no longer a public body, but a private club. Columbia University agreed to drop the practice, and Jews and others went on to win wider acceptance to higher education as both students and faculty. By 1971 an estimated 10 percent of faculty members at American institutions of higher learning were Jews, as was an estimated one-third of the faculty at Harvard—adding to my kvell-worthy statistics.

Ending college admission quotas, however, has not been without strife. Opposition to affirmative action erupted, followed by backlashes against programs to ensure diversity in college admissions. I dare not dip my toe into those controversies— writing about what it means to be typically Jewish is contentious enough. However, I will note that charges of discrimination by WASPS could paradoxically be seen as progress. Now instead of being the perpetrators, they consider themselves the victims of the practice. Also noteworthy: many recent complaints about college admission quotas are coming from Asian Americans, a group sometimes referred to as "the new Jews."

By the way, when Asian Americans meet with success, they probably put down their teacups and kvell. But do they have a word to describe this particular form of pride? Religion scholars argue that Jewish kvelling is unique, and I don't argue with religion scholars when I agree with them. The very existence of the term *kvelling* makes me kvell.

Jewhooing

Academics who study such things have another name for the activity thousands of other Jews and I engage in while watching TV or reading a paper: "Jewhooing." The word, reputedly coined by historian Susan Glenn, is defined as "the social mechanism for both private and public naming and claiming of Jews by other Jews." It was derived from the now-defunct website

Jewhoo!, a take-off on Yahoo! To survive, Jews have learned to be very adaptable. The particular website died, but that hasn't stopped Jews from Jewhooing.

Did you know that designers Michael Kors and Isaac Mizrahi are Jewish? The brother-and-sister acting team of Maggie and Jake Gyllenhaal? Yep. The late basketball coach Red Auerbach? Check. We even have our own real-life superheroes. *The Amazing Spider-Man*'s Andrew Garfield and *Wonder Woman*'s Gal Gadot may play imaginary characters but in real life are members of the tribe. (Who else? Check out this book's study guide for a fun game you can play identifying other celebrities who are and aren't Jewish.)

Glenn and some other academics realize that all ethnic groups participate in varying ways in inventorying their own, but they believe the extent of Jews seeking out fellow Jews is different. "It is more than simple ethnic pride," claims religion professor David E. Kaufman. Echoing my kvelling over the word *kvelling*, Kaufman asks, "What other group, for that matter, has a term like Jewhooing?"

For Kaufman, the sheer number of published lists of Jews who done good says something about us. "What other ethnic group has so many bookstore shelves devoted to its popular heroes?" Those of us of a certain age will remember *Great Jews in Sports*, the popular bar mitzvah present given to convince young boys that, along with their reputed brain power, Jewish boys could be athletes (though they were never to forget education, education, education!—education always comes first; even *Great Jews in Sports* is a book).

This book joined the ranks of *Jewish Heroes and Heroines of America*, with the self-congratulatory subtitle **Extraordinary Jewish Americans**. Not to be outdone, *The Golden Age of Jewish Achievement* added the laudatory subtitle *The Compendium of a*

*Culture, a People and Their **Stunning** Performance.* And to make sure that during such list making one-half of the Jewish people were not forgotten, there for our kvelling pleasure came the two-volume encyclopedia *Jewish Women in America: An Historical Encyclopedia.*

As a librarian, I am well aware that Jews are not the only ethnic group to produce self-aggrandizing compilations of greatness. But, like Kaufman, I have noticed that Jewish list books predominate among all the ethnic titles. Simple economics may provide one explanation: publishers are prone to produce more of these kinds of volumes because Jews are heavy book buyers (something else to kvell about).

The online world, too, overflows with lists of famous Jews. The reader-generated Wikipedia maintains an entry entitled "Lists of Jews," featuring more than sixty categories of renowned Jews. Under the letter *A* alone you'll find Jewish Academy Award winners, actors, architects, Asian Jews, astronauts, atheists, and anarchists. There and elsewhere on the web are lists of fictional Jews, chess-player Jews, kabbalist Jews, Oceanian Jews . . . Someone even optimistically created an entry for Jewish U.S. presidents. May it be a long list someday.

Conflicted Kvelling

Identifying successful Jews is a sure way to keep me kvelling . . . except when I'm searching lists of rich and powerful people in the world and experience what I call "conflicted kvelling." No, Jews don't "control the world," as the antisemitic tract has it. But I hope no one else notices that on *Vanity Fair*'s 2010 list of one hundred most powerful people in the world, more than half—fifty-one—are Jews, including Facebook's Mark Zuckerberg, Google's Sergey Brin and Larry Page, and former New York City mayor Michael Bloomberg.

No, Jews are not obsessed with money. But I hope no one else realizes that of the fifty people on the billionaires list that same year, ten are Jewish. Along with the technology giants mentioned, they include casino magnate Sheldon Adelson and investor George Soros.

I also have "kvelling with reservations" (KWR) about Jews who have been influential in evangelical Christian movements. Not all Christian sects or even all evangelicals proselytize, of course. Many of my former fellow theology students, for instance, fervently believed in the saving grace of Jesus Christ, but not one of them ever attempted to convince me to accept him as my personal savior. But—as most Jews know firsthand—many devout Christians do see converting Jews as their divinely sanctioned duty, so I am predisposed to evangelical wariness. Therefore, Jews such as Howard J. Phillip, described as "the titan of conservative Christianity," who worked with Jerry Falwell to form the Moral Majority, gets a squishy KWR at most. Over the edge is Moishe Rosen, who founded the proselytizing group Jews for Jesus—but after all, at one point he did employ more than one hundred people . . . don't you need *sekhel* (intelligence) for that?

Talking about influencing Christianity, one other Jewish man arguably made the greatest impact of all: Jesus Christ. What a difference! I wonder if his mother *shepped nachas*. And then another one of us, Paul, a.k.a. Saul, used his *Yiddishe kop* to spread Christianity worldwide. So successful were his writings, Jewish thinker George Steiner dubbed him "the greatest Jewish journalist in the history of Jewish journalism."

I also have to KWR about Jews' significant influence on non-Christian religions. That takes *sekhel*—and chutzpah. As Rodger Kamenetz, author of *The Jew in the Lotus*, notes, JewBus (Jewish Buddhists) have had an outsized impact on American Buddhism. Along with founding Buddhist meditation centers and Shambhala Publications, they compose an estimated 30 percent of the faculty teaching Buddhist studies at American universities. The joke about an elderly Jewish woman who treks to the Himalayas underscores this Jewish influence. Waiting in the long line of people about to consult their beloved guru, she learns that each person can offer the holy man only three words. When it's her turn, without missing a beat she states hers: "Sheldon, come home."

Machers Make It Happen

No doubt about it: Sheldon is a *macher*, and Jews value one who attains this distinction. No exact English word precisely captures the term, but a *Forward* column attempts its translation as "someone who, often with no official position or title, makes it his [or her] job to get other people to do things."

I remember hearing the word for the first time when I was six years old. My mother had been elected president of her B'nai Brith chapter and I was pulled out of school to attend her installation luncheon. To this day I remember sitting at the lavishly set table, tugging at my scratchy tulle dress and trying to keep from spilling my water glass. When my mother approached the lectern, my father leaned over to me and whispered, "We should be so proud of Mommy. She's a real *macher* now." I wasn't sure what that word meant, but I could tell from Daddy's beaming smile it was a good thing.

Though the word can carry a twinge of disparagement, like calling someone "a big shot," it is ultimately a compliment. You wouldn't call someone a *macher* at work; you'd call the person executive material. A blowhard who talks a good game but doesn't get anything done doesn't qualify. To be a *macher*, you need to accomplish something—a harkening back to the Yiddish origin of the word, *makhn*, meaning "to make" or "to do."

Several of this book's Jewish jurors qualify as *machers* in my eyes. One woman transformed a moribund Hadassah chapter whose members were literally dying off into a thriving, growing organization. Another helped organize a series of Jewish-Muslim dialogues. A third turned a suggestion for a synagogue-based theater group into an annual production that even makes money for the congregation, so you could say she performed a double mitzvah.

Generous Jews

One of a *macher's* most respected actions is organizing and implementing successful fundraising campaigns. Making their tough challenge just a little easier is the fact that for many Jews, giving is equated with living as a Jew. A scene in a Letty Cottin Pogrebin novel brings the point home. One Jew is chastising another for his lack of religious commitment. "Tell me one thing you do that's Jewish," the first man challenges. The second man responds, "I write checks."

Jews, it turns out, are among the most generous givers of all Americans. A 2013 study by the philanthropic research group Jumpstart found that approximately 75 percent of American Jews had given to charity in the last year, compared to 63 percent of other Americans. Even more kvell-worthy was the giving pattern of low-income Jews. Two-thirds of Jews earning under $50,000—compared to half of non-Jews with similar earnings—gave to charity. More astounding, 40 percent of those Jews earning under $20,000 yearly made charitable contributions, as compared to 25 percent of non-Jews in the same income bracket.

Though they may not have been aware of it, these Jewish donors are continuing a long-standing Jewish tradition. According to the Talmud, "Everybody is obliged to give charity; even one who himself is dependent on charity should give to those less fortunate than himself." At the other end of the income spectrum, nearly half of the wealthiest people in America who signed the Giving Pledge—a commitment to donate a majority of their funds to charitable causes—were Jews.

Despite widely held myths to the contrary, Jews give generously to both Jewish and non-Jewish causes. In fact, those who give to a Jewish organization are more likely to also donate to non-Jewish charities. Ironically, the only institution to which Jews don't "out-give" their non-Jewish neighbors is their own religious congregation. Half of Americans donate to a church or ministry, compared to 40 percent of Jews who support synagogues. (Then again, other religious groups don't have nearly the array of associations from which to choose, such as Jewish Federations, Jewish Community Centers, Jewish day schools, camps, and more.)

Political Influencers

Politics is yet another area where Jews have exerted an outsized influence. Wherever Jews settled, whenever possible, they became actively involved in politics. As the *Encyclopaedia Judaica* recounts, Jews "held powerful positions in Ottoman politics in the late Middle Ages; Jewish ministers held office in medieval Spain; and Jews served as court advisers in Holland, Germany, and Sweden." In the nineteenth century the novelist Benjamin Disraeli served as England's prime minister. Although he'd been baptized by his father, the British statesman never ceased to proclaim his "sympathy with and admiration for the Jewish people," and he demonstrated this in 1848 by supporting Lionel de Rothschild's right to be seated in Parliament. Also in the 1800s Sir Julius Vogel was elected prime minister of New Zealand, and Vabian Solomon prime minister of Australia. Even the heavily Catholic city of Dublin elected Robert Briscoe, an Orthodox Jew, as mayor in 1956.

As for America today, Jews have become "the most highly politicized ethnic/religious group" in the country, says Ira Forman, an expert on Jews and politics. In light of their population size, Jews are overrepresented among political opinion leaders, political party donors, elected federal officials, political journalists, political consultants, and political appointees. The chair of the Federal Reserve Board, often referred to as "the second most powerful person in the world," has included Jews Alan Greenpsan, Ben S. Bernake, and Janet Yellen. Several Jews have served on the Supreme Court, including current justices Ruth Bader Ginsburg, Stephen Breyer, and Elena Kagan. In 2000 Senator Joseph Lieberman was on the vice president ticket, and in 2016 Senator Bernie Sanders made a serious run for the presidency. More than two hundred Jews have served the U.S. Congress, recently among them Debbie Wasserman-Schultz, Chuck Schumer, Eric Cantor, Barbara Boxer, Dianne Feinstein, and Barney Frank. Renowned Jewish government officials have included Secretary of the Treasury Henry Morgenthau Jr., Secretary of State Henry Kissinger, and Secretary of Commerce Oscar Straus. Moreover, Jews such as the Socialist New York congressman Meyer London and Wisconsin's Victor Berger, as well as the Confederate's Judah Benjamin, were influential in American politics even in the nineteenth century.

The reason for this outsized involvement in politics is—no surprise—another matter of hot debate within the Jewish community. Some have credited the extensive system of Jewish communal nonprofit associations, where activists learn to master the organizing skills essential for influencing the political process (see chapter 8, "Joining"). Others trace it to the Jewish imperative to pursue social justice (discussed later in this chapter). No matter the reason, however, few could argue that Jews have influenced the political process whenever and wherever they've had an opportunity to do so. There's a lot to kvell about.

Granted, other groups also like to boast about "what *our* people did for history." In *My Big Fat Greek Wedding*, for instance, the father constantly crows about the Greeks' contributions to Western civilization, much to the bemusement of his daughter. But this doesn't negate the fact that kvelling is typically Jewish. Indeed, cataloging and crowing over the outsized impact of the Jewish people may qualify as one of *the* quintessential Jewish behaviors.

Truth: we Jews love to kvell. Or is it: we Jews have to kvell? In either case, allow me to indulge in just a bit more subject-specific kvelling.

Influencers on Arts and Culture

Jew and the arts? To paraphrase Rodney Dangerfield, "We don't get no respect," or at least we don't get the respect we deserve.

Jews are famously funny (see chapter 5, "Laughing"). The late comic Steve Allen—who, despite rumors to the contrary, was not Jewish—claimed that 80 percent of comedians he worked with were Jewish. Monty Python sang of Jews' outsized impact on the entertainment world in *Spamalot*'s "You Won't Succeed on Broadway if You Don't Have Any Jews." (By the way, the producer of *Monty Python and the Holy Grail*, the classic Monty Python comedy film on which *Spamalot* is based, is also Jewish.) Among the Jewish entertainers who have become household names are Barbra Streisand, Leonard Bernstein, Itzhak Perlman, George Jessel, Sammy Davis Jr., Walter Winchell, Groucho Marx, Howard Stern, Sid Caesar, and Mel Brooks.

Another non-Jewish comedian, Colin Quinn, attests, "Without the Jews, the whole country would be like Branson, Missouri." Though I have yet to visit that tourist attraction, I agree with

Quinn's observation that "Jews read, love the theater, museums. The place doesn't even need to have any Jews living there to be supported by them." As evidence, he offers, "The Maurice and Florence Rosenthal Center for Art is in *Wyoming*."

The overrepresentation of Jews at cultural activities was made real to me at a film discussion group I attended. As we sipped lattes and discussed the indecipherable foreign film we had just seen, a participant mentioned that one of the movie characters reminded her of her Jewish grandmother. This led to the realization that all but one of us were Jewish, even though the film had nothing to do with Jews. At least, I don't think it did. I still don't know what it was about.

Jews also flock to lectures. Taking classes is a typically Jewish activity according to an Israeli survey; one-quarter of respondents say they take classes outside of professional training. As for American Jews, according to the 2013 Pew survey, half of Jews claim that being intellectually curious is essential to being Jewish. This is apparent at my local adult education center, where Jews attend in far greater numbers than their proportion of their population. (How do I know? See chapter 6, "Detecting.")

Serious about Social Justice

Even Jews who never go to synagogue and consider themselves "secular, not religious" crow about Jews' involvement in social justice issues. Albert Einstein did his own share of kvelling when he admitted, "The pursuit of knowledge for its own sake and an almost fanatical love of justice . . . these are the features of the Jewish tradition which make me thank my lucky stars I belong to it."

Jews were especially prominent in the civil rights movement. Rabbi Abraham Joshua Heschel and dozens of Reform rabbis marched alongside Martin Luther King Jr. Many ended up in jail and required representation by civil rights lawyers, an estimated 90 percent of whom were Jewish. Jews constituted at least 30 percent of the white volunteers on the freedom buses to the South, and two young Jewish New Yorkers, Michael Schwerner and Andrew Goodman, lost their lives to the struggle.

What would the sixties have been without Abbie Hoffman, the political activist who founded the Yippies (the Youth International Party), or Jerry Rubin, the anti-war leader who became an icon of the counterculture?

Indeed, there have been so many influential Jewish activists, they warrant a separate category on Wikipedia. Jewish activists were at the forefront of both the gay rights and the women's movement. Harvey Milk, the first openly gay official elected to the San Francisco Board of Supervisors, was Jewish, as were Betty Friedan and Bella Abzug, founders of the National Organization for Women and the National Women's Political Caucus.

Of course, Jewish involvement in social justice considerably predates 1960, extending all the way back to BCE (Before the Common Era—or as a convert to Judaism suggested to me: Before the Common Error). "Justice, justice shall you pursue," demands the Hebrew Bible's Deuteronomy. The biblical prophet Amos proclaims that justice must "well up like water, righteousness like an unfailing stream." The prophet Micah insists that we are to "do justice, love goodness, and walk modestly with your God." Some scholars believe that Jewish law was the only premodern legal system that did not permit torturing prisoners.

Rabbi Gideon D. Sylvester believes the pursuit of justice constitutes the very core of the Jewish people's mission. Like Superman in the cartoon world (among the many fictional superheroes created by Jews), in the real world, when injustice reigns, Jews believe it is up to us to act.

Naturally, this propensity to provoke has not endeared Jews to the locals. "Nobody loves his alarm clock," quipped Jewish essayist Maurice Samuel. I once heard it said that dictators have historically despised Jews because they found them "indigestible." Unlike other citizens, Jews refused to dissolve into the population, staunchly remaining apart and questioning official decrees. Hitler complained that "the Jew invented conscience," which turned out to be a tragic compliment. Freud credited his "Jewish nature" for his ability to "take on the side of the opposition." Writer Lisa Schiffman notes that "Jews never follow directions without asking why."

Today, Jews continue to be in the forefront of social justice issues. Jewish actress Julia Louis-Dreyfus used her Screen Actors Guild acceptance award speech to denounce President Donald Trump's immigration policy. Many prominent Jews, including Philip Roth and Stephen Sondheim, signed a PEN America writers' and actors' open letter demanding that the immigration order be rescinded. Jews have also spearheaded efforts to battle climate change. Of the more than one thousand organizations that supported the 2014 People's Climate March in New York City, nearly one hundred were Jewish. The Jewish Social Justice Roundtable engages more than fifty organizations animated by Jewish tradition and values in collaborating to advance social justice in the broader society. Fighting poverty, ending hunger, saving the environment, and promoting human rights are just a few of the causes that have been supported, if not led, by Jews.

Education, Education, Education

Chapter by chapter in his book *The Coloring Book*, comedian Colin Quinn skewers different ethnic groups. But he opens the section about Jews with "I'm cautious with this one, because

I know that Jews are the only ones who are actually going to read this book."

Quinn is spot-on about associating Jews with literacy, books, and education. Kvellers delight: Jews on average have attained the highest level of education of any religious group—and not just in America, but in the entire world. According to a 2016 Pew survey, the worldwide average number of schooling years for Jews is 13.4 years, compared to 9.3 for Christians, 7.9 for Buddhists, and 5.6 for Muslims and Hindus. Almost two-thirds (61 percent) of Jews worldwide have had higher education, compared to 14 percent of non-Jews. In every region of the world, only 1 percent of young Jews have not been educated, compared to 13 percent of the rest of the population.

And Jewish feminists worldwide should rejoice: Jews also have virtually no educational gender gap. Notably, for the younger generation of Jews, females on average have a year more of schooling than males.

The statistics on educational attainment in the United States are similarly astounding. According to a 2005 American Jewish Committee study, Jews surpassed all ethnic/racial and religious groups in education. Two-thirds of Jews held at least a four-year college degree, compared to fewer than one-quarter of non-Jews.

And the Jewish dedication to education pays off—literally—in terms of household wealth. According to a 2015 Federal Reserve study, the median net worth for a U.S. householder with less than a high school education is $37,766, compared to a stunning $689,100 for a U.S. householder with a bachelor's degree. This discrepancy is so huge I had to double-check it. In large part it can be attributed to home ownership, a significant proportion of household wealth.

By 2014 a Pew Research study showed that American Hindus and Unitarian Universalists had caught up with Jews on education, but Jews still topped the list for household income; four in ten Jews reported living in households with annual incomes of at least $100,000, compared to one in three Hindus.

Nice Jewish Boys and Girls

Not only because they're good providers, many Jewish men and women are also perceived as good marriage partners. Historian Jonathan D. Sarna explains the phenomena this way: "Jews [today] are much more in danger of being loved to death than persecuted to death."

For verification, look at the growing number of non-Jews on the Jewish singles network JDate. The exact number of non-Jews using the site is unknown, but according to a *New York Times* article, users have noticed an increased presence of gentiles. So prevalent are non-Jewish members, the site added the category "Willing to convert" as a profile option.

Non-Jews give this kvell-worthy reason for signing up: they think Jews make good mates. "It comes down to the old idea of the nice Jewish boy or girl," *New York Times* writer Sara E. Richards says. One Christian man said Jewish women "hold onto tradition, take care of themselves—they just seem to be more put together." One Catholic woman used JDate because she thought Jewish men "seemed to be a little bit nicer and have their values intact." After her son's wedding to a Catholic woman, one of this book's jurors learned that the bride's father had encouraged the relationship all along. "He kept telling her, 'Stay with this guy. Jewish men make good husbands.'"

The Chosen People

Choosing a Jewish life-mate is one thing; chosenness is another. The very concept of Jews being "the Chosen People" is the number one topic Jews will only kvell about internally, if ever—and never share with the neighbors.

One of my Jewish jurors shuddered to hear the words: "That whole 'We're better, God chose us concept' is disgusting." Another cringed, "To me it is simple arrogance, elitism, and an example of racial prejudice gone amuck." Still another juror greeted my question about her belief in chosenness with silence. "Are you still there?" I said into the phone. "Yes, yes," she said. "I don't know what to say. It just doesn't resonate."

Yet many other Jews understand chosenness in a non-triumphalist manner. The Conservative movement, for example, interprets the Chosen People concept as realizing, together, the prophet Isaiah's vision of the people Israel as "a light to the nations." The movement's official statement of beliefs, *Emet Ve-Emunah*, explains, "Far from being a license for special privilege, [chosenness] entailed additional responsibilities, not only toward God but also to . . . fellow human beings. . . . For the modern traditional Jew, the doctrine of the election and the covenant of Israel . . . obligates us . . . to build a just and compassionate society throughout the world."

In their book *Jews: The Essence and Character of a People*, Arthur Hertzberg and Aron Hirt-Manheimer point out that "the prophet Amos defined chosenness not as merit but as responsibility, even as affliction. God expects Jews to live creatively, decently, in the moral vanguard of humankind. Chosenness is the ever-present and inescapable discomfort caused by conscience."

In other words, Jewish chosenness is a call to action. Rather than a heavenly version of "God likes you better," Rabbi Alan Lurie explains, "it's more like a parent telling one child, 'The room needs cleaning, I choose you to do it.'" Philosopher and journalist Bernard-Henri Levy sees it as "both glory and weight, election and burden."

Other rabbis assert that the commonly held conceptions about chosenness are misguided, because the Jewish people, not God, did the choosing. As one midrashic story has it, God offered the Torah to other nations of the world, but only the Jews said yes.

Nonetheless, chosenness has been called offensive, divisive, outdated, and the cause of antisemitism. The phenomenon of Jews questioning and "un-choosing" to believe in the concept appears to have started in the Enlightenment, which enlightened human beings to the possibility that all people could be equal. Even the esteemed Mordecai Kaplan, founder of my own Reconstructionist denomination of Judaism, rejected the notion in the 1940s, insisting it was potentially racist and alienating to both Jews and non-Jews alike. In typically Jewish fashion, many Jews joke about it. The Yiddish writer Sholem Aleichem's quip is typical: "God, I know we are your chosen people, but couldn't you choose somebody else for a change?"

Maybe God did. After all, Jews are not the only ones with a supposed divine preference. Mormons claim they are God's chosen. Canadian aboriginals believe the Creator selected them to protect the land since time immemorial. As interfaith counselor Dawn Kepler notes, "Every people are chosen. Every faith brings a new message."

Indeed, chosenness is complicated. Despite numerous Jews' discomfort with the idea of God choosing "us" over "them," many Jews also tend to be uncomfortable about rejecting this special status. This creates a dilemma because of the lingering notion of what religion professor David Kaufman sees as a "none-too-subtle suggestion of Jewish distinctiveness." Without chosenness, Jews are left with the frightening possibility that they are not different from everyone else. As Kaufman puts it, Jewish exceptionalism is "a communal *raison d'etre* for group survival." *Oy.* Talk about *tsuris* (trouble).

Bagels and Beyond

Moving on . . . did I mention all the delectable edibles Jews have brought to the masses? Even in places Jews have never heard of you can find bagels and a schmear. Bagels were on the agenda at Jewish *Forward* editor-in-chief Jane Eisner's private meeting with former U.S. president Barack Obama. When asked for his flavor preference, he responded, "I was always a big poppy seed guy."

Along with bagels, Jews brought to America our famous rugelach (sweet dough encasing cheese, chocolate, or raspberry filling) and mandelbread, though everyone now calls the latter biscotti, giving the Italians credit. If you had a sandwich for lunch today, you can thank the Jews. The Hillel sandwich, that combination of *maror* (bitter herbs) and *haroset* (sweet apples and nuts) eaten between matzah at the Passover seder, is reputed to be the first iteration of this hand-held meal.

Jews have also had an outsized impact on chocolate. Rabbi Deborah Prinz, author of *On the Chocolate Trail,* writes that the Jews were historically connected with growing, processing and crafting chocolate and directly involved in trading the cacao beans that helped spread it around the globe.

And, I might add, that influence extends to eggplant parmesan, which, according to Jewish culinary expert Tina Wasserman, was invented by Jews. Although long considered a quintessentially Italian dish, Jewish cooks in Italy invented the meatless version as a delectable kosher alternative to the standard meat-and-milk varieties.

Living Long and Prospering

Also kvell-worthy is how long we Jews get to stick around to eat our gustatory delights. Jews live longer than our non-Jewish counterparts. According to one British survey, Jews live an average of five to six years longer than gentiles, and "there may be nearly three times as many Jewish centenarians as in the general UK population."

Longevity may be literally in our genes, dating all the way back to biblical times. According to Genesis, the "perfect" lifespan was 120 years, the age when Moses purportedly died. Joseph supposedly got to 110, while Abraham beat them all, making it to the awfully ripe old age of 175. Good old Abe even fathered a child, Isaac, at age 100, thousands of years before the invention of Viagra, and Abe's wife Sarah became a mom at 90, without one visit to a fertility clinic.

The Best Beliefs

Before I began my religion studies at a Catholic institution, like a fish doesn't know it is swimming in water, I hadn't even realized how many of my actions, thoughts, and feelings were typically Jewish. Only then did I come to appreciate—and kvell over—our differing beliefs about life.

THE PELVIC ISSUES

For some in the Catholic world, "the pelvic issues"—celibacy, abortion, birth control, gay and lesbian sexuality—were not to be talked about. Whenever a conversation veered in one of these directions, the professors, who were also priests, began pacing, fidgeting, straightening their ties. "Interesting observation," they would say, like skilled politicians, nodding their heads and then spinning the subject to safer ground.

In contrast, by and large Jews encourage verbal wrangling over contentious issues. Even the Christian "seven deadly sins" are not that big of a deal to Jews. Rabbi Harold S. Kushner shocked an interfaith gathering by saying that none of those transgressions—lust, gluttony, greed, sloth, anger, pride, and envy—would even make it to his top one hundred because "they all happen inside a person, not between one person and another and have no impact on the real world until translated into deeds."

Similarly, remember when Jimmy Carter confessed to reporters that he had "committed adultery in his heart" over attractive women in the crowds that greeted him? For some Christian denominations, this was a big deal. For Jews, no problem. Carter claimed he didn't act on his lustful thoughts, and according to traditional Judaism, what you do is far more important than what you think or feel.

Expanding on the point, Jewish women are particularly outspoken about sexual matters. Comedians Sarah Silverman and Susie Essman are known for bawdy monologues. Holocaust survivor Dr. Ruth Westheimer, author of *Dr. Ruth's Guide to Good Sex* and age eighty-nine as I write, is still encouraging satisfying sexual encounters—and even climaxed her career by endorsing the Eroscillator vibrator. Kate Siegel's *CrazyJewishMom* blog, which became the best-selling book *Mother, Can You Not?* featured screenshots of the sexually explicit text messages sent by her Jewish mother, Kim Friedman. Among the choice messages sent were reminders to Kate to do her Kegel pelvic exercises, warnings of her boyfriend's possible low sperm count, and the flat-out "Did u have sex last night???" I wonder if an Italian, Irish, or Korean mother would send such texts to her daughter?

SEX

Archie Bunker told this joke on the TV show *All in the Family*:

> The priest says to the rabbi, "Why don't you ever eat ham?"
> The rabbi says, "It's against my religion. Why don't you
>   ever go out with a girl?'
> The priest says, "It's against my religion."
> The rabbi says, "You oughtta try it; it's better than ham."

I kvell over the Jewish approach to sex. In general, Judaism approves of it! Yay! And more than that: the Talmud says a woman is entitled to divorce her husband if he isn't performing his requisite manly duties, instructs men in how to pleasure their wives, and encourages frisky females. According to the Talmud, "Any man whose wife demands he perform his marital duty will have children greater even than the generation of Moses." Quite the opposite of "Not tonight, honey."

Non-Orthodox Jews should take note: adhering to Talmudic stipulations often results in observant Jews having more sex than the rest of us. One 2009 study found that observant married Jewish women are having sex three to six times per week, more than twice the average for all married women. And here's a "*frum* fact": Orthodox Jews have more sex than non-Orthodox Jews. According to a 2015 Israeli study, half of the ultra-Orthodox report having sex at least once a week, compared to 42 percent of the general Israeli population.

Liberal Jews can still take heart (and other body parts): another 1998 study found that Jews are also "doing it" 20 percent more than Lutherans or Presbyterians.

One man I know credits his decision to become a rabbi to sensual verses in the Torah. Back before prayer was banned in public schools, one of his teachers would start each class with a reading from the Christian Bible. When he requested opening with a prayer from the Jewish Bible, she invited him to select one. The teenage boy read this text: "Your rounded thighs are like jewels. . . . Your breasts are like two fawns. . . . Let me climb the palm, let me take hold of its branches; let your breasts be like clusters of grapes." From the ensuing shock of the teacher and delight of his classmates he then knew he was meant to lead our people.

NON-ASCETICISM

There are no Jewish monks or monasteries. As Rabbi Joseph Telushkin notes, "Although some individual rabbis have been ascetics, the Talmudic Rabbis, and most subsequent Jewish scholars, believed that God put human beings on this world to enjoy it." Jews are encouraged to relish (literally and figuratively) the acts of eating, drinking, loving, and living, albeit all in moderation. "Eat your bread in gladness, and drink your wine in joy. . . . Enjoy happiness with a woman you love," urges Ecclesiastes. The Talmud goes further, warning, "In the future world, a man will have to give an accounting for every good thing his eyes saw, but of which he did not eat." Life is to be enjoyed, not suffered through.

Philosopher George Steiner goes as far as to accredit our survival as a people to the fact that "Jews have signed a pact with life."

NON-REDEMPTIVE SUFFERING

My Catholic colleagues taught me the term "redemptive suffering"—theological speak for "grin and bear it." Throughout history and continuing today, many Christians believe they must endure whatever trials and tribulations life throws at them in this life in order to reap rewards in the next one.

Though notions of an afterlife—the world to come—are also threaded throughout Jewish sacred texts, by and large Judaism is focused on "this world" of the "here and now." Despite what Rabbi Telushkin describes as the Talmud's "categorical assertion of an existence beyond this one," opinion polls show that less than half of Jews believe it. "You live on through the good works you perform on earth and in the memories of loved ones," the oft-repeated mantra of my *bubbe*, succinctly summarizes the view of many Jews.

Jewish preference for the here and now over the world to come is also seen in the story of Rabbi Yochanan ben Zakkai, who said that if you are planting a sapling and learn that the Messiah has come, you should keep planting. You can always go welcome him afterward. Sound advice. My grandmother, may her memory be a blessing, would probably have put it this way: "*Nu*. Finish your digging. We've waited this long for the *Mashiach*. Now he can wait."

What is more, Jews do not believe that any merit, or inherent redemption, comes from suffering just for suffering's sake. A good example is the Jewish joke about two young students who were discovered goofing off when they should have been studying. As punishment they were ordered to walk with dried peas in their shoes for ten days. When they met each other afterward one student was limping in great pain and the other appeared fine. "Didn't you do what we were ordered?" asked the first. "Of course I did," said the second. "I just boiled the peas first." For Jews, suffering is not to be endured, but to be cleverly avoided or complained about.

DISPOSITION TO DISCUSS

The silent variety of suffering is the very opposite of a typically Jewish behavior. Instead, Jews prefer to employ what could politely be called our disposition to discuss. Quoting comedian Quinn, "The worst thing you can say to a Jew is, 'I don't want to talk about it.' Jews like to talk it through, yet they still all have digestive problems."

After becoming engaged to a Jewish man, a non-Jewish friend asked me, "Why do you guys argue so much?" The first time she was invited to his family's house for dinner she was stunned. "In my midwestern Protestant family, we were taught to speak politely to each other," she recalled. "But they were yelling at each other, pounding on the table. I was actually scared." After a few more visits, she realized that this was her new normal.

Yes, in many Jewish families—including my own—it is normal to discuss, deliberate, and debate (and that's just the *d*'s). Table pounding is not always involved, but Uncle Mel sending the silverware flying is not that unusual. As one quote has it, a Jew is someone who can't take "yes" for an answer. I do kvell over the Jewish propensity to verbally challenge one other—the antithesis of my experience in studying Catholicism.

The underlying assumption behind Jewish verbal exchanging is all the more astounding. Jews have a deep respect for rationality, "a profound trust in the human mind," says Swedish Jewish thinker Barbara Lerner Spectre. "Judaism can be a headache, but its capacity for reasoning is marvelous," notes philosophy professor Daniel Herwitz. Unlike other religions that rely on divine revelation, Jews assume that with enough thinking and talking, we humans can figure it out—no matter what *it* is. You gotta love a religion that views people so optimistically.

JEWISH WISDOM

I kvell that Judaism is so darn wise. Not to say that we are the only religion to possess wisdom. I just kvell over our own kind.

I especially admire the wisdom of our forefathers and fore-mothers to locate so many major holiday celebrations in the home. Shabbat dinners, Passover seders, Hanukkah celebrations, all take place around the family table, not the synagogue *bimah*. Even shivah, the condolence ritual, is held in the mourner's home. Locating these events in the home lends creativity, inno-vation, and, well, "hominess" to the celebration. For instance, one of my Jewish jurors relayed this most creative alteration to a Jewish home-based ritual. One year her friend's plans to host a seder fell through at the last minute, and she couldn't round up enough Jews for her own celebration. Substituting for guests, her dog and her stuffed goat joined the small group, donning *kippot* and singing *Had Gadya* in rather unusually animated voices. The only hitch was opening the door for Elijah—the dog spotted Elijah, barked ferociously, and scared him away before he could drink any of his proffered wine.

Basing Jewish religious traditions at home also gives women incredible power over these traditions. Women of the house frequently insisted upon keeping kosher at home long after the other inhabitants wanted to forsake it (see chapter 4, "Nosh-ing"). The (non-Jewish) British scientist and writer C. P. Snow traced the source of the Jewish people's outstanding accom-plishments directly to what he called "the Iron Maiden of Jew-ish Life, the Jewish Mother."

I'm also impressed by the wisdom behind the synagogue-based bar and bat mitzvah tradition. Is there a more terrible time of life than that of being a twelve- or thirteen-year-old? What a marvelous idea to honor and recognize a child at this stage of development.

The ceremony is even the envy of non-Jews. Relaying his experience of attending a Eucharist study breakfast for mem-bers of Britain's House of Commons and House of Lords, Rabbi

Mark Winer recalls that "several Parliamentarians mentioned feeling 'holy envy' regarding bar and bat mitzvah, explaining how they agonized over developing programs to make young people want to be more socially responsible. In bar and bat mitzvah they saw an ancient tradition which could imbue in young people that very sense of ownership." Author Corinna Nicolaou, a self-proclaimed "none" who writes of her search for a religion, describes bar and bat mitzvah as "a life-affirming rite of passage, a shot of pure joy coming just as the young person needs it most." After my daughter's bat mitzvah, an African American work colleague scheduled a lunch date with me to discuss how she could create a similar ceremony for her adolescent daughter. How's that for imitation being the highest form of flattery? Indeed, other non-Jews have created a "faux mitzvah," replicating the ritual without any religious component.

A Commonsense Religion

Also kvell-worthy is Judaism's unique emphasis on pragmatic solutions to daily living. The famous philosopher Georg Wilhelm Friedrich Hegel noted this difference in what he thought was an antisemitic slur: "God arrives, and in his right hand he is holding the holy texts of the revelation and the promise of heaven; in his left hand, the Berlin newspaper. The Jew chooses the newspaper." To me, the Jew chose correctly. After all, the promise of heaven is, well, a promise to be had who knows when? Today you have to know if you need to grab an umbrella on your way to work.

Similarly, the following two jokes highlight Jewish levelheadedness:

God announces that he has given up on humanity and will flood the earth in ten days.

The priest tells the Catholics, "It's God's will. Forgive each other and await the end."

The minister tells the Protestants, "It is God's will. Pray and await the end."

The rabbi tells the Jews. "Ten days. That's more than enough time to learn how to breathe under water."

A barber cuts a Catholic priest's hair and refuses to take any payment for his services. "For you, Father, there is no charge."

"Thank you, my son," says the priest, quickly returning with a rosary as a gift for the barber.

Then the barber cuts a Protestant minister's hair and once again refuses to take any payment. "For you, Reverend, there is no charge."

"Thank you, my son," says the minister, quickly returning with a Bible as a gift for the barber.

Finally, the barber cuts a rabbi's hair and, again, refuses to take any payment for his services. "For you, Rabbi, there is no charge."

"Thank you, my son," says the rabbi, quickly returning with another rabbi.

The Whys behind the Kvelling

Enough with the kvelling. Though it's hard to pull myself away from my addiction to acknowledging Jewish accomplishments, I'm going to step back and ask, "Why?" Why have the Jews excelled in myriad fields?

The answer is—there is no unanimous answer. Far from it. (Did you expect anything else? Jews can't agree on who has the best bagels in town. Why should this be different?)

The void allows me to jump in with some explanations of my own, beginning with our perennial status as strangers in a strange land.

ALWAYS OUTSIDERS

The history of the Jewish people is a history of being outsiders. Recent social scientists are finding the silver lining to this status: looking in from outside leads to innovation. As the late historian William H. McNeill put it, significant social change results from interactions with strangers, especially those possessing new and unfamiliar skills. The contact is not always pretty, and the old players often get upset by the novelty. Often a "painful ambivalence" follows as people are pulled between imitating the new and preserving the old. Ultimately, however, the result is often innovation and creativity benefiting the entire community.

EDUCATION, EDUCATION, EDUCATION (YES, AGAIN)

The reasons behind Jews' exceptional educational attainment are also kvell-worthy. Jews have prized education from their very beginnings. As education expert William W. Brickman writes, "The Jewish people have an educational tradition as old as history." The parental requirement to teach one's children appears within Judaism's most fundamental prayer, the *Shema*. Since much of this education was traditionally conducted as biblical and Talmudic study, Judaism required that children be literate at a time when few other cultures promoted reading.

Antisemitism, ironically, may have also motivated Jews to excel academically. African Americans often quote the maxim "Blacks must be twice as good to get half as far." So, too,

Jews knew they needed to outperform and outsmart hostile neighbors to survive.

YIDDISHE VERSUS *GOYISHE* KOPS

Here's one of those chicken-or-egg quandaries: do Jews excel at education because they are smart or are they smart because they excel at education? Or, put another way, is there such a thing as a *Yiddishe kop* (Jewish head)?

If you're seeking a surefire strategy to get a group of Jews talking, ask them that question. If they're anything like my Jewish Jury, they will immediately commence an animated, exhilarating, and contradictory exchange.

Especially fascinating to me was how the discussion began: with unanimous agreement that there is no such thing as a Jewish versus non-Jewish way of thinking. "It's just a stereotype and we're all the same," said one juror, as all the others nodded in agreement.

"Except for—" one juror tentatively began. "I guess a *goyishe kop* might mean someone having no common sense."

"And using a *Yiddishe kop* could mean being clever, finding different angles or seeing more than one side to something," said another. Before they knew it, the group was discussing various traits and behaviors that two seconds ago they proclaimed did not exist.

One juror attributed her *Yiddishe kop* to the strategy she employed as a schoolgirl to inform her mother about a math test. "I knew if I told her I got a ninety-eight, she would demand to know why I had missed two points. So, instead I told her, 'I'm so upset with myself. I missed two points on the test.' As expected, instead of berating me, she comforted, 'That's okay, honey. You'll do better next time.'"

Proud to Be a Jew

All of this Jewish wisdom makes me proud to be a Jew, which turns out to be another typically Jewish sentiment today. When the Pew researchers asked American Jews in 2013 if they were proud to be Jews, a remarkable 94 percent of Jews said "yes."

Helen Telushkin, mother of Rabbi Joseph Telushkin, summarized it beautifully: "When it's not terrible to be a Jew, it's wonderful." And definitely something to kvell about.

3

Dying

"At the age of 88, after a valiant battle with colon cancer, she was escorted by angels to her heavenly home on Thursday."

Reading just the first sentence of the obituary provided all the information I needed. Even though she had one of those last names that might be Jewish. Even though what took her—cancer—is the most prevalent causes of death among most Jews (followed by cardiovascular diseases). Even though making it to eighty plus is particularly common for Jewish women (our average life span is five to six years longer than for non-Jewish women, according to the British census). Describing her demise as "escorted by angels to her heavenly home" was a dead give-away: this lady was not Jewish.

Obituaries are one of countless ways Jews die differently from non-Jews. No, I don't mean that we Jews expire by nontraditional means. Rather, just as there is a Jewish way to live, so too there is a typically Jewish approach to death.

Now, many Jewish death rituals—from covering mirrors to dropping pebbles onto graves—are simply *minhag*s (technically *minhagim*), customs handed down from generation to generation, while others are observed because of *halakhah*, Jewish law. Some death-related practices reveal a Jewish worldview profoundly different from that of our Christian neighbors. Let's start by considering the wording of a typically Jewish obituary.

The Obituary: Live Long, Die Short

Despite the Jewish love affair with words (see chapter 5, "Laughing"), Jewish obituaries tend to be curt. The non-denominational website ObituariesHelp.org explains that Jewish obituaries are "quick, orderly, and unadorned." As the old joke has it, "Death is the one thing Jews can't talk their way out of," so why bother?

Several years ago, when I was composing my husband's death notification, my daughter suggested opening with "He went peacefully, surrounded by loved ones." All of a sudden I was picturing one of those *Little House on the Prairie* scenes with Ma, Pa, and "the young 'uns" staring down solemnly at just-departed, dear old Gramps.

"Oh God no," I protested. "Way too goyish."

As author Hillel Halkin relates in *After One-Hundred-and-Twenty: Reflecting on Death, Mourning, and the Afterlife in the Jewish Tradition*, "Death was never eroticized by Judaism." Sounds kinky, no? Don't get excited: Halkin wasn't talking about cuddling up with corpses; rather he meant that Jews don't harbor romantic notions of death. No loving arms of death will be wrapped around us, carrying us off to a better place at the final moment. Rabbi Neal Gold puts it this way: "Judaism gives all honor to the dead person, but not to death itself."

For Jews, an ideal death is imagined simply as painless. While it is true that the Hebrew term for such a demise also has sexual overtones—*mitat neshikah*, or "death by a kiss"—for Jews this is not a kiss of bliss, but an analogy referring to the lack of distress in demise. The Talmud likens such a pain-free death to "plucking a hair from a cup of milk." If done right, the hair will glide smoothly out of the cup, offering no resistance or obstruction. (Though, for most of us, it will also render the milk undrinkable.)

A totally unscientific survey of death notices in my local Florida (thereby semi-Jewish) secular paper revealed that, like me, most Jews choose to avoid any description of the death scene. Not one mentioned who was gathered at the deathbed. Nor did I see any Jewish deceased who had "returned to her heavenly Father," "met his Maker," or "ascended to heaven."

Deceased Jews, however, may be in store for a different meeting: catching up with their predeceased relatives. In the Torah, the patriarchs' deaths are described as "gathered to his kin," "gathered to his people," or "slept with his fathers." I rather like these images, because reuniting with my departed relatives would provide me with some longed-for conversations. I'd let Dad know he was right after all; eggs are now okay to eat every day. And I'd finally get Grandma's recipe for *lungen*, offal stew. When I asked her for it when she was on earth, she thought I meant *lokshen* and told me how to make noodles.

Some of this book's Jewish jurors, however, weren't so anxious to meet up again with their departed relatives. One woman said she would steer clear of Cousin Harry, who always managed to lose his balance in front of her, thrusting his hands into her bosom to steady himself. Another said she didn't want to hear Aunt Sadie and Uncle Max *still* arguing over whether that terrible snowstorm began on a Tuesday or a Wednesday.

Perhaps it is images such as these that lead so many Jews to discredit the afterlife. According to the 2008 Pew Survey of Religious Beliefs, fewer than 40 percent of Jews believe in heaven, compared to 75 percent of all Americans. And, comparatively, hardly any of us believe in hell: just over 20 percent of Jews think there's a punishing place after death, in contrast to almost 60 percent of the population at large.

Given this widespread disbelief, it is noteworthy that "passing" is a popular phrasing for Jewish obituaries. Perhaps they mean "passed out"—more accurate and closer to a worldly based eschatology. Or perhaps "passed wind," which, I've been told, is often one's final physical act.

To be fair, some Jewish notices state that the person was "laid to rest," grounded in the Jewish tenet that mourners must accept the cold, hard reality of death. "Buried," another preferred description, calls a spade a spade. Others, including the one I settled upon for my husband, simply say, "He died."

In Lieu of Flowers

Most Jewish notices also leave the cause of death unstated. This, however, is not unique to Jews; non-Jews, too, often avoid any mention of what led to the person's demise. Therefore, a good Jewish detective (see chapter 6, "Detecting") will find hints in the donations—another typically Jewish death ritual—suggested "in lieu of flowers."

Flowers are "used primarily at Christian funerals and are considered to be a non-Jewish ritual custom," explains Rabbi Maurice Lamm in his classic book *The Jewish Way in Death and Mourning*. However, Jews did not always avoid funereal flowers. The Talmud describes how flowers—along with spices—were used in ancient days to offset the odor of the decaying body. More recently, Jews who immigrated to the United States at the turn of the twentieth century were known to purchase funereal flower arrangements, according to George Washington University Judaic studies and history professor Jenna Weissman Joselit. But in no time rabbis and synagogue Sisterhood officials began decrying the practice, objecting to what had become "ostentatious, heathenish, offensive displays." Meanwhile, some Jews balked at the cost, while others asserted that flowers were supposed to represent the good things in life to be enjoyed by the living, reflecting the Jewish attitude of relishing life while we have it. As the Hebrew Bible says, "I have put before you life and death. . . . Choose life." The Torah also demands that bodies be buried the same day, which may have been related to the pungency problem the flowers couldn't camouflage.

Regardless of the reason, the use of flowers is now considered "un-Jewish and inappropriate," Joselit explains. Jews are encouraged instead to make a charitable contribution. As a seasoned obituary reader, I've seen my share of those, but my favorite such designation is not traditionally charitable. In the obituary for Theodore Roosevelt Heller, eighty-eight, readers were instructed, "In lieu of flowers, please send acerbic letters to Republicans."

Bye-Bye Body

No matter what words you use to describe it, dying is dreadful—so repulsive, in fact, that Woody Allen quips, "I'm not afraid of death. I just don't want to be there when it happens." Especially repugnant is the dead-body part. As Halkin bluntly puts it, "The putrefaction of human flesh is revolting. We do not want to see it, touch it, or smell it. We quite literally want to wash our hands of it."

Keeping with this sentiment, Jewish practice recommends banishing the body from the mourner's sight. Quickly, if at all possible. "Viewing the corpse is objectionable, both theologically and psychologically," explains Rabbi Lamm. As the Jewish maxim goes, "Better you should remember him alive." Traditionally, someone is required to remain with the body from death to burial, to preserve the dignity of the body, but Jewish community members play this role, to relieve the mourner of the morbid responsibility.

In contrast, Christian traditions—wakes or viewings—expose the expired to all. To soften the impact of these morbid events, morticians (now called funeral directors) apply cosmetics and embalming fluids to conjure up a lifelike person. But no matter how skillfully undertaken (if you will), the task is impossible. The person is not sleeping, resting, or reposing. Rather, that carcass is *kaput.*

Jewish tradition also forbids any attempt to mask the reality of death. As one online death resource puts it, if everyone were Jewish, embalmers would be out of work. Anyone who has ever seen a beloved die knows that it's almost impossible to dislodge the picture of your lifeless loved one from your brain. The day my neighbor's husband died, she was so rattled by the image of him dead in the bedroom, she had to spend that night at her daughter's house. She never set foot in the house again.

I thought her reaction extreme at the time, but when my husband Rod died in our house years later, I understood. It took me years to remember what Rod looked like before he died. I couldn't enter the living room where he perished without picturing him "that way." I tried rearranging the furniture, to no avail. Like my neighbor, I ended up selling the house. (If the new owners had known the haunting history of those two properties, we might have been forced to reduce the price. My real estate agent said I didn't need to reveal that a death had occurred on the premises, unless it was a widely known murder.)

My horrified reaction to the image of Rod's body was the opposite of what I experienced volunteering for my first *tahara* (ritual body washing). Though many liberal Jews rely on funeral professionals to prepare their loved one's body, Orthodox Jews and some liberal Jews turn to a community organization called a *hevra kadisha* (holy burial society) to ritually wash, dress, and pray over the body and to remain with it until burial.

The biblical basis for washing the body comes from Ecclesiastes: "He must depart just as he came" is interpreted to mean that since babies are washed at birth, so should people be at death. The practice also emphasizes the democracy of death. Everyone—rich or poor—gets the same burial shroud (a pajama-like outfit made of the color and fabric seen worn by mummies in horror movies).

The safeguarding practice is meant to show respect for the body. "The dead shouldn't be left alone like a piece of luggage in a locker someplace," says Rabbi Shloma Freed of West Hollywood's Chevra Kadisha Mortuary. According to Rabbi Lamm, Jews originally remained with the body to keep rodents away from the corpse—another image difficult to dislodge from one's brain—and to prevent grave robbers from stealing and selling the body for scientific investigation, a common nineteenth-century practice.

As part of my religious studies program I was given the opportunity to either serve as a *shomer* (watcher) or to ritually prepare bodies according to Jewish law. I volunteered for the *tahara*. Being alone with a body was way too creepy for me.

Unlike the agony I suffered seeing my husband's body, I found participating in the *tahara* a meaningful, spiritual experience. Not at first, though; entering the preparation room, a bizarre combination of a hospital operating room and industrial kitchen, I was terrified. The sign hanging on the freezer door did little to qualm my nerves: "Please put all bodies in head first."

But once I laid my gloved hands on the first body, an elderly Jewish woman I had never met in life, I relaxed. Rhythmically washing her arm put me into a near trance as I began wondering if someone had done this for my *bubbe* (grandmother) twelve years ago. My thoughts went from my *bubbe* to her *bubbe*, and to her *bubbe*, and then to all the *bubbes* who have washed and been washed by Jewish women like me. Much like reciting *Kaddish* (discussed below), all of the generations melded into one.

The Cover-Up

Kevin O'Leary, the tough-minded venture capitalist on the TV show *Shark Tank*, eagerly invests in anything related to weddings and funerals. "When both of those happen," he says, "people make stupid decisions."

Anthropologists, too, have observed a commonality between these two life-cycle events: wedding and death rituals are the most resistant to change. The reason why remains unclear. Some researchers hypothesize that it has to do with both rituals causing irreversible physical changes: the loss of life with death and the loss of virginity after a wedding (or at least previous generations of weddings). I'm not sure I quite buy this explanation, but maybe the why doesn't matter. Sure enough, at the moment of death, I was doing what previous generations have done: I covered the mirrors.

Knowing this, I am confident that my daughter will cover the mirrors when I die, because she saw me perform this ritual on the day Rod died. Though I tried to be unobtrusive and not wake any sleeping family members, the sound of me draping a pillowcase over a mirror in a nearby bathroom woke her. "That's how I knew Dad had died," she told me later.

The Jews are not the only people to engage in the ritual. The hospice nurse who saw me wrapping linen offered to help, telling me, "My people do this, too." I was so shaken, I didn't find out who "her people" were.

No one knows the true origin of the custom, but according to Victorian superstition, the first person to see him- or herself reflected in a mirror after a death would be the next to go. (Perhaps that's the origin of "Don't look now"?) Others explain it as preventing sprits from lingering about. After all, ghosts dwell in the mirrors of haunted houses. We know this from horror movies.

Among Jews, the explanation most often given for the practice is that mourners should not focus on themselves at this time. This restriction prevents us from facing another cruel reality. If you are mourning as expected, you're probably looking pretty awful.

The Star at a Jewish Funeral

A Jewish funeral is blessedly short. Rabbi Lamm advises that it should be "brief, starkly simple, but emotionally meaningful." As Rabbi Joseph Stolz sees it, "Any funeral service lasting more than 15 minutes is a torture and a cruelty."

Along with their brevity, Jewish funerals are known to be unassuming, modest events, especially when compared with those of other ethnic groups. As early as 1928 it was noted that American Jews spent less on funeral expenses than the Irish and Italians. Given the extravagance often on display at Jewish weddings and bar and bat mitzvah celebrations, such restraint is admirable. Along with the lack of flowers, another noteworthy difference is the coffin, which at least traditionally for Jews is a plain pine box. Thanks to our tradition, we can pass up those polished walnut caskets with padded liners and puffy pillows. In Israel, even this feature can be omitted, with bodies buried sans container.

Of greatest significance, however, is the differing focal point of the Jewish funeral. As one death and mourning website summarized, "While the Christian's funeral focuses on the departed, the Jewish focus is on the family." In a Jewish funeral, the afterlife is peripheral; the focus is on praising the deceased for accomplishments while on earth and comforting those left behind. By contrast, Catholic funeral masses emphasize the everlasting life awaiting the deceased.

Throughout our several-thousand-year history, Jews have held differing and contradictory opinions on the afterlife. These differing opinions are possible because, according to Jewish philosophy professor Alvin J. Reines, much of Judaism is "a polydoxy," which is not a dental cream, but means a religion where every person has the ultimate right to determine his or her own beliefs.

So, for example, the Hebrew Bible mentions She'ol, an obscure realm beneath the ground into which the deceased descend. The Talmudic Rabbis make mention of the soul someday reuniting with the body in the world to come. The kabbalists even occasionally embrace reincarnation. However, as Hillel Halkin points out, Judaism never permitted the afterlife to become the centerpiece of Jewish faith. Unlike the texts of other religious people that describe the lives and surroundings awaiting them, the Hebrew Bible does not include elaborate afterlife descriptions. The Talmud claims that doing good in this world for one hour was better than all the life in the world to come.

These days, Jews tend to see immortality in the ongoing life of family and community. And, as Halkin says, for the most part, "contemporary Judaism has preferred to talk about something else."

Working at a Catholic college, I had occasion to attend many a Catholic funeral and can attest to the different afterlife directions. At one funeral for a nun who worked at the college, the priest lovingly described her heavenly destination so beautifully I wanted to jump in the casket and join her.

Another difference: the eulogy is the centerpiece of a Jewish funeral, but technically it is not allowed at Catholic funerals, according to *Our Sunday Visitor* writer Brian Fraga. That said, some clergy will allow "words of remembrance" following Communion that will sometimes sound a lot like a eulogy.

The Jewish tradition of speaking about the life of the deceased dates back to biblical Abraham, who eulogized his wife Sarah. Today's eulogies, Rabbi Lamm advises, should not "grossly exaggerate or invent" positive traits, but authentically praise and honor the person. The rabbi who conducted my grandmother's funeral should have heeded his advice. I remember tittering as he praised her as "a most generous person." I loved and admired my *bubbe*, a strong, no-nonsense businesswoman not to be trifled with. "The General," as my siblings and I dubbed her, had many admirable characteristics, but generosity was not one of them.

Further Funeral Formalities Focusing on the Family

"I want one of those," said my friend Julie, pointing to my shirt. The source of her envy was not a jeweled brooch or elegant diamond. Rather, she coveted my pinned black ribbon. Julie's husband had died around the same time mine did, but her Catholic tradition did not provide her with a means to display a visible sign of her loss. "No one knows what I'm going through like you," she lamented. "I almost wish I could put on one of those Scarlett O'Hara mourning outfits."

The ribbon she desired had been bestowed upon me during *keriah*, the traditional Jewish act or ceremony of rending one's garment at the funeral of a near relative as a symbol of mourning. Indeed this is one of the Jewish funeral's most dramatic moments. According to Jewish law, a gash is made in the chest area of a shirt, vest, or blouse, symbolizing that the mourner's heart has broken. The ritual can be traced back to the Bible— Jacob, David, and Job all rent their garments upon hearing news of a death—although some scholars believe it originated as a substitute for the ancient pagan custom of mutilating one's flesh and tearing out one's hair. (Ouch. Thanks, Judaism.)

These days, liberal Jews attach a black ribbon instead of actually tearing clothing. Although it was not technically required, I chose to continue so displaying my grief for thirty days to notify others—and remind myself—that my life was not yet normal. My daughter continued to wear hers, too. When she returned to college, her teachers and fellow students responded so positively, she renamed it her "be-nice-to-me button."

Another Jewish funeral ritual focusing on the family is the requirement that close relatives of the deceased be the first to throw earth on the grave. The ancient Rabbis insisted the grave be filled immediately to indicate that the burial was complete and thus initiate the next phase of mourning (see text to follow). According to Jewish tradition, having the mourners actively participate in burying their loved one forces them to accept what has happened so they can begin letting go. Some have likened the ritual to throwing cold water onto the face of a hysterical person—here making the mourner wake up to the reality of the loss. Mourners may, however, use the backside of the shovel, a representation that their burial task is decidedly different from how they would otherwise wield a shovel in their day-to-day lives.

Though doing this for Rod was heartbreaking, I also found it effective. Hearing the thud of earth on the casket dispelled any illusions that Rod still lived, thus beginning my healing process.

One final burial ritual that focuses on those closest to the deceased is the mourner's walk. To acknowledge that the family members are now journeying through a different path, attendees form two lines at the conclusion of the graveside ceremony. The family members pass through to honor the grief they are about to endure.

Rocks On

At the conclusion of the Jewish burial service, many people stop by the nearby graves of other people they knew, though some believe stopping by on the way out dilutes the mitzvah of attending the funeral. Regardless of when the "visit" happens, most Jews will place rocks on their headstones. (In Florida, though, realism sometimes overrules ritual; certain cemeteries only allow marbles, because stones interfere with the lawn mowers.) One Jewish juror told me that by enacting this ritual her fiancé got to know a majority of her dead relatives before meeting most of the live ones.

The source of placing stones on headstones is unknown, but several explanations have been proposed. Some theorists believe it originated as a visual marker to let the *Kohanim* (Priests) know of the burial site—important information because the Priests were forbidden to have contact with the dead (a restriction some descended from this class continue to observe). Others contend that small rocks were positioned on headstones to keep restless souls from escaping (perhaps to haunt a philandering ex-husband or meddling mother-in-law) or to prevent demons and golems from entering the coffin. Others conjecture that the custom was akin to an exclamation point for the headstone, underscoring that the person would not be forgotten.

Another distinction of Jewish cemeteries is the Hebrew lettering on the headstones, usually including the deceased's Hebrew name. Since I don't know Hebrew, I can only hope that whatever else it says on my husband's and father's graves is something nice. (I often wonder how people can get tattoos in Chinese when they don't know that language. Talk about trust!)

You'll also find different iconography on Jewish and Christian headstones. A common Christian image is palms together in prayer. Some Jewish markers, though, depict hands with fingers split in the Priestly Blessing position, indicating that the deceased was a descendent of the *Kohanim*. For Trekkies, it's better known as the "Live long and prosper" sign, originated by Leonard Nimoy, who remembered seeing it used in his synagogue.

Some Jewish cemetery regulations present contemporary challenges. For example, no unmarried men and women will be placed next to each other. Complying with this restriction can become as tricky as arranging a seating chart for a wedding.

There is also a tastefully separated section for suicides and intermarrieds. Before Rod converted, we investigated buying plots at one Jewish cemetery that had such a parcel hidden behind a border of bushes and flowering plants, separate from all the other sections reserved for the area synagogues. As it turned out, my congregation's allotment was several sections away from the non-Jewish part. "No way! I'm not going way over here," he insisted. "Are you going to be over there with all our friends and wave at me over here? No thanks."

Fortunately, his conversion averted this problem, and we buried him with the rest of my family, so now he and all my dead *mishpachah* (family) can wave at me together.

Nowadays, however, with more than half of Jews marrying non-Jews, some Jewish cemeteries are reconsidering the ban or separation of non-Jews, just as they are being forced to reevaluate the cremation prohibition.

All Fired Up

"Low-cost, dignified cremation services, provided by the area's oldest family-owned cremation services." Thus touted a quarter-page ad from Cremation Service of the Palm Beaches, which would have been unnoteworthy if not for its publication source:

the *Jewish Journal.* Unthinkable for Jews several years ago, cremation is now routinely advertised along with Judaica gift shops and kosher markets.

National statistics on Jewish cremation are not available, but according to Mindy Botbol, president of the Jewish Funeral Directors of America, and local Jewish cemetery surveys, cremation is growing in popularity among Jews. In areas with large Reform populations, an estimated 15 percent of Jews are choosing this option. In Orthodox communities, however, 99 percent are still opting for traditional burial.

Cremation is growing in popularity among non-Jews as well, both because of environmental concerns (cemetery burial plots permanently rob the earth of natural land—though certain cremation methods can pollute the atmosphere) and cost (a cremation averages $1,650, and a traditional burial $7,300, according to the Cremation Association of North America).

That said, according to Rabbi Neal Gold, the high cost of funerals is nothing new. Despite the Talmudic precept that rich and poor should be treated equally in death, those lacking in funds often found burial so outrageously costly, they would abandon the body and run away. To discourage such behavior, in the Talmudic period, Rabbi Gamliel began using rough burial cloth—sometimes cloth worth "only a single *zuz*"—and the people subsequently followed his example.

Some Jews, though, continue to find cremation abhorrent. "After the Shoah, the thought of burning bodies is just unbearable to me," says Rabbi Jeremy Kalmanofsky. "I just can't do that to my relatives, or to myself," one Jewish juror told me. "Perhaps it's my Jewish guilt coming out." The daughter of Holocaust survivors, she knows that burning would be too painful an association for them.

Nevertheless, responding to this growing preference among Jews, some Jewish cemeteries are now allowing space for what are called "the cremains," the ashes left when a human body is cremated.

Speaking of space, other twenty-first-century postmortem disposal methods include being shot into orbit (assuming no fear of flying) or being cryogenically preserved (if you don't mind the cold; not me—that's why I moved to Florida).

Other people are trying to persist in perpetuity by preserving their online presence. Facebook now allows you to live on after death through a "legacy contact," a person you designate who can continue your page after you are gone. Others are aiming for something grander: "electronic immortality," basically cryogenics for your mind. Futurist Ray Kurzweil predicted in 2013 that "in just over thirty years humans will be able to upload their entire minds to computers and become digitally immortal." *Oy vey iz mir.* I have enough trouble not saying what I'm thinking now, let alone censoring my thoughts from the grave.

Mourning by the Numbers

Regardless of the option chosen, once a body has been disposed of, most Americans tend to believe mourners should "get over it" as quickly as possible. Jews, however, have a different approach, acknowledging that it takes a full year to recover from a loss. During that time mourners will have endured all of the special celebrations—birthdays, anniversaries, holidays, dinners at Aunt Minnie's—without the loved one there.

Accumulating thousands of years of wisdom, the Rabbis constructed a graduated system of rituals and restrictions to move people from incapacitated grief to normal life.

One of the first stages is known as shivah. Literally meaning "seven," shivah refers to the number of days that people

come to the house of mourning, offering comfort, condo-
lences, chronicles (of the deceased), and casseroles. The spiritual idea is that just as God created the world in seven days,
the person who died was unique and lived in a human world
unlike any other. Jews thereby honor that individual world for
seven days after death.

Most Reform Jews don't observe shivah for a full week. When
Rod died, I opted for only two days, but they turned out to be
among the most memorable days of my mourning year.

The membership committee of Ramat Shalom synagogue
will be glad to know that I will always remain a member of
the congregation. They can thank their handling of my husband's shivah for this resolve. I was especially impressed that so
many congregants who participated were barely acquaintances.
Though our previous interactions had largely consisted of a
nod at services and *Shabbat shalom* at the *Oneg* afterward, here
they were, handing me a pan of rolled cabbage and telling me
what a great guy Rod was.

Some people consider shivah the Jewish version of a wake,
but it couldn't be more different. Unlike a wake, the body has
already been buried. Shivah begins immediately thereafter,
when the mourner is expected to be debilitated and incapable
of caring for him- or herself. Even the Baal Shem Tov, reputed
to be among the wisest of men, was said to be too incapacitated
by his wife's death to carry on.

The Jewish community assumes responsibility for bringing the
mourning family members everything they need—food, drink,
comfort, even daily religious services. Food, of course, plays
a dominant role, as the classic joke about the man at death's
door reveals. The delicious aroma of his wife's mandelbread
baking perks him up, and he asks her for some. "No way," she
says. "It's for the shivah."

Anyone raised by a Jewish mother knows you are never to enter a shivah house without bringing something for the mourners to eat. Especially important is the "meal of condolence," the first meal for family mourners following the burial. By tradition, the family should be served this meal while separated from everyone else, like the mourner's walk, emphasizing that they are traversing a new path and deserve special treatment from the community.

At Rod's shivah, I received enough bagels, kugels, and coffee cakes to cater a bat mitzvah. I could barely fit all of the fruit baskets, vegetable trays, casseroles, briskets, and lasagna trays in the refrigerator. I still have a blue Tupperware container belonging to someone. If you are missing yours, please let me know.

One Jewish juror made a shivah call at night to a house she had never been to before. Turning down the street, she couldn't read the house number, but saw a carload of people heading to one of the houses. She followed them, threw open the door, and yelled from the foyer, "Someone come take this babka. It's still warm from the oven."

When no one responded, she proceeded to the living room, where a throng of astonished young people looked up at her from the bong pipe they were smoking.

"Oh, I guess you aren't having a shivah," she said.

"Next door," pointed one bearded young man. "But want some before you go?"

Unfortunately, some shivah participants forget that the purpose of the gathering is to comfort the bereaved. One incensed Jewish juror told me that at her father's shivah, "One woman asked me to bring her decaf tea. Another wanted a baggie to take home some *rugelach*. Don't these people know they are supposed to be bringing me food, not the other way around?"

In short, shivahs are not to be treated like festive events, although sometimes that's exactly what happens. Historian Joselit found references to restaurants offering Jewish "funeral parties." Indeed, I've seen ads from delis announcing, "We cater shivahs."

Though few contemporary Jews are aware of it, Jewish tradition provides one further ritual to conclude the shivah period: a symbolic walk. Since it is assumed the mourners have been sequestered in their homes for the duration, at the official end of shivah all those within the house of mourning are encouraged to walk outside together, symbolizing their return to the outside world.

At the conclusion of my father's shivah, I suggested to my mother that we observe this ritual. "I've never heard of such a thing," she said, but she was willing to humor me. She yelled up to my sister and daughter, "Come downstairs. Nancy wants us all to take a walk."

They, too, found this request strange but indulged me. We gathered at the threshold, linked arms, and set off. Two steps out the door, my daughter began singing, "We're off to see the Wizard"—we were observing shivah in Kansas, where my mother and sister live, after all—and we all joined in. Though I doubt having mourners zigzag down the sidewalk, skipping and singing, was what the Rabbis had in mind, we enjoyed our official end to shivah. On second thought, perhaps that is exactly what the ancient sages had in mind.

According to Jewish tradition, *sheloshim* (meaning "thirty" in Hebrew) is the next official mourning period. During this thirty-day period after the death, mourners are not supposed to wear new clothes, attend parties, or get their hair cut or colored. (No wonder it is not widely observed.) Men are not supposed to shave if the males in the surrounding culture are clean-shaven, but if other men in the community sport beards, they are to get rid of theirs. The intent here, like that of the torn garment, is to visibly differentiate the mourner from others—to remind the mourner, and all those around him, that life with the loved one has been shredded apart and will never be put together like it used to be.

Kaddish: In God We Trust

Just as shivah is sometimes confused with a Christian wake, so the Jewish mourner's prayer, *Kaddish*, is often equated with the Catholic Mass for the dead. But the comparison is—well—dead wrong. As historian Joselit explains, "Safeguarding the souls of the deceased and ensuring their eternal rest has nothing to do with *Kaddish*. Rather than summoning up thoughts of heaven and hell, *Kaddish* speaks only of God, not death."

Essentially, this ancient Aramaic prayer expresses the mourner's faith that although distressed, he or she still believes in God and in living. *Kaddish* has also been called "an echo of Job," a reference to the biblical Job's declaration "Though He may slay me, yet will I trust in Him."

According to tradition, the obligation to say *Kaddish* for eleven months falls to the male who has lost a parent. Today, however, many Jews, both male and female, routinely recite *Kaddish*, and not just for parents, but for other family and friends as well. Those Jews who recite *Kaddish* for their closest relatives—adult children who have lost parents, parents who have lost children, spouses who have lost their wives or husbands—frequently attend daily services to fulfill this commitment.

This practice was already commonplace in the twelfth century. By the 1900s, historian Joselit notes, even harried businesspeople "took time out from their worldly affairs and raced to the synagogue" to say *Kaddish*. Wise to the fact that many Jews were coming for this explicit purpose, the rabbis moved the prayer to the end of the service, so that none of us can fulfill our obligation and then make a quick exit.

When writer Corinna Nicolaou visited synagogues, churches, and mosques in a search for her own religion, she took note of the impact of reciting *Kaddish*. Standing or hearing the names of those being memorialized called out seemed to her "a sorrowful lamentation, the shaking of a metaphorical fist at the cruelty of death." She could also feel the congregation's enveloping support and how the *Kaddish* prayer tied the mourner to millions of other Jews in the past, present, and future.

The prayer even inspired writer Leon Wieseltier to pen an entire book about his year reciting the devotion, earning him not only a spiritual connection with his father but a National Jewish Book Award.

I, too, recited *Kaddish* for nearly a year after my husband and my father died. (Alas, no writing awards followed.) Perhaps because I didn't associate Rod with the synagogue, saying the mourner's prayer for him didn't move me as it did when I recited it for my father. During the year of Dad's death, whenever I would stand and begin mumbling the words, images of him would flicker through my mind. Sometimes I pictured myself as a child standing next to him at High Holiday services, him smiling down at me as his hand rested on my head. More often I would see him in other settings—hunched over his worktable in the garage or *shvitzing* (sweating) as he tended his beloved vegetable patch.

One time, a vivid recollection came to me. My father was hanging up yet another weather gauge in the backyard. He was enthralled by measuring devices. Each new instrument he bought was bigger, gaudier, and uglier than the next.

"You are *not* putting that up there for the neighbors to see," my mother insisted.

"This is the last one. I promise," he said.

Later, of course, he bought another.

Smiling at the memory, I wished I still had one of those tacky devices to remind me of him each day.

Well, my *Kaddish* observance began daily, anyway. My synagogue didn't offer daily services, so I tried to organize an afternoon service each weekday. But just try drumming up the required ten people for a minyan (quorum)—one of whom has a key to a liberal synagogue—on a Tuesday afternoon at 4:00 p.m. Impossible. Abandoning the effort, I explored other synagogues' daily services.

I began attending services at Orthodox congregations but found it impossible to summon thoughts of my father while segregated in the women's section. Many famous Jewish feminists trace their early activism to the outrage they experienced while being similarly ostracized. Though females were not allowed to do so, at age thirteen Bella Abzug insisted on saying *Kaddish* for her father. "The congregants looked askance, but I did it anyway," she recounted, crediting the experience with teaching her "to be bold, be brazen, and be true to your heart. People may not like it, but no one will stop you."

I switched to attending daily services at a Conservative synagogue for a few months but eventually found it too difficult to incorporate daily services into my schedule. From there I reduced my *Kaddish* obligation to three times weekly, and that eventually decreased to once a week. Sometimes even this was too much, so I would substitute taking a walk while thinking about Dad. For each Dad memory I had during those walks, I gave credit to the ritual of *Kaddish*.

New Headstone: Heading On with Life

Many Jews conclude the year of mourning by erecting a headstone at the grave and then "unveiling" it with a brief graveside service. The tradition of thus marking the burial spot of loved ones goes all the way back to the book of Genesis, where we are told Jacob marked Rachel's grave.

Though the unveiling ceremony is traditionally held eleven months after the death, it can take place anytime after the thirty-day *sheloshim* period. Few people are aware that one of the original reasons for the nearly yearlong waiting period was to give the family time to save up for the grave marker. Headstones can be expensive.

Like funerals, the unveiling ceremony is usually brief. Often it is conducted by the family without clergy. All of the unveilings I have attended included reminiscences of the deceased, removal of the cloth covering the headstone, and recitation of *Kaddish*—followed, of course, by a nice meal at a nearby restaurant or someone's home.

Yahrzeit: Lighting Up Memories

If you ever wonder if you are in a Jewish person's home, here's a dead giveaway: look around for a yahrzeit candle. (For other tried-and-true methods, see chapter 7, "Dwelling.") Though most American Jews no longer observe communal mourning rituals such as Tisha b'Av (which commemorates the Temple's destruction), Rabbi Lamm believes that marking individual deaths "is observed by almost all Jews."

Jews observe yahrzeit (from two German/Yiddish words meaning "year" and "time"), commemorating the anniversary of a death, by lighting a small juice-glass-sized candle that burns for twenty-four hours. As far back as the 1900s, Joselit reports, the candles could be seen "perched atop the refrigerator or the living room mantelpiece, flickeringly recalling the memory of the dearly departed."

I began lighting a yahrzeit candle the year after my father died and found glimpsing at it throughout the day consoling. As I put groceries away, grabbed a cup of coffee, or dried the dishes, I thought about Dad. So effective was the ritual, I began lighting a candle each year to mark the death of Rod's mother and father. Even though they weren't Jewish, I didn't think they would have minded. Of course, I now light one for my beloved husband too.

With all these dead relatives, I seem to be buying and lighting memorial candles all the time—surely an indicator of aging, right up there with graying hair and slipping memory. I always put my candle on a plate for safety, just like my mother did, as most likely her mother did, these death rituals passing from generation to generation. But my mother never told me what to do with the empty jar. I usually just throw mine away but feel guilty about it.

While lighting yahrzeit candles is a home-based ritual, many synagogues get involved in the observance by sending reminders to mourners as the date approaches. Of course, they also encourage memorial donations to the temple to honor those loved ones. Beginning in the 1920s, synagogues also began mounting memorial electric tablets with individualized light bulbs that could be lit on death anniversaries. Many of these synagogue plaques have become pivotal—and profitable—memorial practices, lighting the way to not just remembrances, but increased finances. Indeed, these memorial gifts can be so lucrative, aging populations begin to look like assets to synagogue treasurers.

Yizkor: Four More Times to Remember

Yizkor, Hebrew for "to remember," gathers Jews together in the synagogue to recall the lives of loved ones. Like *Kaddish*, the traditional obligation to participate fell only to a son or daughter whose parent had died, but observance can now be extended to memorialize any beloved one who has died. Four *Yizkor* services are held each year—on Yom Kippur, Sukkot, Passover, and Shavuot—but most contemporary Jews participate only on Yom Kippur.

As a child, I was shooed away from the sanctuary at High Holiday services during this portion. Then, anyone with a living parent was barred from *Yizkor*—the restriction motivated by the superstition that a child of any age attending this service of remembrance would hasten a parent's death. In many contemporary synagogues, the ban is no longer upheld.

In addition to having yahrzeit lights, many synagogues produce *Yizkor* books, also known as "rolls of remembrances," as means for members to publicly remember those who are no longer with us. Congregants concomitantly make a donation, and the funds honor their deceased relative in large part by facilitating future good deeds. In my family, I could see Mom's memorial funds going to feed the poor and Dad's supporting the synagogue choir. Mine, of course, would sponsor a Jewish book fair—with plenty of copies of *Typically Jewish* available for sale (20 percent off if you buy today).

Living On after Death

Woody Allen explains immortality this way: "I don't want to achieve immortality through my work; I want to achieve immortality through not dying. I don't want to live on in the hearts of my countrymen; I want to live on in my apartment."

Still, as we advance in years and begin experiencing frequent losses—my mother has been known to attend two funerals in one day—most of us realize our finality and strive for ways to live on after we are gone.

Jews are prone to providing financial support to an institution or cause—hence the popularity of synagogue donor plaques—but non-Jews, too, buy into such an imaged immortality. In his book *Old Age*, Michael Kinsley notes that many cultural buildings implant floor tiles with the names of contributors who hope that, in the future, as people walk across, "maybe one or two out of thousands will devote a couple of seconds wondering who the hell you were."

Other physical manifestations often chosen as permanent markers of our time on earth include tombstones, books, artworks, and sculptures. Children carve names into trees. Teenagers spray-paint billboards. As a senior citizen, I long to scrawl my initials into the sidewalk cement drying outside my house.

Beyond tangible objects, Jews seeking the vestiges of immortality tend to accept the validity of the oft repeated saying, "You live on through the good deeds you did on earth and in the memories of loved ones." Perhaps especially since we don't put much stock in the afterlife, we concentrate on what we do in the here and now. Many of us work for social justice causes or give charitable contributions, hoping to leave this world a better place than when we entered it. And some of us invest $360 in a plaque that lights up once a year in synagogue in hopes that someone may remember: you lit up my life.

For many Jews, our family connections most of all provide us with the sense of a lasting legacy, enhanced as they are by our religion that links the generations. I find solace in the thought that my daughter will rise to recite *Kaddish* in the synagogue just as I did for my father. *L'dor vador*, "from generation to generation," our tradition reaches across time, uniting the past, present, and future with this one simple prayer. As a wise observer remarked, "Death sustains the life of American Judaism."

Ironically, at the time of death, it is often the secular agnostic among us who returns to the synagogue to observe traditional Jewish mourning rituals. One thoroughly secular Jewish woman I know who had not "done anything Jewish" for decades was so comforted by the *keriah* ribbon, she continued to affix it to her blouse religiously every morning of the *sheloshim* period. One of my Jewish jurors began attending Friday night services when her mother died. Pleasantly surprised to find that she *enjoyed* coming, she continued going after the required mourning period. Another juror used reciting *Kaddish* for her mother to work through some of the issues and resentments that had plagued them in life, paradoxically healing that relationship after her mother's death.

I, too, turned to Judaism to honor my father's memory. And to this day I take great comfort imagining my dad, me, and my daughter all reciting *Kaddish* in the synagogue across the years. Confronting death, we will live a more Jewish life. Likewise, my omitting any mention of Rod's death scene from his obituary, writing a check to the American Cancer Society instead of ordering flowers, and bringing a baked chicken to a shivah house are all expressions of my Judaism.

I thank the God I don't believe in for providing me the opportunity to live my Jewish life through all of these lively death rituals.

4
Noshing

When my husband-to-be ordered his dessert, I knew I could marry him. Up until that moment, I wasn't so sure. I had been raised to think Jews and non-Jews were two different species that could never be successfully combined (see the introduction).

I'd taken his suggestion that we stop for coffee after the movie as a hopeful sign. As Jackie Mason notes, "You can tell the difference between Jews and gentiles after a show. All the gentiles are saying, 'Have a drink? Want a drink? Let's have a drink!' While all the Jews are saying, 'Have you eaten yet? Want a piece of cake? Let's have some cake!'"

And here we were, sitting in a booth at Green Acre's Coffee Shop, when he made his life-altering menu selection. "I'll have the cheesecake," he told the waiter. I beamed at my future husband for ordering something so typically Jewish, thus revealing his inner *Yiddishe neshamah* (Jewish soul).

Non-Jews (and some Jews) may wonder how something as mundane as a dessert selection could be fraught with so much meaning. But food items are often laden with social cues we don't even realize. "Latte liberals" and "Joe six-pack" are just two examples of how symbolism can be attached to a comestible.

Jewish versus Goyish Edibles

Which foods, you might ask, are laden with meaning along with calories? Lenny Bruce fashioned an entire comedy routine designating such Jewish versus goyish edibles. Among his inherently Jewish foods: pumpernickel, macaroons, fruit salad, and black cherry soda. His goyish list included white bread, lime Jell-O, Kool-Aid, instant potatoes, and all Drake's cakes. Sure enough, my non-Jewish father-in-law downed a Drake's cinnamon bun every day, while all of the Jews I knew bought Entenmann's.

Apple pie is goyish too. When I offered to bring one to a new neighbor she said, "I thought you were Jewish."

Daniel Sack, author of *Whitebread Protestants*, admits few items could count as "Protestant food" beyond "grape juice, Wonder bread, Jell-O, three-bean salad, Coke and pizza." Unlike that paltry list, when I asked this book's Jewish Jury to list food associated with being Jewish, I couldn't write fast enough: bagels, gefilte fish, kugel, *cholent*, kishka, blintzes, kreplach, chicken soup, matzah balls, tzimmes, chopped liver, *gribenes*, latkes, challah, strudel. These Jewish foods are beloved not only by Jews, but even their pets. Erica Jong pronounced her poodle as a "Jewdle" because the dog loved "not only biscuits, but bagels, smoked salmon, and chopped liver."

Jews are so closely identified with certain food products, in grocery stores I play the detecting game of "Is this person Jewish?" by analyzing people's carts (for more "Detecting," see chapter 6). In one recent round I proclaimed a man as goyish when I spotted Jimmy Dean sausages and French's mustard in his cart. I'm pretty sure that Jews who eat pork don't buy Jimmy Dean's, and all the Jews I know prefer Grey Poupon. On the other hand, I knew the elderly woman in the spice aisle was "one of us" when into the cart went onion salt, garlic salt, and paprika, the go-to spices of Jewish women of my mother's generation (and, um, me).

Using food items to distinguish Jews from non-Jews is nothing new. During the Inquisition, crypto-Jews (Jews who disguised their Judaism by posing as Christians) were frequently "outed" as Jews by the foods they cooked. According to historian Hasia Diner, Jewish children in the 1930s complained about being made fun of because they brought matzah for lunch at Passover. On the other hand, food writer Janna Gur was the envy of other kids in Latvia because her classmates loved "those funny Jewish crackers."

Shikkers We're Not

You can spot Jews in the grocery store, but the liquor store not so much. As Jackie Mason reminds us, Jews are big eaters, not drinkers. Since biblical times, Jews have been known as moderate drinkers in comparison to the surrounding population. In the 1800s, when various ethnic groups established themselves in America, the differing patterns became apparent. The Irish established bars, the Italians started liquor-friendly social clubs, and the Jews created delis. In Europe, Sigmund Freud was so convinced that Jews were immune to alcoholism, he reassured a concerned Jewish patient that alcohol was only a problem for the gentiles. Fast-forward to contemporary America. On Rod's "goyish" side of the family, alcoholics abound. On my Jewish side, there have been none, though we have plenty of other problems, I guarantee you.

While of course Freud was wrong—Jews too can be alcoholics—studies from the 1950s through today do consistently show Jews reporting fewer alcohol problems and having lower rates of alcoholism compared to other groups (though rates of Jewish drug abuse are the same as for other groups). Israel reports lower per capita alcohol consumption than the United States or other Western nations. And fewer Israelis die of cirrhosis of the liver, commonly associated with excessive drinking, than citizens of Western Europe or the Americas.

However, as so often occurs with Jews and statistics, the numbers have been fodder for debate. One 2015 Canadian study noted that "empirical evidence on this topic remains limited." Jonathan Katz, director of Jewish Community Services in New York, notes that the same studies showing that Jews, especially males, are less apt to have alcohol-use disorders are cited as evidence that some Jews *do* in fact have drinking problems.

Several theories have been proposed to explain why Jews aren't big drinkers. One theory has it that drinking is not alluring because alcohol is an essential part of Jewish religious ritual. The Talmud proclaims, "There is no *simcha* without wine!"— and indeed we have wine for *Kiddush* every Friday night, four cups of wine during the Passover seder, enough wine until Jews can't distinguish Haman from Mordecai on Purim. Indeed, studies have found that for most Jews the alcoholic beverage of choice is the Jewishly blessed wine, but alcoholics tend to abuse other beverages.

And let's face it. The sickeningly sweet Manischewitz wine we sip from *Kiddush* cups would turn anyone off the stuff. As a child, I remember seeing wizened old men at an *Oneg* table alternating shots of shnapps with mouthfuls of pickled herring. Some of my Jewish jurors remember the same scene enacted with slivovitz, a powerful plum liquor of Romanian origin. Either way, it was not an attractive sight.

Jews were also historically disproportionately represented in the alcohol trade, which ironically may provide another explanation for their sobriety. Having worked in my mother's catering company, I can attest that being around food all day makes you lose your appetite. Perhaps being surrounded by booze and boozers leads to abstinence.

Other researchers posit genetics as the explanation, buoyed by the recent discovery of a DNA mutation linked to lower rates of alcoholism. Evidently some 20 percent of Jews have a gene that produces "more unpleasant reactions to alcohol" than those lacking the gene—the latter consisting of almost all (other) white Europeans. A less pleasurable drinking experience to start understandably correlates with a decreased risk of alcoholism.

Here's another theory with some statistics behind it. Half a century ago, studies of the drinking patterns of Jewish men in New Haven, Connecticut, and Jewish and non-Jewish male college students concluded that many Jews drink less because they think Jews drink less. In other words, because drunkenness is associated with "the goyim," being sober becomes part of Jewish identity.

And then there is my own theory: Jews drink less because it interferes with their love of food. Unlike marijuana, which gives you the munchies (or so I've heard), alcohol can have the opposite effect. "Liquid lunch" describes a meal that is sipped rather than chewed. The 1960s' "three-martini lunch" rarely included corned beef on rye and a pickle. Instead of downing a cold one and expanding their beer belly, Jewish guys would rather devour an oily latke and deal with the protruding paunch.

Jews—Foods R Us

In one episode of the 1973 TV show *Bridget Loves Bernie,* the non-Jewish Bridget runs to the bathroom after being forced to overeat by Bernie's Jewish mother. Watching in horror, Bernie's father dooms the union: "A gentile, a Catholic, and a frail stomach! That combination could ruin any marriage."

Indeed, Jews—particularly secular Jews—will go so far as to define themselves by the foods they eat. Today we have "gustatory Jews"; as far back as 1911, this brand of Jewish identity was called "kitchen Judaism" or "bagels-and-lox Judaism." Though said in jest, the expressions reveal an underlying truth: food is not just about recipes or calories, but Jewish tradition. Some nonreligious Jews who have zero knowledge of Torah and never attend services unless there's a cousin's bat mitzvah nonetheless "feel Jewish" when sipping matzah ball soup or crunching on half-sour pickles.

Preparing and enjoying traditional Jewish dishes often take on greater urgency for intermarried Jews. In her memoir *The Bridge Ladies*, Betsy Lerner recounts that even when her mother was well into her eighties, she insisted on making gefilte fish from scratch every year for Passover. Lerner supposes that having a half-Jewish, half-Catholic granddaughter motivated the extraordinary effort. How her mother thought homemade gefilte fish could compete with chocolate Easter eggs was never considered.

Grandma Lerner's reaction was not unusual. Many Jews, especially Jewish women, count on emblematic Jewish dishes to provide not only culinary sustenance, but identity sustenance too, as I do with my twentysomething daughter, whose lack of Jewish identity incessantly worries me. She never participates in anything Jewish and mainly has non-Jewish friends. Often when we drive past the synagogue near her house, I announce, "And there's the synagogue." "Yep, there it is," she says, smiling, then changes the subject.

And then . . . last year, a week before Hanukkah, she called. "Can I get your recipe for latkes and brisket?" she asked. "I just got back from a Christmas party and decided I want to have some people over for Hanukkah." Elated, I rushed my mother's recipes to her. The day after Hanukkah she triumphantly reported that everything turned out delicious. (The exact words on her text were "OMG. It was sooooooo good!!!!") Okay, so my daughter may not go to shul, but at least I know she can make a mean brisket and latkes.

How, you might ask, could my daughter's desire to make potato pancakes reassure me that I had raised a Jewish child? The answer can be found in the unique relationship Jews have with food. I'm sure an Italian Catholic momma would rejoice if her daughter asked for her meatball recipe, and her religion does not even esteem food as much as mine. Jews have revered food from the very beginnings of our peoplehood. In the biblical pre-exilic days, people had to sacrifice their most prized possessions at the Temple, and those were all good things to eat: grains, fruits, and animals for slaughter. One rabbi I know irreverently calls the Jewish deity of this time period "the Barbeque God" because the Priests would grill the offerings on sacrifice days. Just imagine the mouth-watering aromas . . .

In the savory words of historian Diner, for Jews, everything connected to cooking and eating "throbs with sanctity." Michael Wex's delightful book about Yiddish food, *Rhapsody in Schmaltz,* notes that Jews pay "almost compulsive attention to virtually every aspect of food." Not just ingesting, but also preparing, cooking, cleaning, and complaining about food are part of our religion. So important is eating, in our holiest text God issues menus, ingredients, side dishes, cooking instructions, and food pairings.

Likewise, the Talmud warns that in the final judgment, people will be punished if they "failed to partake of the good foods." Each will have to "give a reckoning and account for everything that his eye saw and did not eat." Enjoying a good meal was so important to the epicurean Rabbis, a man was allowed to divorce his wife if she burned his soup.

Those same naughty Rabbis also coupled food and sexual references. They described sex euphemistically as "tasting the dish" and tut-tutted, "He who eats matzah on the day before Passover is like a man who has sex with his fiancée in her father's house." Homemade matzah must have been decidedly more delectable in those days. Does anybody have the recipe?

And here's something to chew on: almost every Jewish holiday is associated with one or more foods. Many of these traditional foods carry symbolic meanings, too. For example, the Yiddish word for carrots, *mehren*, means "to multiply," so dishes using this vegetable are consumed in the hopes of increasing one's blessings. According to kosher cooking expert Lise Stern, other holiday foods originated as a play on words in Hebrew or the native tongue; for example, the **Sephardic Holiday Cooking** book offers, "As we eat this leek may our luck never lack in the year to come." Continuing this tradition, some English-speaking Jews have been known to munch on a raisin and celery stalk in hopes of securing a "raise in salary."

Here's how the Jewish calendar moves from holiday to holiday along its fabulous food trajectory.

SHABBAT

How do we "remember the Sabbath day and keep it holy," number four of God's top ten commandments? In large part by enjoying good food as dictated by God. Relishing the enjoyment of delicious dishes on this day is considered a double mitzvah (commanded good deed).

In late nineteenth-century and early twentieth-century America, Jews who observed the day of rest tended to enjoy the day at home (despite repeated rabbinical exhortations to pray in shul). As historian Joselit explains, the Sabbath was not experienced in "devotional terms, but in domestic, culinary, and sentimental ones." Joyous eating on that one day provided Jews with a "powerful sacred food experience," says historian Diner. Especially for hungry refugees and immigrants, the Sabbath was drooled over—including on the days leading up to it. Meat and chicken were luxuries saved for and savored at the *Shabbos* table. To deliver these dreamed-about dishes, the mother of the house would scrimp, save, shop, and slave away. The *cholent* (casserole) she put in the oven the night before included not just meat and potatoes, but huge helpings of Judaism, family, holiness—and even ancient tradition. Archeologists have discovered biblical-era earthenware that evidently was used to cook food underground—the roots of the Jewish pre-Crock-Pot method of slow cooking.

Challah was so important to the Jewish way of life, details about its preparation appear in our holy books. In the Temple days, Jews brought challah dough to the Priests as part of their salary. In remembrance of this practice, the Torah commands "taking challah" (*hafrashat challah*), the ritual of separating an olive-size piece of dough to be burned or disposed of. By commandment, women are the required challah discarders.

Performing this act must have been incredibly painful during times of scarcity. Even when I'm completely satiated I can't stomach the thought of wasting half of a deli tuna sandwich. Imagine what it must have felt like for the women who preceded us to barely have enough to eat, inhale the aroma of the dough, and promptly toss part of it away. Talk about discipline! Practicing this self-control each and every week must have proved advantageous when even harder times ensued. Some could even argue that their self-restraint helped sustain the Jewish people. Way to go, foremothers!

ROSH HASHANAH

Apples with honey and honey cake are among the most famous Rosh Hashanah foods, all associated with the sweetness hoped for the new year. Round items, such as the aforementioned apples and challahs, evoke the yearly cycle. The sliced carrots in the tzimmes (compote) remind us of coins or richness in the new year.

The Talmud mentions five items that "every man should make a habit to eat on New Year: pumpkin, fenugreek, leek, beets and dates"—and, underscoring the Jewish love of word-play (see chapter 5, "Laughing"), each is a play on words. The Hebrew word for pumpkin or squash, *karah*, means "to call out or proclaim," as in the accompanying prayer, "May our merits be proclaimed before You." Fenugreek in Hebrew is *rubia*, which (they say) sounds like *yirbu*, the word for "increase," as in "May our merits increase." Leek, *karti*, sounds like *keret*, "to cut off," as in "Our enemies should be decimated." Beets, *salek*, means "get rid of," and dates, *tamar*, supposedly sounds like *yitamu*, "removed," which is what should happen to the wicked of the earth.

So here we have early examples of Jewish humor (discussed in chapter 5)—Jews skewering their oppressors through food puns. Can you *beet* that?

Sukkot

The holiday of Sukkot is "the Jewish calendar's 'eat local' poster child," says food writer Leah Koenig. Commemorating the forty years the Jews wandered in the desert and lived in temporary shelters, we build a hut called a sukkah, decorate it with fresh fruits and vegetables, dine inside on stuffed foods that symbolize the flowing abundance of the harvest season—cabbage, grape leaves, zucchini, squash, and kreplach (dumplings), along with honey-dipped challah—and sleep in the transient shelter al fresco.

HANUKKAH

"There are no dietary rules regarding Hanukkah, just culinary traditions," says Lise Stern. Based on the legend of the miracle of the rededicated Temple's lamp oil lasting for eight days—which Rabbi Bob Alper reminds us is a mythical story and not fact—many Jews honor the holiday by eating foods fried in oil. However, by Stern's way of thinking, this connection "is a valid excuse, I mean reason" for eating latkes (fried potato pancakes) and *sufganiyot*, the jelly doughnuts especially popular in Israel. Some Eastern European Jews also serve latkes with *gribenes*, onions fried in goose fat—a heart-felt celebration.

TU B'SHEVAT

Mention the word "seder" (literally "order"), and most Jews think of Passover. But the holiday of Tu b'Shevat, a.k.a. "the Jewish Arbor Day," comes with its own ordered eating ritual: consuming three symbolic groupings of fruits and nuts, as well as four cups of wine. Different communities evolved different rituals, but most include eating groups of fruits with pits (cherries, apricots, olives, dates, plums), fruits and nuts with outer shells (pomegranates and almonds), and entirely eatable edibles (figs, grapes, apples, pears, berries).

Sounds pretty juicy, right? It is . . . except when it's not. At my childhood synagogue I remember being forced to eat something called *bokser* (carob fruit), which *Webster's* dictionary defines as "a dry pod used for feeding animals and sometimes eaten by man." The *Forward* explains carob fruits as "flattish, 4 to 6 inches in length, hard as nails to bite into, and yield—if you haven't meanwhile broken all your teeth—a substance that smells like limburger cheese."

PURIM

You know it's Purim when bakery cases fill up with the filled-in cookie known as hamantashen. Literally "Haman's hat," the triangular pastry is said to represent the headgear or ears of the

Purim story villain, Haman, who attempted to annihilate the Jewish people. The pastry dough usually enfolds a gooey paste of apricots, prunes, or poppy seeds (*mohn*), but creative cooks have been known to stuff the middle with a honey-date or lemon-lavender combo. And, to comply with the cravings of modern Jews, you'll also find whole wheat and gluten-free varieties.

As evidence that we Jews take our holiday foods seriously, I submit to you the scholarly disputation known as the Latke-Hamantashen Debate. Originating at the University of Chicago in 1946, this ongoing annual Purim pastime pits academic luminaries against one other arguing the burning question: Which is superior—latkes or hamantashen? For seventy years now, legal expert Alan Dershowitz, economist Milton Friedman, psychologist Steven Pinker, and critic Alan Bloom are among those who have gathered in the halls of Princeton, Harvard, Berkeley, and Stanford to defend their delicacy. Former Israeli-Palestinian peace negotiator Aaron David Miller concluded one such debate saying, "The real significance of the Latke-Hamantashen Debate is that it cannot be resolved, but it's simply too important to abandon."

As I said, this is serious stuff for Jews.

PASSOVER

Half of this chapter could have included foods Jews believe absolutely, positively must be included in the Passover "festive meal," those much-anticipated words in the Haggadah answering that ancient childhood question, "When do we eat?" Jews are not the only people who demand selected foods be eaten on certain holidays. My beloved husband, of blessed memory, would never let me forget that fateful year my cousin failed to put mashed potatoes on her Thanksgiving menu. Every following year as the holiday approached he would complain to anyone who hadn't heard it before (and many who had), "Can you believe it? There were no *mashed potatoes* on Thanksgiving!"

To avoid any such dire omissions on Passover, the Rabbis standardized the holiday's required edible elements. The seder ritual traditionally includes a shank bone (the paschal lamb, symbolizing the meat the Israelites were commanded to roast), egg (symbolizing continuity, birth, and rebirth), bitter herbs (to remember the hardships slavery inflicted on our ancestors), *haroset*—a mixture of fruit and nuts (representing the bricks and mortar made by slaves), parsley or other greens (the spring season), matzah (the unleavened bread baked by fleeing Israelites), and salt water (the tears shed by our enslaved ancestors). Many Jews have added an orange to the seder plate to supposedly commemorate a heckler's comment hurled at Jewish feminist professor Susannah Heschel that "a woman belongs on the *bimah* (pulpit) as much as an orange belongs on the seder plate." Though oft repeated, this story has been debunked, with alternative explanations now given including the orange representing marginalized people or the fruitfulness of the Jewish people.

In addition to the orange, others have incorporated the Sephardic custom of scallions, with which participants whip each other like slaves. I encountered this ritual once at a women's seder. After I turned to the seven-year-old girl sitting to my right, we joyously commenced a beating frenzy with the green onions. When I turned to the patrician-looking woman on my left, she disdainfully warned me, "Don't you dare touch me with that thing. This blouse is silk and cost me a fortune."

SHAVUOT

So important is eating to our people, some scholars believe that dining out was the Israelites' first national activity. While waiting for Moses to return from the mountain with the Torah, what did they do? They ate! Later, the Rabbis proclaimed the holiday of Shavuot to celebrate the people's receiving the Torah.

What do we do today to honor this occasion? We eat! Dairy foods are traditionally served at this holiday, though the reason is subject to debate. Some say meat is to be avoided because of its associations with the forbidden Golden Calf. Others believe the meal is milk-based because the Torah—like a mother's milk—is life-giving.

Typically, Jews dine on blintzes and cottage cheese, along with that iconic Jewish dish, kugel. This classic Jewish casserole of noodles or potatoes, eggs, and fat is so ubiquitous I once heard it said that there are more kugel recipes than there are Jews in the world. It even inspired a bumper sticker, "My bubbe's kugel can beat up your bubbe's kugel," which will most often be found on a Toyota Prius. (See chapter 7 for other "Jewish cars.")

The word "kugel" derives from *kugeltopf*, the German word for "sphere"—the shape of the original cooking dish. When kugel started, it was placed on top of a cooking stew; only later, when relocated into its own rectangular pan, did it become its own dish.

For dessert, cheesecake is the Shavuot favorite. According to my husband, this sacred sweet course was never to be defiled by adding flavors or fruit. That first taste of plain cheesecake was heavenly—which might explain why it is associated with God giving us the Torah.

By the way, on almost every Jewish holiday, there for the eating—and sniffing—is the omnipresent gefilte (stuffed) fish. When the poet Andrew Lustig was asked, "What is that?" he replied, "I don't know. I don't like it. Nobody does. But we eat it because it's what we do." In truth, Jews used to grind up carp or another inexpensive fish, then mix in bread, egg, onion, and spices, because it was cheap to make and helped stretch meager portions.

The Bible Says So

Of course, Jews are not the only ones who associate holidays with certain foods. What would Christmas be like for Christians without a honey-baked ham or Easter without marshmallow Peeps and colored eggs?

But celebrating those holidays with food is not biblically sanctioned the way it is for Jews, particularly on Passover. Our Holy Scripture demands that we commemorate the dramatic Exodus from Egypt—and dictates exactly what and when we eat. "Seven days you shall eat unleavened bread," instructs Exodus. And we are commanded to "observe the Feast of Unleavened Bread. . . . You shall observe this as an institution for all time, for you and for your descendants." According to the 2013 Pew survey, three-fourths of Jews fulfill this requirement, making Passover seders the most observed of all Jewish rituals.

Ironically, even Yom Kippur, the holiest day of the year, during which Jews don't consume any food or water from sundown to after sundown, is all about eating (or the lack thereof). What is the most common exchange between two Jews before and on this day? They don't say, "Have a good repentance day." No; they say, "Have an easy fast."

According to some interpretations, enjoying a full meal the day before the Yom Kippur fast is not only an obligation; it is a mitzvah. The Torah offers confusing instruction for "the ninth day" (the day before Yom Kippur), dictating that "You shall practice self-denial" (meaning you should fast), followed by "You shall observe this your Sabbath" (meaning you should eat). The great biblical commentator Rashi came down on the *let's eat* side, recommending that we stuff our bellies the day before to help intensify the effects of the fast; having a light nosh, he said, would reduce the impact of our sacrifice.

So, on Erev (literally "evening" or the evening before) Yom Kippur I envy traditionally observant Jews, who get an excuse to consume as many sanctified calories as possible.

Food and the Jewish Life Cycle

Along with celebrating holidays, Jews are required to celebrate life-cycle events and sacred moments with food. Beginning with biblical Abraham, who "held a great feast" to mark the weaning of his son Isaac, the Rabbis later established the tradition of the *seudat mitzvah,* or "a mitzvah meal," according to which Jews are obligated to eat joyous meals at weddings, circumcisions, baby namings, and bar and bat mitzvah celebrations. There is no required menu for such events, although historically some rabbis argued that meat was required. However, in our "I don't eat red meat" times, some are questioning this part of the mandate.

Though not biblically required, certain foods have traditionally been associated with different life-cycle events. According to Israeli journalist Molly Lyons Bar-David and ethnographer Yom-Tov Lewinsky, at circumcisions and weddings it was customary to provide fish, meat, cakes, and cookies. Brides and bridegrooms were honored with—what else?—chicken soup; the *gildene yoikh,* or "golden broth," as it was dubbed, was often the food of choice for newlyweds breaking their daylong fast after the ceremony. When I was growing up the *de rigueur* culinary offerings at bar and bat mitzvah celebrations were tuna salad, chopped herring, challah, and a nearly tasteless puff cookie called air kichel.

In recent years this formerly modest repast has expanded into seven-course meals. After one bar mitzvah ceremony I attended, I gorged myself on all the delectable dishes on the buffet table, only to be ushered into the dining hall for the sit-down meal. Indeed, some clergy decry that these ostentatious food events are no longer fulfilling the original requirement. Instead of providing sustenance to the congregation, they are simply feeding parents' egos.

Guess Who's Coming for Dinner?

Not only does our tradition specify when to eat joyously; it dictates with whom we partake our repast. Jews are supposed to share meals with others. In keeping with this mandate, the first recorded dinner party was hosted by none other than our patriarch Abraham, who asked others to join him in his tent, though naturally Sarah had to cook. Their actions set the stage for the mitzvah of *hakhnasat orchim*, the requirement to bring in guests.

But not just any guests would do. Especially valued was feeding poor people. "Let the doors of your home be wide open, and may the needy be often in your home," says the Talmud. According to shtetl custom, the poorest members of a community were to be welcomed guests at feasts and weddings. Historian Diner reports that Jewish immigrants knew that they were expected to bring home "strangers, visitors, poor people, and anyone without a meal."

What is more, how you treat the waiters who bring the food is part of Jewish law. The sixteenth-century Shulchan Arukh (code of Jewish law) stipulates that "a person should immediately offer to the waiter anything that is being served that has an aroma. . . . It is a particularly fine practice to give the waiter something immediately from each kind of food."

And as anyone who has ever taken a meal at a Jewish home knows, "*Yiddishe* mommas" always prepare way more food than can possibly be consumed. This Jewish propensity to overproduce for Shabbat and holidays became a running joke between

Rod and me. A few hours before the guests were to arrive I would invariably decide I needed to add to the menu.

"Honey, I'm running to the store. I don't think the kugel and potatoes are enough. I'm going to pick up some rice."

"Good idea," he would tease. "There's no way you have enough, considering that we are having two people over."

Rod understood: I was simply continuing the tradition I had been taught by my Jewish mother.

The Psychological Effects of a Pre-occupation with Foods

Even Jews who don't observe all the Jewish traditions are sometimes still preoccupied with food. At least that was the conclusion of one 1938 scholarly journal that found that young Jewish mothers who did not keep kosher continued to exhibit "the psychological effects of a preoccupation with foods" that persist for generations.

Even in the Holocaust, Jewish food proved to be sustaining. The book *In Memory's Kitchen: A Legacy from the Women of Terezin* reproduces the recipes women exchanged in the concentration camp. They would "cook with their mouths," recalling what they missed most, "pots, pans, kitchen, home, family, guests, meals." As the book's introduction reminds us, "The food and foodways we associate with the rituals of childhood, marriage, and parenthood, moments around the tables, celebrations are critical components of our identities"—and helped these women survive desperate circumstances.

This understanding is even more meaningful when you consider that for much of Jewish history, food has been our people's only constant. Expelled from place to place, with no country to call our own, Jewish food—those precious recipes for chicken soup, *kasha varnishkes* (buckwheat groats with bowtie noodles), and kreplach (dumplings) handed down from generation to generation—essentially became our homeland. In the words of writer Julie Michaels, "The dishes set upon their tables helped define them as a people."

Food and Death

Enjoying good food is so important to Jews that when death approaches, it is often the last thing on a Jew's mind. Catholics may demand a priest, but Jews call for takeout. One Jewish juror recalled how her dad, dying of congestive heart failure, wanted her to smuggle a pastrami sandwich into the hospital, but she told him she would never make it past the eagle-eyed nurses' station. One Boston deli owner reported that customers would come in on respirators "for that last taste of deli before they die."

And for Jews, getting a good meal doesn't end with the end of life. The book of Isaiah forecasts that in the idyllic end of days God will make for all people "a banquet with rich foods, choice wines, and fat things full of marrow." According to the Talmud, at the end of days, the Messiah will serve up the great legendary fish, the Leviathan, at a banquet for the righteous. Rabbi Neal Gold quips, "Even in messianic times, Jews will be eating smoked fish."

Kvetching

Because food is so important, Jews can be exceptionally demanding about the quality and quantity of what they ingest. Just as every Jew has a synagogue they won't step foot in, so can they name a brand of bagel they would never let grace their lips. In his book about keeping kosher in America, Roger Horowitz pronounces, "For Jews, arguments about food matter as much as the meal itself."

Like the food itself, the Jewish tradition of talking/pontificating/complaining about the food goes all the way back to the Bible. As Michael Wex jokes, the Israelites never complain "unless they have a chance to speak." Wandering in the desert, they grouse about craving fish, vegetables, and melons. To calm them God sends manna, which the Bible says tasted like "the fatness of shmaltz" or "rich cream." But even that wasn't good enough. They still complained, according to the biblical book of Numbers. "They whine before me and say, 'Give us meat to eat!'"

And the Jews continued complaining about food for thousands of years, as can be seen from the joke about the waiter who approaches a table of Jewish women and asks, "Ladies, is *anything* all right?"

Holy Grunting

For Jews, the tradition of complaining about food does not end at the table. What happens afterward, or rather didn't happen, is also cause for concern.

Constipation has been a Jewish problem for thousands of years. The word "kvetch" derives from the Yiddish word *kvetshn,* meaning "to press," and has been linked to what we know as "straining at stool." It is no coincidence that tzimmes, the traditional Passover compote, is made with prunes—the alimentary necessity to counter matzah's binding effects.

Bowel movements were so prized by the ancient Rabbis, they drafted a special prayer called the *Asher Yatzar,* which not only praises "the miracles of our bodies," but specifically thanks God for "fashioning man with wisdom and creating within him many openings and cavities." Observant Jews still recite this prayer every time they relieve themselves. Anyone who has ever suffered through a bout of "blocked openings and cavities" will surely appreciate the inclination to praise God for eliminating the problem.

In the Talmud, the sages even discussed the laxative qualities of the aforementioned manna. Some argued that "everyone born of woman eliminates what he has eaten," while others believed "the manna will never come out of you." You gotta love a religion that argues about the digestive effects of a God-sent comestible.

You also gotta love a people that when they're stuck up, they're not too stuck up to laugh about it. Borscht Belt comedians made the rounds with jokes such as these:

> "If Jews ran Atlantic City, the slot machines wouldn't
>   have cherries, they would have prunes."
> "When you win three in a row, you go to the crap table.
>   Later, they will clean you out one way or another."

Closely related to constipation (anatomically speaking) is the malady of hemorrhoids, which writer Michael Wex notes has been called the "Jewish affliction par excellence." The *Jewish Encyclopedia* of 1906 describes hemorrhoids—those painful, itchy veins protruding from your rear—as being more common to Jews than to any other people. Indeed, in some Jewish communities a Jew *without* hemorrhoids was considered a curiosity.

The condition was so universally dreaded, in the Torah hemorrhoids are listed among the curses that God would send to the unfaithful along with pestilence and plagues (thankfully they were left out of the recitation at the seder table). One's heart goes out to the Ashdodites, to whom God sent an outbreak of hemorrhoids to all people, "young and old." And pity the poor Philistines, who were instructed to "make figures of your hemorrhoids . . . thus you shall honor the

God of Israel, and perhaps He will lighten the weight of His hand upon you."

It is not known exactly why Jews suffer from these two afflictions (and whether they do so more than the general population), but most likely exercise and diet are the culprits. According to medical experts and fitness trainers, the bottom line for avoiding constipation and hemorrhoids is drinking lots of water, eating fruits and vegetables that are high in fiber, and getting enough physical exercise. For much of history the traditional Jewish diet lacked fresh fruit and raw vegetables. One 1914 Yiddish source warned that "human beings cannot eat raw vegetables." And historically, Jews have led sedentary lives, primarily studying, praying, sewing, and talking (the last usually conducted sitting down, unless the speaker was especially agitated). Culturally Jews have prioritized mental activities—especially Torah study—over physical ones. There's even a name for this: "the yeshiva tan," the pale complexion that results from never venturing beyond the house of study. In Chaim Potok's novel *The Promise*, one *yeshivah bucher* (student) questions another student's Orthodox status: "You're a funny kind of yeshiva student. You swim and you're tanned. I've never met a yeshiva student like you."

Why Jews Love Food

Given these gastronomic conditions, one would think Jews would eschew voracious eating. Why didn't that happen? The answer can be found in two words: Jewish mothers. (It's always the mother's fault, right?)

In this case, it's largely the truth: historically Jewish mothers were charged with providing sustenance for their children. Of course, mothers of all races, religions, and ethnic groups must provide food for their offspring; "food is love" is not an exclusively Jewish idea. But, as historian Diner stresses in her book *Hungering for America*, the Jews who immigrated to this country were ravenous, but not starving. Those totally deprived of food were too weak to immigrate; those who barely had enough to eat boarded the boats. And unlike other ethnic groups, the Jews arrived as families. Feeding the hungry children became the new immigrants' paramount responsibility, especially the mothers'.

Indeed, the first words a Jewish child of that generation often heard were "*Ess, ess mein kind*" (Eat, eat, my child). Though it's been more than sixty years, I still carry the distinct image of my grandmother saying it to me. After placing a bowl of her famous mushroom barley soup in front of me, she would sit down across from me at the table, fold her arms over her ample bosom, and watch me eat. "*Essen, essen*," she would smile. I was happy to please, for I was "a good eater," one of the highest compliments one could earn in my family. My sister, on the other hand, was the dreaded "picky eater" deemed to be "all skin and bones."

Diner explains that having a child who wouldn't eat was considered the worst tragedy a Jewish mother could endure. Frequently, battles would ensue, especially once children realized the power food wielded them over their parents. One child brought her mother to tears by refusing to eat. "What did I ever do to be tortured like this!" her mom cried. "I can't bear to watch."

One academic study conducted of immigrant children found that "Jewish children aged two through five tended to be significantly fussier than those of other ethnic groups: forty-eight percent refused two or more foods, compared with only 18 percent of Polish and 16 percent of Negro youngsters of the same age." By the 1910s writers, rabbis, and community leaders repeatedly asked, "Why are Jewish homes such hotbeds of discord?" The answer could usually be found in the importance of food to the mother, combined with new confrontations within the family over maintaining the rules of kashrut (see the forthcoming section).

Is It Kosher?

The first Christmas I spent with Rod's family, his sister served a delectable roasted lamb dinner. Years later I learned that their traditional Christmas meal had always featured honeyed ham, but when they found out Rod's new girlfriend was Jewish, they altered the menu. I appreciated the gesture not only because of the respect it accorded me, but because like many Jews I don't like ham. I don't keep kosher, but ham is still not kosher to me.

Confused? Much of what surrounds kashrut (the kosher laws) can be perplexing. Most non-Jews (and many Jews) assume that keeping kosher means not eating pork products, but the no-pork rule is just a tiny portion of the regulations stipulating what Jews can and cannot eat. Kashrut dictates what categories of foods are forbidden, such as pork and shellfish; how meat must be slaughtered and prepared; and what foods cannot be eaten together, such as milk and meat products. Keeping a kosher home usually means observing all of these restrictions and maintaining two separate sets of dishes: one for anything with meat and the other for milk-based meals.

As the previous paragraph demonstrates, it is difficult to condense what kashrut means into one or two sentences. Whenever I tried to answer my Catholic classmates' questions about keeping kosher, I'd see their eyes glaze over halfway into the meat and milk part. One rabbi I know admits to shoving his *kippah* (head covering) into his pocket before entering a grocery store, lest he be accosted by shoppers bombarding him with kashrut questions. One time he was delayed twenty minutes because an elderly woman shoved a can in his face and demanded, "Tell me what this 'U' in a circle means." (The one-minute explanation: the symbol is a *heksher* [ritual permit] from the Orthodox Union certifying the item as kosher.)

It all began a couple of thousand years ago, when the Rabbis interpreted the Bible's complicated dietary decrees, and their rulings became Jewish law for all future generations. Through much of Jewish history, keeping kosher wouldn't necessarily have been easy, but Jews by and large lived in their own segregated communities, where kosher practice was a way of life. When Jewish immigrants arrived in America in the late 1800s, however, the practice came to be perceived as undesirable, especially because the new arrivals wanted to eat like their fellow Americans. Many Reform Jews began to harbor doubts about the practice, believing that "Judaism was a matter of what one thought and how one behaved rather than what one consumed." Between 1914 and 1924 the consumption of kosher meat in the Greater New York area fell by 25 to 30 percent. Per one estimate, by 1936 only 15 percent of the nation's Jews were still strictly observing kashrut, 20 percent observed "some of the laws," and 65 percent ignored virtually "all of the laws most of the time."

According to historian Diner, for many families these decisions were fraught with conflict. One of the first flash points within families was deciding where to live. Especially as Jews began settling into remote communities, the wives complained bitterly about the hardships of maintaining a kosher household. "Yossel, I love you, but I can't live like this" remarked one Jewish woman who had moved to Ohio. "I just can't do it. There isn't even a bit of kosher food. I want to go live in the city." Confrontations also erupted once the children began attending public schools and were enticed by forbidden foods such as ham and cheeseburgers. And there was that dreaded designation of being different. At Passover one girl complained to her father that she was taunted at school for eating matzah. "Let them stare their eyes out," he scoffed in Yiddish in response.

Often these conflicts were resolved through compromises. Some Jewish families began observing what came to be called "selectively *treif* behavior," where they would avoid certain blatantly nonkosher foods, like pork, while continuing to enjoy hot dogs and chop suey "whose *treif-ness* was less overt." Some separated not just meat from milk, but public from private consumption, continuing to keep kosher in the house, but devouring forbidden foods when eating out. Some decided to eat only kosher meat at home but abandoned the requirement to separate it from dairy. Still others ate nonkosher meat but never paired it with a glass of milk. My aunt continues this practice to this day, claiming that meat and milk "don't go good together."

By the time all the *mishegoss* (craziness) had settled, American Jews had created what historian Jenna Weissman Joselit calls "that singular American invention: 'kosher-style.'" Scoffed at by some as "a Judaized version of having your cake and eating it too," kosher-style eating lets Jews continue certain traditional food practices without adhering to kosher dictates.

My own mother got caught up in the growing kosher-style controversy. Her 1958 cookbook, *Mom's Best Recipes: 151 Jewish-American Dishes*, included some nonkosher Jewish recipes, such as chicken stuffed with white bread that is made with milk and strudel filled with unspecified (and thereby potentially nonkosher) soda crackers. The rabbis cried fowl, demanding that anything Jewish also had to be kosher. To quell the complaints, four years later she produced a follow-up cookbook, *Grandma's Kosher Recipes*.

Despite many rabbis' objections, American Jews continued to forsake kashrut. These days, according to the 2013 Pew survey, three-fourths of American Jews do not keep kosher, and surprisingly, 20 percent of these non-kosher-keeping Jews are Modern Orthodox Jews. Many Jews who do report keeping kosher maintain the kosher restrictions at home but eat nonkosher out, a compromise that inspired rabbi-turned-comedian Bob Alper to quip, "At least their dishes will go to heaven."

A new trend in kosher keeping is the "ethical kashrut" movement, which expands biblical kosher mandates to value how food is grown, prepared, and eaten. Advocates of this approach assert they are returning kosher to its original intent: the Hebrew word *kasher* means "fit" or "proper." As food activist Alix Wall puts it, "I only allow organic, humanely treated, grass-fed meat into my home. That to me is the new kashrut."

In the 1970s Rabbi Zalman Schachter-Shalomi coined the term "eco-kosher" to emphasize living harmoniously with the earth as a Jewish commandment. Eco-kosher integrates into kashrut concerns about agricultural practices, recycling, and the environment. As Rabbi Arthur O. Waskow asks, "Is it eco-kosher to eat vegetables and fruit that have been grown by drenching the soil with insecticides? Is it eco-kosher to drink Shabbat Kiddush wine from non-biodegradable plastic cups?"

Some Jews insist upon the ethical treatment of animals as part of kosher eating, explaining that the Rabbinic concept known as *tza'ar ba'alei chayyim*, the prevention of cruelty to animals, forbids inflicting pain or distress on any animal. In the book of Numbers, for example, an angel rebukes Balaam for smiting his ass—and the same animal gets a pass on the Sabbath thanks to the biblical requirement that along with humans, "your ox and your ass" are to rest.

According to traditional kosher rules as well, animals may be slaughtered for food, but the method must be as quick and painless as possible. Writer Lise Stern explains, "The sages determined that cutting the animal's throat in one smooth, fast stroke, severing vital arteries, was the most merciful method of killing an animal." However, many argue that the slaughter practices deemed most humane in ancient times have been overtaken in contemporary times by more merciful methods that have not been adopted within kosher meat production; meanwhile, new methodologies for raising, transporting, and killing animals, such as shackling and hoisting them prior to slaughter, are technically kosher but deemed inhumane. The result, Rabbi Elliot Dorff says, has been an "unwelcome dichotomy" between animal welfare and ritual slaughter. Many meat-eating Jews ask themselves if it is more important to uphold the rules of kashrut by eating kosher meat produced inhumanely or to fulfill the spirit of kashrut by eating nonkosher organic meat produced from animals that are grass-fed, transported, and slaughtered more humanely. To help resolve this dilemma, the Conservative Rabbinical Assembly now awards a Shield of Justice (Magen Tzedek) to establishments that not only observe kosher laws, but also adhere to ethical animal, worker, environmental, and corporate standards.

Other Jews see the matter differently. "There is no such thing as 'humane slaughter,'" argues Roberta Kalechofsky in her book *Vegetarian Judaism.* Jewish vegetarian proponent Richard H. Schwartz maintains that several Jewish texts point to vegetarian practice. In the very first dietary law, in Genesis, God says, "I give you every seed-bearing plant . . . and every tree that has seed-bearing fruit; they shall be yours for food." The Israelites' demand for meat instead of manna made God angry. After relenting and sending them meat, a plague followed. Rabbi Lawrence Kushner advises Jews to "consider foods in light of their impact on society, the environment and your health, and quit eating meat."

Those of us who remain carnivores could counter these rabbinic opinions with the Talmudic pronouncement "There is no *simcha* without meat!" Indeed, the contradictory statements provide us grist for what almost all Jews love: a good grappling over the matter while gathered at the table.

Sacred Table

An eighty-five-year-old Jewish woman I know took two apartments in my mother's independent living facility because her dining room table wouldn't fit into one. After she tore down the wall between both units, she proudly continued her Shabbat tradition.

So holy is the act of eating for Jews, the table at which the family gathered has been symbolically linked to the ancient Temple altar. When the Temple was destroyed in 70 CE, the place for celebration, ritual, and thanksgiving was transferred from the holy mount to the Jewish home. As Rabbi Neal Gold explains, this relocation "turned every home into a sanctuary and made every Jew a priest. Every dinner table became an altar."

I never considered my dining room table holy, but I would never part with it. When my daughter was growing up, I regularly hosted large Friday night dinners to "give her some Judaism." Often I invited my Catholic co-workers and demonstrated a Jewish Sabbath. The guest list for these dinners began expanding and soon exceeded the seating capacity of our apartment-sized table. Seizing the problem as an opportunity, my husband decided to attempt constructing a new dining room table. Evidently, the man was meant to be a woodworker, as he produced an elegant wooden table expandable to seat fourteen. So impressive was his handiwork, I insisted we hold a "table blessing" to inaugurate the first meal upon it. The Reconstructionist rabbi I asked to conduct the ceremony readily agreed but told me that

Jews bless not things, but actions. (The traditional blessing over the bread does not bless the bread directly; it praises God for "bringing forth bread from the earth.") Thus, on the celebratory day, the rabbi invited the guests to mention the activities they hoped would take place at the new table. Eating, drinking, talking, laughing, reading, and studying were shouted out. My cousin sidled up to me and whispered another activity Rod and I could engage in. The rabbi never publicly blessed that undertaking, though it would have been looked upon favorably by the Rabbis, as discussed in chapter 2, "Kvelling."

Sacred Jewish Deli

The table is far from the only setting where Jews celebrate their religion with food. Like other ethnic groups, Jews enjoy getting together in commercial establishments, but instead of gathering at a bar to drink, they traditionally gather at the deli to dine.

"It is difficult to overestimate the importance of the delicatessen," historian Ted Merwin asserts in his chronicle of the Jewish deli, *Pastrami on Rye*. In fact, before the State of Israel's establishment, the deli served as "the metaphorical homeland for the Jewish soul"—a place where Jews could enjoy being Jews in public. That, of course, came with its own brand of typical Jewishness. When you entered, Merwin notes, all the waiters and counter people would yell at you, creating a "hubbub [of] casualness, conviviality, and sense of community." Food writer Joan Nathan avers that eating in one of these establishments constituted "the Jewish experience in America."

Especially for secular Jews who abandoned religious practices, the deli became their equivalent of a holy institution. Michael Wex ryely (get it?) notes, "The less faith a Jew has in the Bible, the more meaning pastrami acquires." One deli devotee recalls, "My parents didn't send me to Hebrew school, but they did send me to the deli every Sunday." Eating traditional Jewish foods revived a sense of Jewish identity not found anywhere else.

Acknowledging the symbolism of the restaurants, politicians routinely stop by for a photo op—their attempt to stuff that Jewish deli's renowned gargantuan sandwich into their mouths. When Tim Kaine was running for vice president, he knew where to reach the ethnic populations in my area of South Florida. To connect with Hispanics, he stopped at Pneuma Church in Miami. For hand-shaking with African Americans, he went to the Faith Center Church. But to find Jews, he stopped at Toojay's Deli. He didn't win, but at least he did it right. George McGovern, on the other hand, spoiled his deli opportunity, asking for a glass of milk with his chopped liver sandwich.

Since my daughter and I live in different cities, one of our rituals when we meet is eating a special meal at a Jewish deli. She does the moving these days, so prior to my arrival she will scout out all of the available choices in her new environment. "When I found this place, I just knew I had to bring you," she tells me as we enter the winning choice. You can almost hear the klezmer music in the background as our shorts and T-shirts magically transform into nineteenth-century Russian peasant garb and patrons at other booths become *balabustas* (beloved hausfraus) wearing floor-length skirts.

Nostalgia has been defined as "the sentimental longing or wistful affection for the past," which perfectly describes what many of us are hungrily taking in along with chopped herring.

Artisanal Ashkenazi:
No Longer an Oxymoron

Alas, despite the nostalgia they engender, many Jewish delis are closing. Famous New York institutions such as Stage Deli, Carnegie Deli, and Milgrim's are no more. Especially as customers forgo heavy, cholesterol-laden dishes for healthier fare, the traditional deli is being left behind with the shmaltz (chicken fat).

Nutrition experts suggest that a variety of colors on a plate usually indicates a healthful meal. For instance, salads, fresh vegetables, and fruits constitute a riot of greens, reds, and oranges. But most of the foods identified with Jewish eating—kugel, *kasha varnishkes*, latkes, and bagels—are all the same color: a dull brown.

To meet customer demand for more healthful choices, those delis that have managed to stay in business have changed their menus. Along with the traditional offerings, they've added healthier ingredients and re-concocted the old recipes for a trendier taste. My local Jewish deli now offers latkes made with kale—and traditional latkes with bacon. Napkin Friends in Seattle has made over latkes into a panini-like pressed sandwich. Joe and Misses Doe's in New York offers a celery soda cocktail consisting of gin and celery syrup. At Kutsher's, also in Manhattan, you can enjoy borscht salad made with beets and goat cheese—a dish that would have elicited from my grandmother the untranslatable Yiddishism conveying disgusted disapproval, one of her all-time favorite words: *feh.*

Then there's the multicultural fusion component of changing customer—and cook—demographics. Just as the old Levy's ad campaign claimed, "You don't have to be Jewish" to eat in a Jewish deli, deli customers are of various backgrounds. Many delicatessens are integrating diverse culinary cultures. Los Angeles's fast-food Mexican spot J&S invites customers to savor a pastrami quesadilla. Mission Chinese Food in New York and San Francisco melds pastrami with a traditional Chinese dish to inaugurate kung pao pastrami, a stir-fry with peanuts, celery and peppers. At New York's Kitty's Canteen, purveyor of Jewish soul food, you can enjoy fried chicken made with matzah meal with a "bisgel," part bagel, part biscuit.

Many of these cultural amalgamations result from intermarried chefs. Laura Frangiosa, the Italian owner of the Avenue Delicatessen in Philadelphia, married a Jewish man and created Jewish wedding soup using matzah balls instead of sausage. Matzah balls also bounce over to a Jewish-Japanese restaurant, Brooklyn's Shalom Japan, where they land in a ramen rice dish created by the married owners Aaron Israel (Jewish) and Sawako Okochi (Japanese).

While their creations may be novel, fusing different cultures' cuisines is nothing new for Jews. Moving from place to place, Jews were always adapting new cooking styles and mixing in local ingredients. As far back as the 1900s, Yiddish cookbooks published in America included recipes for Italian and Chinese dishes.

And one doesn't need to be a professional chef to blend food traditions. Many intermarried families are incorporating traditional foods from various cultures into their Jewish home cooking. One Jewish juror reports that her extended family's Hanukkah celebration includes not just her own homemade latkes, but also spaghetti and meatballs prepared by her son's Italian mother-in-law and rice and beans from his Cuban grandmother. Sounds delicious, though not exactly a balanced meal.

Such fusions of food cultures may turn out to be emblematic of the future direction of Judaism. Especially for younger Jews, embracing one's heritage is no longer an either/or proposition. Jewish food—and much else—can continue to adapt and embody other cultural flavors.

For Rod's sake, however, I hope they keep the traditional cheesecake as is.

5
laughing

My cousin almost married a guy she had been dating for six months. He was good-looking and intelligent, came from a wealthy family, and had embarked on what was bound to be a successful banking career. But at the last minute she called it quits, admitting that he lacked one attribute crucial to her: he wasn't silly enough.

Wackiness is not only required for my relative's suitor; it's also requisite to being Jewish. A 2013 Pew survey found that almost half of American Jews answered the question "What's essential to being Jewish?" with the response "Having a good sense of humor." More important than observing Jewish law, being a part of the Jewish community, or even—get this—eating Jewish foods is having a funny bone. Caring about Israel and working for social justice beat out humor, but by just a bit. Evidently, most Jews would find a comedian doing a charity benefit in Tel Aviv a thrice-blessed Jew.

It's been said that if you want to understand African Americans, listen to their music. I submit that if you want to discover the essence of Jews, consider their comedy. Over the past forty years, an estimated 80 percent of America's leading comedians and writers have been Jews, even though they've constituted a tiny fraction of the population. And many are household names. Consider Wikipedia's entry for Jewish comedians—these are just from the first three letters of the alphabet: Judd Apatow, Roseanne Barr, Jack Benny, Milton Berle, Shelley Berman, Lewis Black, Fanny Brice, Albert Brooks, Mel Brooks, George Burns, Lenny Bruce, Sid Caesar, Myron Cohen, Billy Crystal.

Steve Allen, himself a non-Jewish comedian, called American comedy "a sort of Jewish cottage industry."

And even that's too small a take. Funny Jews are not just an American but a worldwide phenomenon. While researching *Kvetching and Shpritzing: Jewish Humor in American Popular Culture,* author Joseph Dorinson was astounded to discover Jews among the top humorists in Russia, Germany, Canada, France, Great Britain, Austria, and Australia. Among just the Canadian and British entertainers are Sasha Baron-Cohen, Howie Mandel, Marty Feldman, David Steinberg, Rick Moranis, and Eugene Levy.

Why are there so many Jewish comedians?

"Why not?" to employ that classic Jewish conversational technique of answering a question with a question. Truth is, no one knows the definite answer, and as E. B. White warned, if you dissect humor like a frog, the thing dies, but (like everything else Jewish) there are plenty of opinions.

Torah and Talmud Tittering

"A Canaanite, a Jebusite, and an Israelite walk into a bar. . . ."

Okay, those words may not actually appear in the Hebrew Bible, but they could have. Jews have been jokesters since Genesis. Unlike the Christian Bible, in which Paul likens "foolish talking and jesting to fornication and uncleanliness," the Torah regales in humor. The Hebrew Bible mentions the root word "to laugh," *zehok* or *sehok,* fifty times. And besides "to laugh," the verb is also variously defined to mean "play, enjoy, insult, mock, fondle, rejoice, or scoff."

Sarah, the founding mother of the Jewish people, guffaws at God's promise of progeny at her and Abe's old age. "Now that I am withered, am I to have enjoyment—with my husband so old?" She laughs so heartily when God assures her that she will bear a child at age ninety, Abraham names her child Isaac, meaning "laughter."

And antics appear in Talmud. To illustrate the teaching "All aspects of our lives are guided by the Torah," one of Rav's students hides under the great master's bed, listening to him making love to his wife. When the student is discovered, Rav yells at him, "Get out!" to which the student mildly offers, "It is a matter of Torah, and I have to learn." Elsewhere, the Talmud warns that all foul language is forbidden. However, Rav Huna bar Manoach said, "A Jew is permitted to tell [an idolater], 'Take your idol and stick it up your rear end.'"

Wordplay is also sprinkled throughout the Hebrew Bible and Talmud. The Bible alone presents more than five hundred examples. For instance, Samson fights the Philistines with "heaps and heaps" (*hamor hamortayim*) of the jawbone of an ass (*hamor*). In the Talmud, Abdan is supposed to show Rabbi Yishmael ben Rabbi Yose honor (*yekara*) but instead makes fun of his weight (*yukra*). And in another story, when Honi falls into a seventy-year sleep (*shinta*), he's covered by a mound of earth (*shunita*).

The Talmud prizes humorists too. In one tale, when Elijah the prophet is asked who in the marketplace belongs in the world to come, he points to two men who, upon inquiry, are revealed to be jesters. "We make sad people laugh. And when we see two people in a quarrel, we use humor to make peace between them."

What is more, the sages taught that humor, along with one's "cup, purse, and anger," reveal a human being's essential character. In other words, to learn the truth about the people in your life, pay attention to how they act when they're drunk, how they spend their money, what incites them to rage—and what makes them laugh.

The Clergy Comedy Connection

How's this for a reason many of the rabbis I know like to crack jokes? According to Reconstructionist Rabbinical College's David Brodsky, the Talmudic Rabbis encouraged humor while engaging in Torah study. Long before the days of Toastmasters, the sages lauded Rabbi Rava, who "before beginning his classes would say something humorous."

Studying Torah can evidently be so funny, some rabbis and cantors became professional comedians. *Mohels* (ritual circumcisers), too, are known to make cutting remarks while performing their duties. (I have been told they work for tips. Groan.) I'm not sure how many priests or ministers go from Vespers to Vegas, but among the several rabbis and cantors segueing from standing on the pulpit to doing stand-up was the trailblazing Jackie Mason. Growing up in a family of rabbis, including three of his brothers, Mason first joined the "family business" as a cantor. By age twenty-five he had also become a rabbi, but he left the synagogue three years later, explaining, "Someone in the family had to make a living." One of his rabbi-brothers deadpanned another reason: "As a rabbi, he was a joke." *People* magazine put it this way: "Mason was too much of a ham to remain a rabbi."

Recently, a trio of comedic Reform rabbis—Molly G. Kane, David Segal, and Matt Soffer—went on the road, performing their "Three Rabbis Walk into a Bar" show of stand-up, sketches, and musical comedy in clubs from New York City to Aspen, Colorado. "We believe in saving the world for our children," they say, "but not for our children's children. Children shouldn't be having children."

Then there's Modi—otherwise known as Cantor Mordechai Modi Rosenfield—one of New York City's top comedians, according to the *Hollywood Reporter.* Like many of his predecessors, he got his start in the Catskills hotels. Modi acknowledges that in his comedic line of work it's harder to find a Jewish girl to date. When he tells a non-Jewish girl he's a comic, she lights up. "But," he explains, "when I tell a Jewish girl that I'm a comic, she says, 'Is that all you do?'"

Is there some clandestine connection between being clergy and comedian? According to comedian Sarah Silverman, whose sister is a rabbi, these two vocational choices are related. "The truth is, we both kinda preach. We both take in our surroundings and try to mirror it."

Rabbi Bob Alper, another clergy-cum-comedian, has his own theory about why Jews, clergy or no, are so drawn to humor: "We Jews love language, and comedy is an art built on love of language." Comedian Marty Feldman adds, "The pen is mightier than the sword, and considerably easier to write with."

In my experience, Jews agree that interpreting, reading, debating, and talking about words is as delicious as a warm bagel, and much less fattening.

The Bad *Badchen* Theory

Theater professor Mel Gordon offers a different theory for the prevalence of Jews in modern comedy. In the seventeenth century, he says, entertainers known as *badchens* (rhymes with "Maude wins")—"ragtag insult artists known for abusive, unpleasant, and rude in-your-face repartee"—were one component of a vast performers' network in Jewish communities throughout the Ukraine and Poland. The Cossacks had launched devastating pogroms on Jewish communities, massacring tens of thousands of Jews. Theorizing that the Jewish community's wayward behavior—especially its mimicking of gentile carnivalesque practices like dancing and drinking on Purim—might be responsible for its own afflictions, the Council of Elders decided to attempt to return the Jews to God's good graces: they issued an edict outlawing performances by all types of merrymakers, including jokesters, jugglers, and showmen. *Badchens*, however, were excluded from the ban, because "they were neither funny nor popular." The result, according to Gordon, was a significant boost in hyper-aggressive jousting and obscene effrontery within the Eastern European Jewish world—which, over the generations, evolved into contemporary Jewish humor. To this day, many associate caustic humor, most often directed at members of the audience, with Jewish comics.

Perhaps no one represented this type of humorist more than "the insult comic," Don Rickles, who was famous for berating his audiences. A transcript from one of his live shows reveals just how brutal his attacks could be: "Right in the front they got *ficata* Arab over here, a boozed-up gypsy broad over there, three kids in heat over here, a German pain in the ass over here, two Japs that passed away, trick or treat hobby with the turtleneck sweater, Ma Fricket sitting over there waiting for the Pillsbury bake-off, the Spanish guy planning to attack the Mexican and two Pollacks on the end waiting for their truck to be fixed."

Oy. I'm not laughing. Two Jews, three opinions evidently applies to Jewish humor, too.

Gimme Your Monologue

Other funny Jews believe their humor grew out of a fundamental need: protection from the gentiles. As Mel Brooks notes, "If your enemy is laughing, how can he bludgeon you to death?" Or, as writer Abe Burrows remembers, "Other kids threw rocks, I made jokes." Another rabbi-turned-comedian, Simcha Weinstein, notes that the mean kids in school were less prone to beat him up when he unveiled his "hidden super power"—humor.

Years later, while attending "rabbi school" (yeshiva), Weinstein realized that he had been subconsciously tapping into a long Jewish tradition. Living in hostile environments, Jews often found that a well-placed barb could ward off violence. Throughout Jewish history "suffering inspired humor, which in turn can be used to fight oppression."

Along with turning their humor against external threats, Jews also found that directing it inward proved an effective protective measure. An oft-repeated joke encapsulates this strategy. "Goys don't need to attack us. We can do a better job ourselves." Eastern European Jews who faced bitter discrimination especially availed themselves of this type of self-directed attack, dubbed by post-Freudian psychiatrists as "psychic masochism."

Lenny Bruce exploited this type of humor in his bit about the antisemitic smear that Jews killed Christ. "Why did you kill Christ? It was one of those parties, got out of hand. We killed him because he didn't want to become a doctor."

Playing off the tainted association of Jews and money, Jack Benny employed the cheapskate shtick. When a robber sticks a gun in his face and demands, "Your money or your life," he responds, "I'm thinking. I'm thinking." And there's the joke about an elderly Jewish man who is hit by a car. The ambulance driver carefully places him on the stretcher and asks, "Are you comfortable?" "Thank God," the old man answers. "I make a good living."

Unrelenting Irreverence

Another funny-Jews theory attributes our tribal humor to Jewish irreverence. After all, piety, defined as "a belief or point of view accepted with unthinking conventional reverence," is not a particularly popular notion in a religion that encourages thinking, doubting, and even questioning everything. Including God.

Unlike creedal religions such as Christianity that demand adherence, Judaism allows—and even encourages—Divine questioning. "I believe it is not only permissible, but a religious obligation to question the existence of God," asserts Rabbi Harold Kushner. After our patriarch Jacob wrestled with God, his name was changed to Israel, and the people Israel have been wrestling with God ever since.

The stats show that Jews are awesome God wrestlers. Barely one-third say they believe in God, compared to three-fourths of Christians (2013 Pew study). According to one rabbi's 2012 survey, three-fourths of Jews don't even have a "traditional" view of God; they define God not as a celestial being, but as hope, healer, provider, or love.

Differing opinions about God should come as no surprise. As writer Marjorie Ingall notes, "We are a people who cannot agree on who has the best pastrami, so why would we agree on the notion of the Divine?"

Still, most Jews would find common ground with Henny Youngman, who quipped, "I once wanted to become an atheist but gave it up. They have no holidays."

God-Awful One-Liners

Because so many Jews feel comfortable questioning divine doctrine, the topic of God's existence has become prime material for Jewish comics. Consider the following godly one-liners.

"Not only is there no God, but try getting a plumber on
the weekends."—Woody Allen
"God isn't dead. He's just getting a second opinion."—
Milton Berle

"Oh, God, help me. If you don't, I'll ask my uncle in
New York."—Anonymous

"Dear God, you help total strangers. So why not
me?"—Anonymous

And there is the classic story of Chaim, who topples from a
mountaintop and becomes ensnarled in a tree branch. Dan-
gling above the abyss, he calls out, "Help, Help."

A great voice from above booms out, "My son, do you
have faith in Me?"

"Yes. Oh, yes, Lord," avers Chaim.

"Then let go of the branch," bellows the voice.

"What did you say?"

"Let go of the branch," repeats God.

A pause, then Chaim asks, "Is anyone else up there?"

The Jews are not only skeptical about the existence of God;
they also question God's unlimited saving power. In one Sholem
Aleichem story, Tevye calls out, "With your help, God, I nearly
starved to death."

Since Jews have license to question their own God, some Jewish comics have taken liberties with other deities, too, especially
poking fun at the majority Christian religion. Along with the
standard, "Jesus saves, Moses invests," are the following Christian jibes:

How to do you know Jesus was Jewish? He was thirty, still
living at home, and went into his father's business.
Naturally, his mother believed her son was God.

At Easter all of the downtown stores decorated their
windows. The Jewish-owned store owner joined in by
displaying bunny rabbits and colored eggs but added

the sign, "Christ Has Risen, but Horowitz's Prices Remain the Same."

A Jewish man is taken to a Catholic hospital. When asked about his living relatives, he says he only has a sister, who converted to Catholicism and became a nun. "Because she's an old maid, she couldn't be responsible for my bill." The intake nun tells him, "I'll have you know that nuns are not old maids. We are married to Jesus Christ." "In that case, send the bill to my brother-in-law."

Chutzpah Theories

Joking about God takes a lot of chutzpah, a quality never in short supply among Jews. As the Yiddish saying goes, a Jew is 28 percent fear, 2 percent sugar, and 70 percent chutzpah.

It's difficult to find an exact English translation for anyone unfamiliar with the term. "Chutzpah" has been translated as "audacity, insolence, impudence, gall, nerve, effrontery, guts, presumption, and/or arrogance." Supposedly "chutzpah" has been used 231 times in American legal opinions; whether or not these references are by or about lawyers remains unclear.

One of the best ways to describe the quality is to give examples. Guy Kawasaki, marketing manager for Steve Jobs, defined "chutzpah" as "calling up tech support to report a bug on pirated software."

Jews have so much chutzpah, they institutionalized "reverent irreverence," establishing a holiday—Purim—when Jews everywhere can mock their own religion and its leaders. At least once a year, rabbis and congregation leaders worldwide become the butt of Jewish jokes. For instance, there is this classic rabbi barb: A rabbi travels to a faraway restaurant to secretly enjoy a *treif* (nonkosher) dinner. He orders pork, and just as the waiter presents him with a pig with an apple in his mouth, several congregants approach his table. "Wow, is this a great restaurant," he tells them. "You order an apple and look how they serve it."

One classic chutzpah joke tells of a grandson playing on the beach when a huge wave sweeps him under. His horrified grandmother shrieks, "Oh God. I can't bear to live without him. Send Hymie back to me." The son miraculously washes upon land unharmed. Bubbe grabs him by the arm, brushes off the sand, and yells, "He had a hat."

Bubbe hails from a long line of *chutzpadik* Jews, starting with our biblical patriarchs. Abraham deigned to argue with God over plans to destroy Sodom and Gomorrah. Moses, too, had the audacity to demand that God save the people. David took on the giant Goliath in battle.

Why have so many Jews continued in the *chutzpadik* tradition? One theory is grounded in the Jewish cultural makeup. According to social psychologist Ryan P. Brown, societies are either honor cultures or dignity cultures. Honor cultures require members to earn their reputation (a.k.a. "cred") through acts or words. Dignity cultures, on the other hand, automatically extend respect to all societal members. Believing that all people are created in the image of God, Judaism fits the definition of a dignity culture.

According to this theory, members of dignity cultures imbibe inherent self-worth, resulting in a sense of entitlement and self-assuredness. Writer Elizabeth Gilbert calls it "the arrogance of belonging," but rather than self-absorption or egotism, it's "a good kind of arrogance." Those possessing this quality exhibit sturdy assurance and confidence. For example, the non-Jewish writer Corinna Nicolaou recalls that when she was growing up, her Jewish girlfriends, unlike her, "didn't seem uncertain about whether they deserve to be here. They took up their little bit of space in this world with a confidence I hadn't realized was possible."

Others credit the ubiquity of Jewish chutzpah to the Jews' possession of what modern-day sociologists call "human agency." A fancy way of saying "Power to the people," the term refers to the belief that an individual's or a group's action can improve a situation. Despair that nothing can relieve one's misery is the polar opposite. Judaism demands the former: Jews must "choose life"—in the broader sense, choose action over anguish. As Swedish academic and philosophy lecturer Barbara Lerner Spectre explains, a core principle of Judaism is that the world does not have to be accepted as is. When weighted down with crushing burdens—situations all too familiar to Jews—tradition demands that they keep going.

Clinging to hope over despair requires abundant heaps of optimism, another quality that Jews as a whole have never lacked. As Jewish thinker George Steiner sees it, "Jews have signed a pact with life." When this optimism is compounded with confidence, the result is one *chutzpadik* crowd of Jews.

While in the individual arena this trait can sometimes be offputting—"Who does she think she is, telling my daughter to be quiet!"—collectively, chutzpah has been "good for the Jews." And, I would add, "good for humankind." As England's former chief rabbi Lord Jonathan Sacks sees it, "Judaism begins not in wonder that the world is, but in protest that the world is not as it ought to be." Rabbi Harold S. Kushner calls it a "theology of the 'not yet,'": a demand that we see all that is wrong with the world and refuse to accept this status quo.

Starting from this position of protest, Jews believe that people—not God—must take action to address the wrongs of the world. As Pulitzer Prize–winning author Thomas L. Friedman sees it, God gives this very message to the first humans in the Garden of Eden. "From the first day of the world, God entrusted Adam to make the right decision about which fruit to eat. We are responsible for making God's presence manifest by what we do."

Many Jewish comics have sized up the absurd injustices of those in power. Jon Stewart, for one, is a master at "tendentious humor," what Freud called the use of one's wit to undermine another person's authority or idea. Nightly on *The Daily Show* Stewart (a.k.a. Jonathan Stewart Leibowitz), whom Congressman Paul Ryan called "the funniest man in America," became known for "naming what seems most ridiculous about the news." He scorned members of both political parties. Chiding the coverage of the Gore-Bush debate, he quipped, "If George Bush proved he could feed himself, that was presidential, and if Al Gore blinked, he had warmth." So popular was his brand of humor, on election night in 2000 almost as many younger viewers tuned into his show on Comedy Central as watched the results on Fox News.

Stewart's humor joined a long tradition of Jewish political satirists. Mort Sahl and Lenny Bruce, among others, also skewered the news.

In short, Judaism demands that we take action toward *tikkun olam*—healing, repairing, and transforming the world. This begins with the recognition that something needs changing.

Luckily, not just Jewish comics but all Jews appear to be good at identifying the problems. After all, isn't this what kvetching is all about?

Kvetching

In what is undoubtedly the understatement of the hour, one dictionary defines "kvetching" as "complaining, especially chronically." More precise would be constant and excessive complaining, whining, badgering, and nagging, subsiding for brief periods and then repeated. Yiddish expert and stand-up comedian Michael Wex reminds that the word "kvetch" derives from the verb "to strain," as in what you do if you haven't eaten your prunes. (See "Noshing," chapter 4, on this particular Jewish malady.)

Since the beginning, Jews have been kvetching. Wandering in the desert, they bitch at Moses, "Was it for want of graves in Egypt that you brought us to die in the wilderness?" which could roughly be translated as "No, you had to bring us to this *verstunkene* [stinky] place!" Instead of squelching their whining, Moses lets them complain. Thousands of years before the advent of classical psychology, Moses seems to have grasped that humor helps release anger.

Our own Sigmund Freud, who knew a thing or two about psychoanalysis, saw Jewish humor as a mechanism for discharging aggression and anxiety, and self-critical Jewish jokes in particular as a beneficial means of transforming pain into laughter. "I do not know whether there are many other instances of a people making fun . . . of its own character," he said of Jews and humor. One of his favorite jokes stemmed from his own embarrassment over the debts he owed friends early in his life.

A man was sued after returning a borrowed copper kettle with a big hole in it. For his defense, he claimed:

First, I never borrowed it at all.
Second, it already had a hole in it.
Third, I gave it back undamaged.

"Jewish humor is laughter through tears," says humor scholar Dr. Stephen Z. Cohen. "That, and group psychotherapy." Comic

Paul Mazursky notes, "The goyim [non-Jews] don't know how to laugh, they haven't suffered enough."

"Oppressed people tend to be witty," observed the writer Saul Bellow. Consider the joke about a Jewish comedian who is asked if Jewish humor is masochistic. "No," he answers, "and if I hear that one more time, I'm going to kill myself."

Comic Lenny Bruce attributed the prevalence of Jewish humor to the two *t*'s: "tragedy plus time equals satire." Jews have had plenty of both.

Comic Mort Sahl recounted this exchange between two men standing before a German firing squad: "Long live the Holy Land," shouts the first man. "Shah," demands the second. "Don't make trouble."

Comic Rodney Dangerfield made the point in a personal way: "I told my psychiatrist that everyone hates me. He said I was being ridiculous; everyone hasn't met me yet."

"It's hard to be a Jew," goes one of our mottos. Fortunately, when said with a heavy *krechz* (groan), such kvetching can also be funny. One Jewish juror was delighted to see herself being mimicked by her two-year-old granddaughter. Coming in from an afternoon at the park, the tyke eased herself onto the couch, put her tiny hands in her lap, sighed heavily, and said, "*Oy*. Does it feel good to sit down."

Who's Arguing?

Much of this kvetching ends up as comedic monologues, but so does another typically Jewish form of speech: arguing. As a Yiddish proverb has it: "Spare me from gentile hands and Jewish tongues."

Comedian Lewis Black credits his confrontational form of conversational rant to his Russian Jewish family. "After five minutes of yelling and screaming, my grandfather would sit back, totally satisfied, and announce, 'It's a great life.'"

It has been said that kvetching made the Yeshiva University rowing team lose its regatta race. "Maybe next time," coach Reb Moshe suggested, "we should try having six people rowing and only one shouting."

Gentiles encountering the Jewish predilection to—shall we say—vociferously discuss have had various reactions. Philosopher A. C. Grayling believes that the love of argument, combined with theology and tradition, yields the Jewish doctrine that everything can be said.

A Lutheran-born friend of mine who moved to Miami was flabbergasted the first time she overheard a group of young Jewish mothers at the playground. Arguing about the health risks of bottled versus tap water, she recalls, "They were all talking at once, yelling at each other, waving their hands. But they were also laughing. They seemed to be having great fun."

Comedian Colin Quinn quips that Jews can't stop themselves from speaking their mind and always have to have the last word. "The easiest way to lose a Jew is to say you don't want to talk about something," he warns. And the most likely response will be "Why wouldn't you want to talk about it?"

So prevalent is verbal sparring among Jews, our foundational Jewish prayer, the *Shema,* reminds us to listen. No equivalent prayer is needed to encourage us to speak.

The Talmud, too, is filled with "verbal violence" the sages inflict on each other while presenting logical arguments to make their points. Michael Wex contextualizes, "Of the 523 chapters of the Mishnah, only one is without argument about Jewish law. They only disagree 99.8 percent of the time." Writer Marjorie Ingall summarizes, "The Talmud is pretty much a bunch of dudes contradicting one another."

You're Both Right

In her joke book *Don't Mind Me and Other Jewish Lies,* humorist Esther Cohen recalls overhearing this conversation between her mother and her friend Bernie:

> "Would you like a cup of coffee?" her mother asked.
> "Don't bother," responded Bernie. Her mother immediately headed to the kitchen to put on a pot, knowing Bernie really meant, "Of course."

Some philosophers have posited that Jews excel at the ability to simultaneously hold two conflicting thoughts. Jews tend to trust that with enough talking, arguing, debating, and analyzing, the truth will emerge, even if it turns out to be the "on the one hand, yet on the other hand" variety.

Judaism supports this notion. The Rabbis teach that two forces, the *yetzer ha-tov* (good inclination) and *yetzer ha-ra* (bad inclination), dance delicately within us. The *yetzer ha-tov* in us supplies the instinct to form or create, but that's not enough; without the *yetzer ha-ra,* humans would not "marry, beget children, build a house or engage in a trade." Snoring spouses, I understand, are one of the leading causes of murderous thoughts. And anyone who has "begot" a child knows all about struggling to control their "evil inclination," especially when their crying child lurches from the grocery cart seat to grab fistfuls of candy from the impulse rack in the checkout line. And as for "building a house," the word "contractor" evokes immediate rage in every living person who has ever renovated a bathroom.

The Talmud also tells us, "Always let your left hand push away and your right hand draw you near." Many people have interpreted this to mean that, because most of us have a more powerful right hand, when we instruct children, tenderness is a more important quality than discipline. So when you next drop off your child at school, you might want to check on the right- or left-handedness of the teaching staff.

Contradictory Jewish Identity

Into the wit mix we must toss the perennial question of what it means to be Jewish. We ourselves don't know if we are a religion, a civilization, an ethnic group, a race, all or none of the above. Pity the unfortunate library catalogers who are perplexed every time a book about Jews arrives. Should it be placed in the Dewey Decimal classification 296 for Judaism or 305.8924 for Jews? According to the *Harvard Encyclopedia of American Ethnic Groups*, only the Jews, Amish, and Mormons constitute both religions and ethnic groups.

Even our stereotypes are contradictory. As author Marjorie Ingall quips, "We're leftists, but we're capitalists! We're Marxists, but we're money-grubbers!" There is the standard observation "Jews earn like Episcopalians but vote like Puerto Ricans." And Jews can wholeheartedly agree that Jews are no different from other people even as they cling to the notion that Jews are somehow special.

Ingall offers her own upbringing as an example of conflicted identity. "I grew up Conservative, went to an Orthodox day school, and married a Reform Jew. Like many Jews, I can do difference." Psychologists call these dueling doctrines cognitive dissonance, but she sees it as "magnificent fractiousness." Indeed, Judaism is one of the few religions where secular Jew is not an oxymoron, but a description for 90 percent of us.

Tel Aviv is home to a "secular yeshiva" where students learn to critique not only the Bible and Talmud, but also Israeli literature and Zionist history. Jewish writer and philosopher Alain de Botton wrote a book suggesting how nonreligious people like himself could reimagine and embrace religion.

Rabbi Joseph Telushkin tells the joke of a man who returns from traveling to a small Polish shtetl and regales his friend with all the wonders he beheld there.

> "I met a yeshiva-trained Jew who could recite the Talmud by heart. I met an atheist Jew who owned a large clothing store. I met a Jew who was an ardent Communist."
>
> "What's so strange about that?" asks his friend.
>
> "They were all the same person."

This ambiguity cost my daughter a grade in elementary school. When she was in second grade, the class was celebrating "Our Diverse Cultures," and each student was tasked to bring in food that represented a different country. The teacher assigned the countries of Italy, Puerto Rico, Cuba, and Haiti to the children whose ancestors were from those places. She assigned my daughter the country of Israel.

When Amanda explained the assignment to me, I used it as a teaching moment to discuss the difference between being Jewish and Israeli. On the day of the food festival, I sent her off with a plate of mandelbread in recognition of her cultural heritage. She presented the platter of cookies to the teacher, repeating the lesson by saying, "I'm Jewish, but I'm not from Israel." The teacher (obviously not Jewish) looked perplexed. "This has nothing to do with your religion, honey. You were supposed to bring in something from Israel, not something Jewish." Forever traumatizing my daughter, at eight years old she learned our motto: "It's hard to be a Jew."

Perhaps I should have sent her off with a bag of bagels and a shmeer, one of countless words Jewish comics brought to the English language. Terms such as shmuck, putz, chutzpah, klutz, shmooze, and shlep are now uttered from the mouths of midwestern Republican Avon ladies without the slightest recognition that they came from Jewish jokesters. And thanks to Jewish humor, countless one-liners have become integral elements of American speech:

> "Take my wife, please."—Henny Youngman
>
> "Can we talk?"—Joan Rivers
>
> "I don't get no respect."—Rodney Dangerfield
>
> "I would never belong to a club that would have me as a member."—Groucho Marx
>
> "I'm thankful for laughter except when milk comes out of my nose."—Woody Allen

Perhaps it was the milk-spewing humor that inspired Jerry Seinfield's fictional dentist to convert to Judaism in one episode of *Seinfeld*. The reason, posited Jerry: "He did it for the jokes." Evidently the dentist was destined to be a Jew. His reasoning was typically Jewish.

6

Detecting

In desperation the awning salesman flapped his arms this way and that, trying to convey to my husband and me the contours for his proposed patio enclosure. Despite his exaggerated gesturing, we weren't getting it. He tried again, this time drawing imaginary lines in the air. Still nothing. Frustrated, he dropped his arms, sighed, and contemplated another approach. That's when it hit me. "Do you mean it would look like a *huppah* [wedding canopy]?"

"Yes, exactly!" he said, raising his arm, but this time for a triumphant fist bump. But my husband didn't join in the celebratory motion. He was too stunned by my response.

"How did you know he was Jewish?"

"I don't know," was all I could say. To this day, I have no idea how I knew that the screen company representative standing on our back patio was Jewish. No mezuzah or Star of David necklace dangled on his chest. He didn't have a "typically Jewish name," and we hadn't exchanged any Jewish code words. Yet, somehow I knew I was speaking with a fellow Jew.

This was not the first time my not-born-Jewish husband was flabbergasted at my use of "Jewdar" (Jewish radar)—or, as one of my Jewish jurors calls it, "bageling." No matter what you call it, in the more than thirty years Rod and I were together, he could never discern how I did it. And I could never provide him an adequate answer, because I honestly haven't a clue. Somehow smiling and saying, "Nice to meet you," I can frequently "just tell" when my fellow hand-shaker is Jewish.

I am far from alone in my ability to sense out my own. Jewish thinker George Steiner claims Jews recognize each other "on a level that is not just that of rational reflection." On a blog post discussing this radar-like ability, one person claimed having a father who "can pick out other Jews with an accuracy approaching 100 percent. Within minutes of meeting some random person, they are talking about some JCC or synagogue."

A recent widower told me that he and his wife used to play what he called their "Was That Person Jewish Game." While heading home after a party, they would consider all the people they just met, each making a case for Jew versus not-Jew. Invariably, upon learning the religion of the guests later, it would turn out that she—not he—was right. Women's intuition, perhaps?

Most non-Jews appear to be oblivious to this surreptitious scrutiny. The non-Jewish leader of the writing critique group who read portions of this chapter commented, "I never think about someone else's religion. People are people. Why does it matter to you?"

In this chapter, I attempt to answer her question about why. Next, for my late husband's sake, I take a stab at explaining how.

Why Do I Care If You Are Jewish?

One of the most famous Jewish jokes tells of a grandson who rushes home from a Yankees baseball game to announce to his grandfather, "Zayde, Babe Ruth hit another home run today!" to which Grandpa responds, "Yes, but is it good for the Jews?" As *New York Times* columnist Stanley Fish once noted, no one ever asks, "Is it good for the white, male, Anglo-Saxon graduates of Princeton? It's always good for them." Not so much for Jews.

Remnants of Zayde's anxiety reside in many of us, despite the fact that overall things remain "good for the Jews," at least right now in America (see chapter 1, "Worrying). According to a 2014 Pew Research Center poll, Jews are viewed more positively than any other religious group. When asked to rate each group on a "feeling thermometer" from 0 to 100, Jews beat out Catholics, evangelicals, and all other religious adherents. Not surprisingly given the tenor of the times, Muslims ranked at the bottom, garnering ratings even lower than the previously most-despised population group in the country, atheists.

Despite this widespread acceptance, from the long history of Jewish persecution we know that the situation can change on a dime. If—or, for the pessimists among us, when—that happens, it's nice to be among fellow Jews who "have our backs." "All Jews are responsible for one another," commands the Talmud.

I am not naïve enough to think that all Jews would always protect me. Some might not be able to help. Some could ignore me. Others might even expose me. But my feeling of security is not based on a rational calculation. It emanates from a deep emotional level. I simply feel safer among fellow Jews.

Jewdar and Gaydar

Speaking of safety, perhaps it is no coincidence that both Jews and gays employ a mysterious sixth sense to identify members of each respective group. As columnist Jon Carroll notes in a blog post, such detection ability may have evolved among members of both groups as a survival tactic. Especially in the dating arena, misidentifying someone as gay could potentially lead to jail, torture, or even death. Likewise, for Jews, especially at certain times throughout history, confusing friend with foe could have dire consequences. The ability to sort out our own took "almost supernatural instinct," since Jews could look so different from one other and speak different languages. "Get it wrong, go to jail," said Carroll, "like Monopoly, only with real people and the Gestapo."

Feels Good

Today, in (ostensibly) safer times, discovering that you are among "your own kind" feels good. Studies have shown that engaging in acts of group cooperation can increase the levels of oxytocin, dopamine, and other pleasurable hormones in our blood. Much like using drugs, we actually get a little high from our social bonds.

Many of the Jury on Jewishness agreed that they feel different—and yes, in some situations, better—upon learning that the stranger they've just met is Jewish. "There is a shared intimacy you get being with other Jews," one juror says.

Even someone far removed from traditional Judaism can experience such an affinity. The writer Joyce Carol Oates, whose father's mother was Jewish, reported feeling a strange kinship to Franz Kafka and attributing it to her Jewish roots.

One Jewish juror says she feels especially connected to Jews she encounters while traveling. "When I was in India, I met a couple who turned out to be Jewish, and I felt an automatic bond with them. There was a feeling of specialness and safety being with them."

Another juror says it feels like being with family. "It's not that I necessarily even like them more," she explains. "Often I don't like them at all," she laughs. "But I accept them the way I would a relative."

Rejecting Racial Judaism

Her insight resonates, but I find it troubling, because referring to a family of Jews borders on a potentially perilous biologically based Judaism. Our "civilized" (quotes intentional) Western society has repeatedly demonstrated the dangers of defining Judaism as genetically inherited. As one scholar put it, "Using 'blood logic' remains repugnant to many Jews, even though the tenet of a physical Judaism lies deep in the subconscious." As Jews know all too well, one of the most fervent proponents of racial Judaism was Adolf Hitler. As Ari Feldman put it succinctly in the *Forward*, "Race is a word so slippery as to be meaningless, and the hatred it has inspired can in no way be scientifically vindicated."

Even if the term was not so precarious, race does not easily fit the amalgamation of individuals known as the Jewish people. As Judaic studies scholar Dr. Frederick Greenspahn explains, "Judaism at one point was a nationality, at another point it was a religion, at another point it was a race. All of these categories are much more fluid than we tend to think." The inaccuracy of defining a physical Judaism can be seen in the joke about the Jewish couple sitting at the kitchen table reading the newspaper:

> The wife reads aloud to her husband, "It says here that
>   Jewish women have a higher rate of breast cancer
>   than non-Jews."
> "Quick. Go convert," says her husband.

The truth is, certain genetic dispositions and diseases are more prevalent among Jews than non-Jews. According to the Jewish Genetic Disease Consortium, one out of three Ashkenazic Jews in the United States are believed to carry at least one of nineteen Jewish genetic diseases. The Tay-Sachs gene is so prevalent among Ashkenazic Jews that some rabbis were known to require that engaged couples obtain a genetic test to determine if they are possible carriers.

For ninety-nine dollars you can spit into a bottle and discover what percentage of your makeup is Ashkenazic Jew. My rabbi, Andrew Jacobs, was delighted to learn from his test that along with being 92 percent European Jewish, he's also Latin, Middle Eastern, and Norwegian.

But these results confirm only the cellular composition of your body. They can't confirm or deny that someone is truly Jewish. As genetics professor Harry Ostrer explains, the Jews are a people with a "shared genetic legacy." However, not all Jews share the same genes, nor is having a part of that legacy a requirement for being Jewish.

Besides, reducing Judaism to genetics excludes all those wonderful converts, and we dare not leave them out. Many of the "best Jews" I know didn't start out as Jews. All the Jewish jurors agree that converts are among the most active members in their synagogues, Jewish Community Centers, and local Jewish Federations. We need those dedicated, hardworking men and women (especially women) to chair the synagogue Fundraising Committee and serve on the Jewish Community Center Board of Directors. Converts also lessen the incidence of Jewish genetic diseases.

MOT

Jews by birth, Jews by choice—to me they're all MOTS, members of the tribe. To some, the word "tribe" is derogatory—problematic at best, if not outright racist—but in many ways it best describes my connection to other Jews.

Writing about his own Jewish bloodline, *Esquire*'s former editor-in-chief Lee Eisenberg defines a tribe as "a transactive memory system larger than a family." In other words, your mother and father may hold memories for you on a small scale, but your tribe helps place your life story in a longer-term historical context. For many Jews, imagining the ancestral roots of our clan connects us to those who lived before us. And, when used as a code word, MOT allows us to identify others living here and now.

"Nice to meet another MOT," I'll often say upon discovering a fellow Jew. Occasionally my reference falls flat—not because my detecting skills are diminishing; several Jews are unfamiliar with the MOT shibboleth.

The word "shibboleth," by the way, comes from a biblical story. To determine if a fugitive was truly an Ephraimite, the captive was commanded to "say *shibboleth.*" According to Judges 12:6, if he was not able to pronounce it correctly, "they would seize him and slay him." I, on the other hand, have never resorted to violence against anyone not knowing MOT. But you should practice, just in case.

My uncle once used the term at a brunch to celebrate my husband's official conversion to Judaism. Entering the house, Uncle Martin looked around and bellowed, "Rod, Rod. Where are you, you old son-of-a-gun?" Spotting Rod hunched over a trash bag in the kitchen, he sprinted over to him, slapped him on the back, and said, "So, now you're a Yid. *Mazel tov.* Welcome to the tribe."

In a theology class, I tried to describe the bond I felt for fellow Jews to my Catholic classmates. Avoiding the word "tribe," I described it as an intimate sense of kinship. Or, to be more accurate, I *tried* to explain it.

"I just get this feeling of instant camaraderie when I find out someone is Jewish," I stated. They nodded politely, said "uh-huh," but their eyes told me they didn't get it. No one did, except the Nigerian priest with limited English who sat in the back row and rarely said anything. My comment finally inspired him to speak up. "Yes, yes, I know what lady mean. In my country, we feel same."

I appreciated his comment, but having an African support me did little to assuage my unease about experiencing tribal feelings. The very word "tribal" brings to mind racist images of barbaric savages waging war on each other. Besides, in our now more-enlightened times shouldn't we love all humanity equally and leave behind outdated and dangerous preferences for one group over another? Enshrined into U.S. law at least is the notion that all people should be treated equally, regardless of "race, color, religion, sex, or national origin."

Nonetheless, I violate that law emotionally by giving Jews an extra helping of empathy. Or, as that classic *Animal Farm* quote puts it, I treat "some more equal than others." I remember reading in the newspaper that a ten-year-old boy had been killed riding his bike on a busy street. "How awful," I muttered, shaking my head and turning the page. Days later a friend mentioned, "You know that kid who got hit on his bike? Their family used to go to my synagogue."

"He's Jewish?" I felt like someone had punched me in the stomach.

Jews are far from alone in identifying more profoundly with some than others. Understanding this tendency, U.S. journalists often report global disasters with headlines such as "Thousands Killed in China Earthquake, Including Six Americans." Intellectually, U.S. citizens should mourn equally for all the lost lives, but somehow viscerally we relate more to Americans like us.

According to philosophy professor Stephen T. Asma, preferring "our own" should not necessitate an apology. Rather, he finds fruitless the suffering of those of us—especially the political left—who "writhe under a neurotic push-pull" between enjoying attachments to family and tribe and advocating for an open, fair society. To Asma these are not mutually exclusive. We can—and should—have both. Likewise, author Sebastian

Junger tried to reclaim the word "tribe" by so titling his best-selling book. Tribal affiliations serve as motivators for soldiers, he explains, and tribal feelings are key to psychological survival and the human quest for meaning.

The problem comes when we conflate being at ease with "one's own" with repudiating all others. I have heard people complain that black students frequently sit together at their own tables in high school and college dining halls. I don't think this self-selection is motivated by hostility or animus toward "whitey." Rather, from time to time they might simply prefer the comfort and camaraderie of being with their brethren (sister-ren?). My preference for chocolate ice cream is not motivated by my abhorrence of vanilla or strawberry. It just means that, all things being equal, I'll take chocolate (with lots of hot fudge, please).

But preferring our own does not give us license to ignore others. Perhaps cognizant of that tendency, the Talmud requires that Jews give *tzedakah* (charity) to both their own and others. Expounding on this idea, the Talmud established a hierarchy of giving: charity was first to go to women in one's family, then to the men in one's family, then to poor relations, then to close friends, and finally to strangers. "We must sustain the non-Jewish poor and the Jewish poor," the Rabbis demanded.

Maimonides grounded this exhortation in the Hebrew Bible, explaining that because "God is good to all," likewise Jews must give to everyone, both within and beyond the community.

Funny, You Don't Look . . .

Unlike ice-cream flavors, a person's ethnicity can't be determined simply by looking at the color, which leads me to the "how" part of finding fellow Jews. I realize that much of the "is this person Jewish" guessing is based on groundless stereotypes.

Nothing stated about "all Jews" will ever be accurate, and whatever attributes I ascribe to Jews will also be found in non-Jews.

But I still do it. And almost all of the Jewish jurors admitted that upon meeting someone they often consult an internal Jewish checklist. Psychologists have discovered what they call the "own-ethnic bias" or "own-race advantage," the ability of people in a certain ethnic or racial category to recognize faces of their own group better than those of other groups. Hispanics, for instance, can recognize Hispanic and white faces better than those of Asians and blacks; Asians can identify other Asian faces more than those of non-Asians, and so forth.

Though none of the studies I could locate specifically tested Jews, one study conducted by Israeli and Chinese investigators did compare the reactions of undergraduate students at Xuzhou Normal University in China with students attending Hebrew University in Israel. Though the students' religion was not stated, it would be safe to assume that most, if not all, of the Israeli students were Jewish. The study confirmed that the Israelis recognized other Israeli faces more than Chinese faces and vice versa. In this broader sense, it could be said that Jews harbor their "own-ethnic bias."

Visual detection can be tricky, though, because someone's Judaism is often not revealed just by looking. My own daughter missed out on landing a key role in *Fiddler on the Roof* because she didn't "look Jewish," even though she was studying for her bat mitzvah at the time. Besides, anyone who thinks Jews all share similar looks should scan the sanctuary of a Conservative, Reform, or Reconstructionist synagogue in America. I would wager they would spot people of various races and skin tones. Ashkenazic heritage may be the common default for "Jewish looks," but a sizeable proportion of American Jews are Sephardic or *Mizrachi*. So along with the usual Eastern European appearance, we must add looking Spanish or Egyptian.

According to a 2015 Pew survey, 10 percent of Jews are something other than white—4 percent Latino, 2 percent black, 2 percent Asian, and the rest some mix of racial identifications. The Institute for Jewish and Community Research estimates that about 20 percent of American Jews are "racially and ethnically diverse by birth, conversion, and adoption," many of these resulting from an estimated twenty to thirty thousand marriages between Jews and African Americans.

At my childhood shul I don't remember seeing even one non-white person, but the membership at all the synagogues I have belonged to as an adult has included "a mixture" of races. Similarly, on her first visit to a synagogue in her quest for a personal religion, writer Corinna Nicolaou was afraid, as she put it, "her freckles and stubby nose" would make it obvious she wasn't Jewish. To her surprise and that of her Jewish mother-in-law, she blended in undetected.

Interracial adoptions, especially involving children from Ethiopia and China, also contribute to the diversity of the Jewish family. Hard numbers are hard to come by, but one adoption professional estimated that as early as the year 2000 between 15 and 20 percent of children being adopted in Jewish families were Hispanic or non-white, thereby literally changing the face of the Jewish community. So common is diversity, the Jewish Multiracial Network was formed to empower and support Jews of color and multiracial families.

Jews are now such a "mixed multitude," even our religious leaders hail from diverse backgrounds. Rabbi Alysa Stanton, ordained as the first African American rabbi in 2009 by the Hebrew Union College–Jewish Institute of Religion (HUC-JIR), served the majority-white Congregation Bayt Shalom in

Greenville, North Carolina, from 2009 to 2011. Explaining her journey from being raised in a Pentecostal family to becoming a Jew, she says, "I was born Jewish, but not in a Jewish womb."

Rabbi Angela Warnick Buchdahl, senior rabbi of Central Synagogue in New York City and acclaimed as one of *Newsweek*'s "50 Most Influential Rabbis," has a Jewish father and a Korean Buddhist mother. She believes that "ultimately Judaism cannot be about race, but must be a way of walking in this world."

Ethiopian-born Rabbi Dr. Sharon Shalom is spiritual leader of Congregation Kedoshei Yisrael in Kiryat Gat, Israel, and author of *From Sinai to Ethiopia: The Halachic and Conceptual World of Ethiopian Jewry*. He says, "Uniqueness is not the opposite of unity, but rather its synonym."

In Israel the notion of "looking Jewish" has become almost nonsensical, given the significant numbers of not only Ethiopian Jews but also Yemenite, Iraqi, and Uzbeki Jews. Among the country's well-known Ethiopian Jews are Yityish Titi Aynaw, who was Miss Israel in 2013; the Olympic runners Ageze Guadie and Zohar Zemiro; and former Knesset members Adisu Massala and Aleli Admasu, who represented the Labor and Likud parties, respectively.

One need only glance at the stunning photos in Frederic Brenner's 2003 coffee-table book *Diaspora* to see that there is no one way of "looking Jewish." After photographing Jews in such remote places as Gibraltar, Istanbul, and Bukhara, Brenner admitted, "The more Jews I met, the less I understood what a Jew looked like."

If all this isn't enough to demonstrate the variety pack of MOTS, some born-Jews have physical features traditionally associated with non-Jews. Hitler was forced to abort an effort to catalog "Aryan-looking" children in German schools because too many Jewish children qualified for the list. After the war it was revealed that several of the models held up as "pinnacles of Aryan looks" were, in fact, Jewish, as was the winner of the "most perfect Aryan child contest." I know a Jewish man whose grandfather looked so "goyish" (non-Jewish) as a child he was hired as a *Shabbos goy*, a role forbidden to Jews.

My own mother is a blue-eyed blonde, and we have a Jewish red-headed, pale-complexioned first cousin. My brother, on the other hand, is "swarthy" enough to be mistaken for an Italian, which he put to use as a teenager to pick up non-Jewish girls. Aided by a necklace with a Jewish star on one side and Saint Christopher on the other, he would reverse the pendant depending on the religion of his romantic target.

Nonetheless many pernicious stereotypes about what Jews look like still persist. Two Jewish jurors reported being traumatized when non-Jews they met seriously asked to see their horns. This canard is rooted in a biblical misinterpretation: the *karan* (beams) emanating from Moses's face was translated as *keren*, meaning "horns"—which explains the interesting hairdo sporting Michelangelo's *Moses* statue.

"The Jewish look—our noses, our hair, our shape, our coloring—has always haunted us," says writer and social anthropologist Lisa Schiffman. "Are we people of the book or people of the body?" What, then, does a stereotypical Jew look like?

Jewish women are most often associated with two specific physical attributes: "Jewish hair," meaning dark, curly, frequently frizzy locks; and "Jewish breasts," supposedly oversized. Hmmm—on both counts, better rule me out as an MOT.

Jewish men's physical attributes, as defined by non-Jews, have been decidedly not as benign. German antisemitic theories described the allegedly Jewish male body as "unathletic, bookish, ruined by excessive study." Internalizing a similar stereotype, many Jews in the early Zionist movement rebelled against the image of the pale, weak, studious Jew. They were determined to give birth to a new type of Jew in the Jewish homeland: the tough, strong, muscular man (and woman) who would work the fields and fight for their rights. Think Paul Newman as Ari Ben Canaan in *Exodus.*

Speaking of manly men, the most obvious Jewish detection device has been his nether region. According to a 2007 World Health Organization estimate, Jews are among the 30 percent of men in the world who are circumcised. Interestingly, most of the world cultures that circumcise male members' members are found in hot, arid, and/or sandy environments, leading to the theory that irritation caused by *shvitz* and *shmutz* (sweat and dirt) may at least partially explain the practice. Circumcision, in fact, was one of the first prehistoric surgical procedures known to man, along with trephining, which bore a hole in a person's skull to alleviate headaches. Thank goodness for modern Excedrin.

Identifying a circumcised male obviously required uncovering his nakedness. How this was handled varied in time and place. In ancient Greece, which forbade Jewish men from competing in the gymnasia, detecting a Jew was fairly easy, as games were performed in the nude. Therefore, according to the book *Jewish Jocks,* Jewish men who were bent on participating hid the physical mark of their Judaism by "crumpl[ing] their penises into their foreskins and hold[ing] them in place with sutures." Ouch.

The book of Maccabees recounts an even more painful practice Judean males endured: an epispasm, or "reverse circumcision." Also called "foreskin restoration," the procedure was performed either surgically or by stretching the residual penis skin (double ouch). Even so, during times of persecution, including the Nazi era, Jewish men subjected themselves to the painful ordeal to save their and their families' lives. Whoever said Jewish men aren't tough?

Can we now move on to the most common anatomical appendage used to sniff out Jews through the centuries? Derogatory depictions of elongated noses have appeared in literature since the twelfth century, when a crucifixion scene depicted a supposedly Jewish figure with a hooked nose. A 1996 Jewish Museum exhibit, "Too Jewish: Challenging Traditional Identities," however, debunked that long-held, long-nose stereotype. On display were artist Dennis Kardon's *Jewish Noses* sculptures, life-size casts of Jewish noses. As art critic Michael Kimmelman observed, "They were all different, which is to say, of course, that there is no 'Jewish' nose."

Other physical stereotypes took hold as well. The alleged "Jewish foot"—supposedly deformed and cloven—was believed to prove the association between Jews and the devil. One 1876 anthropological study conducted on Poles, Ukrainians, and Jews "proved" that Jews had narrower chests than the population at large. In World War I Germany, flat feet, along with a purported distinctive gait, were supposed "peculiarities" common among Jews. Shorter arms than normal, as well as diminutive legs, were said to cause Jews to limp. Though highly offensive, these stereotypes ironically saved the lives of European Jewish men during the First World War by rendering them unfit for military service.

Tattling Tattoos

At one time, seeing a tattoo would have strongly indicated that the person sporting it wasn't Jewish, but no longer. Quite the opposite, as Ron Dicker explains in his *Haaretz* article "Jews with Tattoos": "The use of body art to express a connection with Judaism began on the fringe but is now moving toward the mainstream."

Many Jews have long assumed their religion forbids any form of body art. However, as Bible professor Nili S. Fox explains, the matter has always been more mottled than a black-and-white prohibition. While the Hebrew Bible does demand, "You shall not make gashes in your flesh for the dead, or incise any marks on yourselves," several biblical figures were "marked" in the Bible, starting with Cain. Furthermore, evidence suggests the practice was more prevalent in ancient times than many realize.

Nonetheless, in more recent times, most Jews came to believe that body art was forbidden and anyone possessing a tattoo would be banned from a Jewish cemetery. However, it turns out this widely repeated restriction is a *bubbe meise* (old wives' tale). "Nothing in Jewish law prohibits a tattooed person from being interred in a Jewish cemetery," explains Orthodox rabbi Chani Benjaminson.

Rather, most religious Jews oppose tattoos because of the Jewish principle of *b'tzelem Elohim*, meaning that we humans are made "in God's image." Because Judaism views the body as a holy, God-given instrument, altering one's body through permanent markings can be seen as an affront to God.

More secular Jewish (and non-Jewish) mothers oppose their children's body ink for a more practical reason: they fear the kids will come to regret it. And in many cases they are right. Supposedly the most frequent request of tattoo artists is to remove an ex-lover's name.

For Jews as well, tattoos are also tainted with the memory of concentration camp victims being forcibly inked with identification numbers. "I would never do that to my father," says one Jewish juror, the daughter of a Holocaust survivor.

Yet some younger Jews are reclaiming the tattoo specifically to memorialize relatives who endured the Holocaust. Joseph Metz, for one, had his grandfather's six-digit Holocaust number inscribed on his own wrist to honor his grandpa's memory. "What was done to him in hate, I do in love," he explains.

Metz is also continuing his grandfather's educational mission of visiting Mississippi high schools to educate students about what happened. "That is why I have this tattoo," he says. "We must never forget."

And other young Jews are using tattooing to otherwise express their Jewishness. One Jewish juror reported that her son was the only member of his Taglit-Birthright Israel delegation who returned from Israel *without* a new tattoo. Most had chosen artwork featuring Jewish images, such as a Star of David or a menorah.

Even one rabbi, Marshal Klaven, spiritual leader of Congregation B'nai Israel in Galveston, Texas, first began inking his body at age sixteen, when he returned from Israel. "I decided to avow my place among my people by tattooing a small Star of David . . . on my left ankle," he explains. At twenty he inscribed a Tree of Life and Torah on his back, because "I wanted to hold fast to my Jewish roots." Since then, Rabbi Klaven has been traveling the country, enlightening Jews about the history and permissibility of the art form within Judaism.

Intellectually, I respect the decisions Jews make to ink their bodies. But I must admit that if I belonged to Rabbi Klaven's synagogue, seeing his tattooed arm cradling the Torah would take some getting used to. Besides the disgust tattoos evoke in me, I just can't disassociate the wearers from Hell's Angels biker dudes. To me, tattooing, like excessive drinking, is "what the goyim do."

Jewish Clothing

Beyond the physical body, historically you could immediately identify a Jew from his or her outer garments. In ancient times, anyone wearing a fabric combining wool and linen would be excluded because the Torah forbids mixing those elements, as it does combining meat and milk. However, I'm not sure if one could discern such a fabric from a distance, so the look of one's tunic might not have been a useful ancient form of Jewdar.

The Talmudic Rabbis also disallowed anyone to dress in "a neglected fashion," whatever that meant. One rabbi explains it to mean that when traveling to a place where he is unknown, "I make myself distinguished through the clothes I wear." Elsewhere the Talmud recommends wearing a nice outfit on the Sabbath. "Your Shabbat clothes should not be the same as your weekday clothes."

But Jews were not to go overboard and get too *fapitzed* (dressed up) either. During the fifteenth century, Jews in the Italian town of Forli promulgated a dress code for themselves requiring them to "walk modestly before our God, and not show off in the presence of the Gentiles."

Unfortunately, periodically throughout history Jews were forced to display identifying markers on their clothing. In 1394, Jews living in the Venice ghetto were required to wear a yellow badge, which was changed to a yellow hat in 1496, and then became a red hat in 1500. (I wonder if a subliminal memory remains in me. I sometimes feel uncomfortable surrounded by members of the Red Hat Society.)

As Jews are painfully aware, in 1939 the visible identifier of Jews became the mandatory yellow star, which the Nazis required be worn by Jews throughout Germany and all newly conquered lands. The badges varied from region to region but were usually black and yellow with a six-pointed star.

Today Orthodox Jews can still be spotted through their clothing: a man's yarmulke (head cap) or hat and tzitzit (fringes), and a woman's long sleeves, below-the-knee skirts, and head covering. Jews who are more in the know can discern specific Hasidic sects from the style of hat or head-scarf color. Two women at my gym *shvitz* (sweat) their way through lunges and crunches wearing stretch pants under their gym skirts and wrist-length shirts under T-shirts. *Oy*. I get overheated just thinking of it.

Lilith magazine ran a 2014 story entitled "Should a Jewish Girl War a Dirndl?" examining the ethics of a Jew donning the German *volk*-style skirt that was popular in Nazi Germany. Jews were actually banned from wearing them in Austria in 1938, so a case can be made that Jews should defiantly adorn themselves with them now—or they should banish the thought of ever putting one on (see chapter 5, "Laughing," on Jewish contradictions and humor).

In my mother's generation, Jewish women favored a certain type of matching blouse and slacks. I considered tailored, preppy clothes as quintessentially not Jewish. My non-Jewish sister-in-law favored shopping at Talbot's, outfitting herself in a classic look that never seemed right for me.

Even the time of year one shops for new clothes can reveal a Jew. Right before the High Holidays, Jews are often found looking for new outfits for the kids. As far back as the 1930s, Jews would purchase new suits and dresses for the occasion. Many Jewish jurors remember religious services as fashion shows, or worse: a competitive version of "keeping up with the Rachels."

A family purchasing new clothes in the springtime, however, might reveal them as not Jewish. While Christians purchase Easter outfits, most of the Jews I know don't buy a new outfit for Passover. Perhaps because the seder is home-based, the pressure is off to show off the new outfit to others.

Jewelry can also be a Jewish versus goyish giveaway, but not always. On his fifth trip to Graceland (don't ask, he warns), writer Rich Cohen spotted a *chai* (stylized Hebrew letters *cheit* and *yud*) hanging from a gold chain among Elvis's fancy jewelry. "Yes, Elvis wore the *chai*," said the tour docent, "to celebrate his Jewish heritage." Supposedly, Elvis had a Jewish ancestor and delighted in the image's representation of the word "life."

Unlike Elvis, some men and women display *chai* jewelry without realizing its Jewish symbolism. As Cohen notes, to the untrained eye, the two intertwining Hebrew letters "can look like a soccer player and the ball the player is about to head." Perhaps sports enthusiasts wear it for good luck on the field, along with the life-affirming sentiment (it couldn't hurt).

Along with *chai* necklaces, many Jewish women are partial to Star of David necklaces, or so was the assumption of a huge proportion of bat mitzvah gift givers, judging from the presents my daughter received for her coming-of-age ceremony. In touring a typically Jewish home in search of Jewish artifacts, religious studies professor Vanessa L. Ochs counted sixteen different Jewish stars in one woman's jewelry box. From her bat mitzvah, my daughter could best that.

Jewish women also wear jewelry featuring the *hamsa* symbol—an eye embedded in the palm of an open hand, said (among other things) to imbue divine beneficence of goodness, abundance, luck, and good health. Many Jews view it as an exclusively Jewish emblem, the five fingers representing the five books of the Torah, the hand imagined as that of Moses's sister Miriam, and the eye associated with the wearer's protection from the evil eye. However, scholars note that the *hamsa* (also called *hamesh, chamsa,* and *khamsa*) has been used throughout history as a Christian, Islamic, and pagan fertility symbol. To Muslims, for example, the five fingers represent the Five Pillars of Islam, and the hand is imagined as that of Muhammad's daughter Fatima.

Hadassah and B'nai B'rith pins (round lapel buttons with the respective organization's logo) and golden lions representing the Lion of Judah organization also adorn the blouses of Jewish women of a certain age, silently broadcasting not just their religion, but also the generosity and service of the wearer. Or, as one Lion of Judah jewelry ad puts it, "There's nothing like being in the same room with hundreds of like-minded women who 'roar.'"

Along with Jewish-themed jewelry, many Jews (like others) have a fondness for gold and gemstone jewelry. But for Jews the accessories are associated with a long history. Precious stones are easily smuggled, which made them attractive contraband for fleeing Jews (see chapter 1, "Worrying"). In medieval times various European Jewish communities enacted laws to curtail public Jewish display of riches. For instance, the Cracow Jewish community limited themselves to two rings on weekdays, four on the Sabbath, and six on the Jewish holidays.

Fast-forward to the present day, when the joke is told about the Jewish woman who insists her portrait include her wearing nonexistent jewels. When asked why, she replies, "So my husband's next wife will go crazy looking for them."

Thanks to technology, we now have one additional source for detecting fellow Jews: cell phone covers. These ever-present devices can proclaim that we are an MOT every time we put phone to ear. "Member of the Tribe" is just one of several Jewish-themed phone cover statements available. For $19.99, your phone can proclaim, "Shmutz Happens" (*shmutz* = dirt), "Chai. How Are You?," "Don't Kvetch," or "Keep Calm. Daven On" (*daven* meaning "to pray").

Those of us who don't purchase one of these proclamations may still be detected as Jews through our phones—specifically by what we say and how we say it.

Nu? Are You Kvelling with *Nachas?*

"Jews wear their identities on their tongues," concluded a 2009 HUC-JIR study of the American Jewish language. With acute listening, you will be able to discern the use of certain words and how those words are put together.

The use of Yiddish terms will usually—though not always—reveal the speaker's Jewishness. According to the aforementioned study, the most common Yiddish terms American Jews of all ages utter include *kvetch* (complain), *shmutz* (dirt), *mazel tov* (congratulations), and *mensch* (good person). Those over sixty-five, but not their kids, use *heimish* (homey), *nu* (so), *nachas* (pride), *macher* (important person), and *bashert* (predestined match).

Mishegoss (craziness) and *shmatte* (rag) are among my favorite Yiddishisms. I wish English had an equivalent to *machetunim*, the term describing one's in-laws' relationships, as in "I'm invited to my *machetunim*'s house for Easter. Is it okay to bring a brisket?"

Shmoozing and *kibitzing* can laxly be translated as "chatting," but that doesn't convey the subtlety of either term. *Shmoozing*, for example, can mean talking someone up to make a sale, and a *kibitzer* has been defined as "someone who gives advice and commentary when you are trying to work."

Jews can also identify each other through their secret code number, eighteen, which stands for *chai* (life) or thirty-six, double *chai*. I often purchase gift cards in these amounts, watching for the reaction of the store clerk. If they respond with a puzzled look when I state the denomination, I know they are not MOTS. I am delighted when they look up from the cash register and say, "*Chai*, right?"

Talking with Our Hands

Gestures made while speaking also provide clues to a person's Jewishness. As the owner of Jack Cooper's Jewish deli observed, "You get people speaking, eating, gesturing simultaneously. If [Jews] could talk with their feet, they'd do that, too."

Still, Jews are far from the only ones who use and identify each other through gesturing. Linguists have verified that different cultures use distinctive hand movements during conversation. One early study found that nonethnic Americans gestured by mainly using the hand and wrist, Italians tended to gesture using the whole arm, and Jews used the lower half of the arm only. Though inconclusive, some scholars believe that using gestures may help speakers with an unusually large vocabulary retrieve forgotten words. Thus the corroborated association of Jews and gesturing is something else for us to kvell about. (See chapter 2 for more.)

Perhaps it was "Jewish gesturing" that helped me one day in identifying Jews on television while channel surfing. Flicking from station to station, I came upon the scene of people gaily talking and laughing, gathered at what appeared to be a nondescript community center recreational room. The television was on mute, so no auditory clues were at hand, yet I knew in an instant that they were Jews. Punching the sound on, I discovered that I was watching a scene from an Israeli kibbutz.

Sounding like a Jew

Along with "reading" their hand movements, another method for recognizing fellow Jews is through their animated conversation. While many ethnic groups communicate with spirited interchanges, as one Jewish Juror puts it, there seems to be something "almost over the top" about the way Jews talk. Sitting quietly, hands folded demurely in the lap would not be the typical posture of a Jewish conversationalist. The Jewish actress Rachel Weisz, who played a Jewish character in the movie *Denial*, calls her accent Jewish Queens, "a kind of call-and-response, Talmudic thing."

Evidently, Jewish children learn this verbal speaking style at a very young age. As a drama teacher at a children's theater, my daughter frequently directs children who are appearing on stage for the first time. Because the theater is in the Oakland, California, area, these young performers represent a variety of racial and ethnic groups, and she has noticed a differing population pattern. "I'm constantly telling the Asian kids, especially the girls, 'Speak Up. Speak Up. We can't hear you.' I never have to say that to the Jewish kids."

The Asian girls may be demonstrating what writer Eric Liu has called "Chinese one-downmanship," where each one tries to minimize her own accomplishments. Definitely not Jewish.

Not everyone appreciates the typically Jewish speaking style, however. The 2009 HUC-JIR study of more than twenty-five thousand English-speaking Jews and almost five thousand non-Jews living in America found that almost half of Jews have been told their speaking style is "too aggressive"; just one-third of non-Jews were similarly advised. Furthermore, one out of three American Jews—compared to fewer than 15 percent of non-Jews—have been informed they sound like they're from New York. Even one-fourth of Jews like me who have never lived in the Big Apple—compared to 11 percent of non-Apple-residing non-Jews—have been mistaken for New York natives. Jews and New York are so closely associated, a reference to that place can stand in for Jewish, as in "New York bagels" or, less innocuously, "New York values."

Despite my midwestern roots, people assume I am a native New Yorker because I speak quickly. According to linguist Deborah Tannen, compared to other ethnic groups, Jews do tend to talk more quickly, take fewer pauses, and interrupt more often. They also engage in what academics call "high-involvement cooperative overlapping," which basically means talking over someone. Jews, though, don't see it as interrupting, but rather as expressing interest in what the speaker is saying.

Sarcasm is yet another speech technique Jews use to great effect—perhaps because this type of speech is prevalent in Yiddish. Moreover, humorist and Yiddish maven Leo Rosten notes that the Yiddish language also conveys nuances of "disbelief, skepticism, ridicule, and scorn." For instance, consider his following examples of typically Yiddish speech:

> Smart, he isn't.
> Already you're discouraged?
> He only tried to shoot himself.

Jewish writer Sophia-Marie Unterman evidently employed this form of speech without realizing it. When she moved to a non-Jewish part of the country, the midwesterners she met were baffled by her speaking style, and her non-Jewish southern boyfriend demanded to know, "Why do you always say the opposite of what you mean?"

Jewish Geography

Determining one's place of origin is another tool Jews use to detect fellow Jews. Being born in New York City can be indicative, because at 10.5 percent Jewish, it tops the list of U.S. cities with the highest percentage of Jews. The Miami–Fort Lauderdale–Palm Beach area, however, is gaining on it, with 9.5 percent. As one joke has it, "There comes a time in every Jewish person's life when they must ask that vital question: Should I move to the Holy Land? Meaning Florida, of course."

But not all Jews are journeying South. The four states with the largest Jewish populations remain New York, California, Pennsylvania, and New Jersey.

In general, American Jews avoid living in the sparsely populated areas of the country, perhaps fearing that all you could get to eat there was a ham and cheese sandwich. Only 4 percent of American Jews reside in rural areas, and those who do probably ended up there because their family owned the local dry goods store or because they were back-to-the-land hippies. The state of South Dakota didn't even have a rabbi from 1982 until 2017, when a Chabad House finally opened in Sioux Falls.

Lenny Bruce once quipped, "If you live in Butte, Montana, you're going to be goyish even if you're Jewish." Shortly after I met Rod I was offered an exceptional job opportunity in Moundsville, West Virginia, a similarly *goyishe*-majority locale. I considered accepting for a full ten minutes—the amount of time it took for me to look up the percentage of Jews in the area. When I later told Rod I had turned down the offer, he was aghast. "It would have been a tremendous career move. Why did you tell them no?"

"Because I'm Jewish," I said to my then bewildered boyfriend.

"But you're not that religious," he replied.

Of course he thousght I was being illogical. He wasn't born Jewish.

Nor did he understand the joy I felt after we were married when a job change—his this time—required us to relocate to Sharon, Massachusetts, a heavily Jewish area outside of Boston. When I first saw one of the local gas stations at Christmastime I was elated. Of the four plate-glass windows across the front of the mini-mart, three displayed frost-painted Hanukkah greetings with menorahs, dreidels, and Stars of David. Only the fourth one at the end perfunctorily announced "Merry Christmas" in tiny letters. How different this was from my native Kansas City. When I grew up in the 1950s, Hanukkah didn't even rate a mention, let alone three-fourths of a gas-station greeting.

Several explanations have been suggested for why Jews prefer dense urban to sparse rural locations. There is our ever-present anxiety about expulsion (see chapter 1, "Worrying"). As writer Thomas Friedman noted, for Jews of his (and my) generation, our parents and grandparents always felt tense at home in America. For them, life was "a suitcase with a false bottom, so you should never get too comfortable." Having other Jews nearby also helped ease their skittishness.

And some Jews may feel more comfortable around other urban dwellers because of what psychologists call the place-personality theory: often we choose to live near others who think and act in similar ways. University of Cambridge social psychologist Jason Rentfrow discovered that personality types tend to be clustered geographically. At least according to his research, Utah's residents have the most agreeable and least neurotic personalities; New York's residents are the most disagreeable. (I do wonder how many Jews he asked; otherwise he might have gotten very different results.) On the positive side, residents of the Big Apple, along with those living in California and Washington DC, were found to be most open, which the study defined as individuals with the personality traits of curiosity and creativity.

Ironically, many Jews report they feel most Jewish when they leave their Jewish-heavy environments. As one Jewish juror explained, it was not until she left New York that she discovered "not all delis have matzah ball soup. Some places don't even have delis." Writer Thisbe Nissen was similarly surprised that outside of New York "not everyone celebrates Rosh Hashanah and Yom Kippur and not all boys are circumcised." Another native New Jersey juror didn't realize the world even included Protestants. "In my hometown, you were either Jewish, Italian, or visiting."

What Kind of a Name Is That?

Along with where we hail from, our names can also reveal who is and is not Jewish. Academics have even devised a technique, called the "Distinctive Jewish Names" or DJN method, a list of predetermined names to help identify the Jews for statistical analysis.

As an intermarried Jew, I realize the stupidity of using last names to identify fellow coreligionists, but I (and most of us Jews) still do so. That's one of the reasons I adopted my maiden name, Kalikow, as my middle name after marriage; Maxwell alone sounded too goyish. Kalikow, to be sure, is not instantly recognizable as a Jewish name, but the final "w" is a clue that the name bearer might be Jewish. Think Gwenyth Paltrow or National Public Radio *Science Friday* host Ira Flatow.

The ability to determine Jewish names is second nature for me but must be learned by those not raised in the religion. When we were dating, my husband-to-be recognized that names ending in the "five standard suffixes"—berg, baum, man, stein, witz—were usually Jewish, but beyond that he could never tell. During our courtship, I tried to provide him with guiding principles. For instance, a name ending in "man" with one *n* usually is, but "mann" with two *n*'s usually isn't. Names ending with "Jr.," "Sr.," or Roman numerals such as II or III are likely not to be found among Ashkenazic Jews, who traditionally refrain from naming children after living relatives. However, Sephardic Jews do, so ignore that rule for them.

Sephardic Jews, I understand, can detect fellow Jews through certain last names. Conversos and crypto-Jews, who converted to Catholicism under duress or hid their Jewish roots, also carry identifiable surnames to those in the know. In these arenas I duly concede my lack of knowledge and detection skill.

First names have also provided us Jewish name detectives with ethnic clues. Not too many Jews name their little boy bundles Jesus or Christopher. I used to think Mary was avoided for females, but I have met several Jews either with that name or its variations such as Marie or Maria, derived from the Hebrew name Miriam. A Jewish friend of mine named her daughter Angela over the protestations of both her parents and in-laws. She tried to convince them of the Jewish origins of angels; they kept telling her, "But people will think she's Catholic."

During the Holocaust the Nazis ordered all Jews to take middle names, Sara for women and Israel for men, which may explain why the post-Holocaust generation opted for nondenominational-sounding names for their children, such as Marianne, Lauren, Ken, and Doug. As writer Lisa Schiffman notes, that generation in turn gave their children names such as Zachary, Samuel, and Elijah. As the humor writer Michael Krasny tells the joke, a man introduces his son to a stranger: "His name is Shlomo." "What kind of a name is that?" the stranger asks. "He's named after his dead grandfather, Scott."

It's not just Jews who were choosing biblical names for their offspring. According to BabyNet.com columnist Julie Andrews, biblical names used to be quite common, "but then we sort of went away from that and into this trend of really being creative, trying to win the competition for most original and even inventing names."

More recently, though, parents—both Jewish and not—are returning to history and tradition. Jewish parents, Andrews says, are finding a lot of comfort in giving newborns Hebrew or Jewishly associated names. The aforementioned actress Gwyneth Paltrow named her second child Moses. According to what *Forward* writer Lisa Keys called her "unscientific but weekend-killing" survey of Jewish baby names undertaken in 2001, Jews give their children "Jewish" names (biblical, Yiddish, Modern Hebrew, or "sounds like your grandparents'" names) 59 percent of the time and "American" names (Samantha, Emily, Tyler, Ryan) the remaining 41 percent. Though the exact monikers change from year to year, as I write among the most popular names for Jewish boys are Ezra, Asher, Levi, Elijah, and Caleb. Jewish girls are being dubbed Ava, Elizabeth, Sadie, Maya, and Charlotte (the last the choice for Chelsea Clinton's baby).

Surprisingly, Harvard University sociologist Stanley Lieberson, who studies trends in American baby naming, found that the resurgence in biblical names has nothing to do with a resurgence of religion. "People who use Old Testament names are, if anything, less religious in their behavior than those who don't," he says.

No matter what name they choose, many Jews still hope their kids' names will someday have an MD after them, which leads to the next detection device.

Jewish Jobs

What a person does or doesn't do is also a major clue to detecting Jews. Doctors, lawyers, accountants—these are just a few of the most Jewishly prevalent and prestigious professions, as is apparent in the joke about a *bubbe* with two grandchildren in tow who runs into an old friend at the grocery store.

> "Oh, are those your grandkids?" asks the friend. "How old are they?'
> "The doctor is three. The lawyer is two."

For Jews of a certain age, those were the career choices par excellence.

For a more updated observation, Andrew Lustig's viral video poem "I Am Jewish" includes the following stanza: "I am asked if my dad's a lawyer. I say 'no . . . my mom is . . . my dad's an accountant."

Jews do indeed pursue these and certain other professions more than others. Five percent of American Jews are doctors or lawyers, compared to fewer than 1 percent of all Americans When she was growing up, one Jewish juror was repeatedly counseled by her mother to strive to marry a Jewish dermatologist—a good Jewish doctor who wouldn't be called in for emergencies on nights and weekends. Accounting continues to be such a Jewish-heavy profession, one joke defines a Jewish CPA as someone who can't stand the sight of blood and stutters.

Evidently, Jews bring not just quantity, but perceived quality to these positions. Two jurors reported that they—and many of their non-Jewish girlfriends—seek out doctors who are Jewish (or at least have Jewish-sounding names). A Jewish attorney I know repeatedly receives queries from potential clients—"You are Jewish, aren't you?"—and assures them he is as they sign the retainer.

Moreover, Jews also tend to become professionals of all kinds. According to a 2007 study, more than half of Jewish men and women hold professional positions, compared to one-quarter of the general population. And another 40 percent of Jews are classified as holding "other professions."

The preponderance of "Jewish professionals/professions" is nothing new. Some scholars attribute this career concentration to Judaism's historical emphasis on literacy. After the Jerusalem Temple was destroyed in 70 CE, the Rabbinic form of Judaism that emerged to replace Temple-based sacrifices required reading, a skill lacking among most people in the world at the time. Literacy, combined with expulsions and restrictions prohibiting Jews from entering certain guilds, crafts, and fields, led Jews to become traders, bankers, lawyers, and doctors—vocations that continue to draw Jews in modern times.

Other occupations traditionally pursued by Jews can be traced to their origins as peddlers, historian Hasia R. Diner explains. Owners of dry goods stores, textile factories, and warehouses grew naturally out of Jews' long-distance selling. Scrap businesses, money lending, movie theaters, and photography studios were also common establishments opened by nineteenth-century former-peddling Jews. Of course, they went into the wholesale business. As one joke has it, what do you get when you cross Arnold Schwarzenegger with a Jew? "Conan the Distributor."

Along with these historical explanations, sometimes occupational choices are subtly influenced by Jewish background. I am a perfect example of this, having become a librarian without realizing until much later the Jewish underpinnings of my profession. Obviously, both librarianship and Judaism revere books. "Turn it and turn it for everything is in it," a saying from the Talmud, could mean that anything you need to know is in there—be it a sacred text or a library book. Opening the ark and bringing out the Torah at services could even be seen as a ritualized book checkout. And since the Torah scroll includes the Five Books of Moses, parading it among the congregation could be considered the world's first bookmobile.

The preponderance of Jews in psychotherapy (on both sides of the tissue box, claims a *Lilith* magazine article) has led to speculation that there may be much about the profession that is typically Jewish. Susan Schnur, both a rabbi and clinical psychologist, believes the Jewish tradition of studying in pairs (*havruta*) may have something to do with it. And let's not forget who originated the entire field. Perhaps, says Schnur, "Freud is a secular Rashi."

Jews are also twice as likely to become teachers than other Americans. Journalism is another attractive vocation for MOTs, though the exact number of Jewish journalists is debatable and potentially controversial in light of antisemitic claims of excessive media influence. According to the *Encyclopaedia Judaica,* Jews have played a major role in journalism since the profession's earliest days, serving not only as reporters, but also as publishers, editors, and columnists. Jews are closely associated with reading and writing (see chapter 7, "Dwelling"), and again we are People of the Book, so it is not surprising that Jews would be drawn to these fields. Moreover, as non-Jewish reporter Jorge Ramos explains, the profession of journalism "is based upon questioning everything," a very Jewish trait (see the conclusion to this book).

Theater is so heavily Jewish it even inspired the hit musical *Spamalot* to claim that you can't put on a Broadway show if you don't have any Jews. My daughter, who has been a "theater geek" since elementary school, just assumed up until adulthood that most people in the world were either Jewish or gay, because almost everyone involved in musical theater was one or the other (or both). Comedian Amy Poehler jokes that when she gives her fantasy award acceptance speech she will thank "her Jewish agents, managers, surgeons, ob-gyns, trainers, and neighbors, and every producer and writer I have ever worked with."

You Do What for a Living?

Jews, however, are not known as big farmers—at least not until Israel's establishment turned this stereotype on its head. Still, in the United States, farming is not favored by MOTs. According to the 2009 Jewish employment study, the number of American Jews in farming in 2000 was 0.22 percent, growing from the 1990 figure of, yes, 0.00 percent.

Dr. Ira Sheskin, an expert on Jewish demographics, notes that many rural, agrarian areas are devoid of Jews—dating back, he believes, to prohibition against Jews owning land in many eras and places. Because Jews were cognizant that they could be expelled at any time, they also tended not to invest in real estate.

Jews are also not known for occupations that involve working with machinery. One Jewish juror admits she was attracted to her husband because he was the first Jewish man she'd ever met who owned an electric screwdriver. My late husband was a whiz at home repairs and even made his own furniture, proof positive to me that he was born a Protestant.

Jewish workers, especially men, tend to avoid construction jobs. Almost 20 percent of American men are employed in construction, but fewer than 3 percent of Jews. One in ten men produce "stuff" in this country, but fewer than 2 percent of Jews work in factories. Likewise, auto repair is not considered a Jewish ability. As a Jackie Mason joke goes, "When a car owned by gentiles breaks down, in two seconds they're under the car, on top of the car. . . . It becomes an airplane and they fly away. When a Jewish-owned car breaks down, the husband says, 'It's in the hood.' The wife says, 'Where's the hood?' and the husband answers, 'I don't remember.'"

Athletics is another career not commonly associated with Jews. As the saying goes, "Jews don't play sports; they own the team." Throughout history, Jews were often banned from participating in sports. According to the book *Jewish Jocks*, during medieval times Jews were forbidden from participating in the great tournaments and jousting battles that were the Super Bowls of their day. When staged in Rome and Sicily, the Italians even mounted Jews like horses in mock jousts.

Once they were allowed to participate, though, Jews did attain success in several sports. According to sports reporter Robert Slater, the Olympic swimmer Mark Spitz "outdid almost every Olympian who had come before him" in the 1972 Munich Olympics, not only winning seven gold medals, but setting a new world record in each event. Baseball had the Jewish people's won't-play-on-the-High-Holidays hero Sandy Koufax, arguably one of the best pitchers of all time and the first pitcher in the major leagues to pitch four no-hit games. Olympic runner Harold Abrahams became the first European to win an Olympic sprint title—the one-hundred-meter dash in 1924 in Paris (watch *Chariots of Fire*)—and Barney Ross was the world champion boxer from 1933 to 1938 (see *Monkey on My Back*). Certain Jewish women, too, have excelled at athletics. Slater acclaims the Romanian Angelica Rozeanu as "unquestionably the greatest female table tennis player ever," and many of us remember kvelling over gymnast Aly Raisman, who won Olympic gold medals in 2012 and 2016.

But despite these accomplishments, Jews are not often associated with athletics. In the classic 1980 movie *Airplane!* when a passenger asks for something light to read, the stewardess suggests, "How about 'Famous Jewish Sports Legends,'" and hands her a one-page leaflet.

You Play Mah Jongg?

How one spends time when not working can also provide clues about Jews, especially if that someone is female. When the Jewish jurors were asked to name activities most often partaken by Jews, they shouted out "eating, shopping, complaining, and playing mah jongg."

Called "a social lifeline for generations of Jewish women," this Chinese tile game has been featured in a Museum of Jewish Heritage exhibit and was the subject of a documentary, *Mah-Jongg: The Tiles That Bind*. History professor Anneliese Heinze even wrote a doctoral dissertation on the subject, which was published in 2015 as *Mahjong, American Modernity, and Cultural Transnationalism*. So vital is the game to devotees, one group's members made a pact that when the last woman in the group dies, it's her job to bring her mah jongg set to the world to come.

Despite receiving several invitations, I have avoided taking up the game, largely because it conjures up childhood memories of hair-teased, overly perfumed middle-aged women spending afternoons at our house. Sitting around the card table in the living room, they blocked the television, preventing me from watching both *Romper Room* and *Whizzo the Clown*. My resentment lingers in the form of mah jongg resistance today.

Last Resort—The Ask

If I can't figure out if a person is Jewish from the many finely honed techniques revealed in this chapter, I resort to my final strategy: asking.

But I never blurt out, "Are you Jewish?" without hastily adding, "Because I am."

Like other Jews I know, I recoil at being asked directly about my religion. "Why do you want to know?" I think—part of me instantly time-traveling to you-name-it-dark-period-in-history-when-revealing-you're-a-Jew-might-irrevocably-truncate-your-life.

Soon after I was hired to work at a Catholic college, my pen hovered above the line on the new-employee form asking for my religion. I left the space blank, reluctant to "come out" as a Jew without knowing why my employer needed to know. As I learned later, the personnel office wanted this information to invite me to join the Interfaith Committee and send me a Hanukkah rather than a Christmas card. Still, I reckoned, I did the safe thing.

And I remain hesitant to reveal my Jewish status to strangers. Such reticence was probably the motivation behind what Rabbi Neal Gold calls the best pickup line he's ever heard. "I officiated at a wedding for a Jewish couple who told me that when the groom first met his future bride, he asked her out with the words 'Are you doing anything on December 24?'"

I will definitely add this technique for detecting fellow Jews.

7
Dwelling

My childhood friend Sami claimed that her mother could drive down a street and divine a Jewish person's house. Her mother didn't rely on any secret clues, such as spotting mezuzahs or recognizing a style of lamp or drapery. Instead, she claimed, her mother could "just tell" if a Jew lived there.

I didn't believe her until her mom drove the Hebrew school carpool. Turning down the street to pick up the last child, her mother shouted, "Don't give me the address. I want to pick out the house myself." Slowly she crept down the street, muttering, "Nope. Nope." Suddenly she jerked the car to a stop. "There it is. That one." Wouldn't you know it? She was right.

Evidently, Sami's mother's Jewdar enabled her to detect not just individual Jews, but where they lived.

The rest of us, lacking this talent, rely on the following methods to identify a Jewish home.

Mezuzahs

For most Jews, the doorway amulet that houses parchments inscribed with the *Shema*, the central Jewish prayer, is the first tipoff to a Jewish home. One Chabad website calls the mezuzah "the Ultimate Protection Agency," an apt description for the biblical Jews fleeing Egypt, who smeared lamb's blood on the doorposts so God knew to pass over their homes and slay all the other firstborn children. Director Cecil B. DeMille so dramatically reenacted this scene in the classic 1956 movie *The Ten Commandments*, sometimes I think it's hearing the sonorous voice of God that compels me to immediately hang a mezuzah on the front door of any home I occupy.

That, along with being unapologetically superstitious. I would *never* inhabit a home without a mezuzah. God only knows—literally—what terrible things would happen if I didn't have one nailed to the door.

Thus I have repeatedly implored my sister (who is neither observant nor superstitious) to affix a mezuzah to her door. She just brushes my entreaty aside: "I've gotten along just fine so far without one."

"But just think of the wonderful things you might have missed out on because you didn't have one," I counter.

Since I cannot prove this, my sister remains unpersuaded. Yet my Protestant-minister friend knows all about the supernatural powers of a mezuzah. When she discovered one fastened to the door of a house she purchased, she was thrilled. "I wouldn't dream of taking it down," she told me. "I bask in the spiritual aura it gives off."

Who knew? Maybe we should start advertising our mezuzahs when we put our houses up for sale. We could even offer to throw the doorpost mezuzah in for free, along with the refrigerator and washing machine.

Not only is displaying a mezuzah typically Jewish, so is how it is hung. As the story has it, a heated debate broke out between the eleventh-century sage Rashi and his grandson about the proper direction to hang it. Rashi believed it must be affixed vertically, while his grandson insisted it be horizontal. Providing us an excellent example of finding middle ground, they compromised. We now position our mezuzahs at an angle between the up and sideways axis. The top of the mezuzah points toward the inside of the room, and the bottom points toward the outside.

This was the direction a non-Jewish painter boasted of knowing, according to one joke. After removing all of the mezuzahs in an elderly Jewish woman's condo, he told her, "Look, I put them all back up exactly like you told me. And I even removed all the warranties that were rolled up inside."

These days, no matter how they are hung, door amulets are not the reliable indicators of Jewish inhabitants they used to be. Technically, a mezuzah should be left in place if the new occupant will be Jewish, but removed if not or if unknown. Regardless, many Jews do leave them, but unlike my Protestant-minister friend, many non-Jews moving in don't notice them. Others might mistake them for nonfunctioning doorbells. Being one of many "constructionally challenged" Jews, if I weren't Jewish, I would have assumed it was some unusual decorative piece of hardware holding my door in place.

Besides, several dwellings in my retirement community sport both a mezuzah on the door and a statue of Mary cradling baby Jesus in the front lawn. An intermarriage perhaps? Or maybe the residents are hedging their bets, spiritually speaking.

Yard Decoration

Since mezuzahs don't always designate Jewish homes, I sometimes resort to other spy methods. During certain holiday times, the search is simple. In December, I just look for homes with Hanukkah instead of Christmas decorations. Along with the standard menorah (which according to Jewish law is supposed to be displayed in the window), I seek other more subtle clues, such as the substitution of blue and white for multicolored lights. This methodology is far from foolproof, however, because some Christians simply prefer blue.

At one time, seeing a Christmas tree in the window would have been a sure sign that no Jews lived within, but no longer. One-third of Jewish homes now decorate a Yule-time tree, and the figure rises to three-fourths in intermarried households.

These days, thankfully, there are new giveaways, such as homes with banners proclaiming the one-size-fits-all "Season's Greetings" or "Happy New Year." Undecorated, unlit homes also offer clues to Jews, though sometimes the dark, unornamented home simply means there's a Bah Humbug curmudgeon inside.

Around St. Patrick's Day, homes festooned with elves and four-leaf clovers are most likely not Jewish. That said, the owners could be descendants of the Loyal Yiddish Sons of Erin, a group of Lower East Side Jewish Irish immigrants who commemorated the holiday with green matzah balls.

Easter provides another opportunity to reveal typically Jewish homes. Bunnies, Easter baskets, and oversized decorated eggs rarely adorn the front lawns of Jewish dwellers (albeit mixed marriages can send mixed signals). One of my Jewish jurors contends that rabbits in general are not typically Jewish, perhaps because they are not kosher. Neither she nor I could think of one Jewish person we knew who owned a pet hare or even a statue of one.

Religious lawn statues such as beatific Marys or blessing saints are also uncommon at Jewish homes. I daresay that the vast majority of Jews in intermarriages would eschew such brazen Christian symbols.

Because I live in South Florida, I occasionally spot an unfurled Israeli flag at a home of Israeli transplants or Zionistic American Jews. However, a neighbor's suv has an Israeli flag on the dashboard, but a bumper sticker that reads, "Save the Babies; Protect the Unborn." My guess: not Jewish.

Typically Jewish Vehicles

Recently I was searching for a Jewish friend's new home. I thought I had sighted the correct house number but noticed a pickup truck in the driveway. *Can't be right,* I said to myself. Somewhere in the Torah it is surely written, "Thou shalt not own a pickup."

Or perhaps it's in the Talmud, which did specify various transportation rules. More interestingly to me, the Talmud dictated the sexual behavior of the drivers. Camel drivers were required to have sex with their wives once a month, and donkey drivers were to do their deed weekly. To my knowledge, contemporary *halakhah* (Jewish law) does not detail sexual schedules according to the modern vehicle operator's type of transport, but perhaps a ruling on Uber drivers is forthcoming.

Jews have thus self-instituted their own set of transportation-related regulations. Your Volkswagen may have been a sex symbol, as claimed in that 1972 bestseller, but for Jews of the Greater Generation, German car makers are to be boycotted. "Even though World War II was years ago, I still can't think of a Jewish friend of mine who would drive a Volkswagen," explains writer Neal Gabler. "For good reason: the Volkswagen was the Nazis' car."

Studies of Jewish auto consumers confirm Gabler's observation. Sheldon Drobny, best known as the force behind Air America Radio, posted an intriguingly titled article, "What Would Moses Drive?" on Salon.com, noting that during and after World War II, Jews avoided not just German makes, but also Japanese cars, out of patriotic fervor. Because of Henry Ford's blatant antisemitism, Jews boycotted Fords, leaving them to choose between the American-made General Motors or Chryslers. Among those makers, the most sought-after model—proof that Jews had "made it in America"—was the Cadillac. The comedian Jack Benny noted this preference when he joked, "When

GM recalled 72,000 Cadillacs one Yom Kippur, I've never seen
so many Jews walking to synagogue."

Within a generation, however, many of these preferences
were abandoned. "Showing that they are truly a tolerant people, Jews forgave their old enemies," explains Drobny. "Many
of the Nazis were dead. The Japanese didn't kill any Jews. And
Henry Ford's heirs aren't anti-Semites." Jews now purchase
"beemers" (BMWs) and Volkswagen bugs without reservation.
As Gabler sighs, "My daughter, my beloved daughter, drives a
Volkswagen."

It is difficult to find recent data on Jewish purchasing patterns,
but a 2006 Gallup poll hints at Jewish auto choices. Fewer than
half of U.S. citizens with postgraduate educations and incomes
of $75,000 or more purchase American-made cars, whereas two-
thirds of those who are less educated and have lower incomes
buy American. Thirty-six percent of self-described liberals drive
Asian cars, compared to just 20 percent of conservatives (more
on Jewish political persuasions to follow).

The Coalition on the Environment and Jewish Life encourages Jews to "purchase with prudence, because buying a car is
a moral choice." Evidently, many Jews are heeding the advice.
Anecdotal evidence suggests (meaning I asked my Jewish jurors)
that Jews seem to prefer energy-efficient, ecologically friendly
models. Hybrids in particular are the new Cadillacs of the
boomer generation, the jurors say. So if I spy a Prius parked in
the driveway, especially one with—or without—certain bumper
stickers, I know I'm on the right track.

Read My Bumper

See that bumper sticker: "The Blood of Jesus"? Or the one over
there: "For God so loved the world . . .—John 3:16." These are
not Jewish-owned cars.

Nor do many Jews display "Pray. God will answer you," even if that reflects their theology. And the metal outline of a fish is rarely affixed to Jews' bumpers, unless the word "gefilte" is inscribed in the middle.

Rather, when the car owner is Jewish, you might find bumper stickers featuring the word "kiss," as in "Kiss My *Tuchis*" (behind), "Kiss My Mezuzah," or "Kiss My *Knaidlach*" (matzah balls). You might also find exhortations written in the negative: "Stop Kvetching," "Thank You for Not Kvetching," along with "If You Can't Say Something Nice, Say It in Yiddish." Underscoring the importance of eating to Jews, some bumper stickers proclaim, "Keepin' It Kosher," complete with a picture of a red-lined pig.

In some parts of the country, stickers from Jewish summer camps are easy giveaways, and political bumper stickers can offer clues to the auto owner's religious persuasion. Since about 70–80 percent of Jews are Democrats, stickers supporting—or opposing—certain candidates as well as political positions may tip the scales of the investigation.

College bumper stickers can periodically provide pointers too. Ivy League school? Outrageously expensive liberal arts school? Good chance a Jew goes there. According to Hillel's "Top 60 Schools by Jewish Population," a university ranking based on estimated total Jewish student population numbers, private colleges such as New York University, George Washington University, Cornell University, and the University of Pennsylvania are among the Jewish favorites. Certain public school stickers, too, may indicate that the driver is a Jewish student. Here in my home state of Florida two schools—University of Florida and the University of Central Florida—are numbers one and three on the public school list. Who said Florida is just for *alter-kackers* (old people)? (Rutgers University is number two. I guess Jews do like Jersey.)

I'd also advise paying attention to parking permits. Stickers from educational institutions and hospitals may signal "Jewish," given the high percentage of Jews who work in these locales (see the stats in chapter 6, "Detecting"). Speaking of occupations, seeing a car jacked up in a driveway tells you it is not a Jewish home. Most Jews don't fix cars. On the other hand, if there's an AAA vehicle parked nearby: could be Jewish.

Jewish Neighborhoods

If you get really lost when searching for a Jewish home, it may help to know if you are at least in a Jewish neighborhood. Sometimes the subdivision's name can be a code. While it is illegal to limit housing to any religious or racial group, housing developers are adept at naming their properties to strategically signal the intended population group. South Florida, for example, is home to neighborhoods known as "The Traditions" and "Sinai Residences," where one ad promises you will find "like-minded individuals with your heritage and family values." Wink, wink.

The presence or absence of certain amenities can also reveal Jewish neighborhoods or the dearth thereof. As Lenny Bruce quipped, "Trailer parks are so goyish Jews won't go near them."

One of the best methods of determining if an area is heavily Jewish is to investigate the public school system. First and foremost, most Jews insist that their kids attend top schools—even in nursery school and kindergarten. Jews prize education and children, and when you apply both stakes in one, it's apparent: premiere schooling is paramount for their progeny. One Jewish juror told me that a non-Jewish friend concentrated her home search to areas with predominately Jewish residents. "If Jews go to school there, it'll be good enough for my kids," she said. One Muslim mother explained that she enrolled her pre-schooler at my synagogue's early childhood program because "you Jews know how to educate kids."

Along with quality education, Jews require other amenities. According to the Torah, while dwelling in the desert after leaving Egypt, the Israelites had to have a sanctuary so God could dwell among them, though opinions differ about exactly what that meant. The Talmud stipulates that Jews should only live in places offering the following ten features: a court, a charity fund, a synagogue, a bath house, an outhouse, a bloodletter (some believe this is a ritual circumciser), a doctor, a scribe, a kosher butcher/slaughterer, and a teacher. For his part, Rabbi Akiva advised that a variety of fruits should be readily available. You will note that half of these provisos pertain to justice, education, and philanthropy, while the other half deal with bodily functions. You gotta love a religion that prioritizes praying with eating, bathing, and toileting.

According to the Jewish jurors, the needed balance of ethereal and physical in the neighborhood continues to this day. When I asked them what features a Jewish neighborhood needs, they listed "a good Jewish deli" first, followed by good schools, a public library, a university, a Starbucks, and a nail salon.

Not on any of my secular jurors' lists was the Torah's number one necessity: a synagogue. This omission might seem odd to outsiders, but I was not surprised. Further discussions with the jurors revealed that they did want a synagogue in the area but wouldn't necessarily join it. As the joke has it, two Jews on a deserted island construct three synagogues so there will be one they both won't set foot in. Besides, for typically Jewish American families, it is the home, not the house of worship, where Judaism comes alive.

The Jew Next Door

Jews also like living around other Jews because that's who their friends are. Or, at least, that used to be the friendship pattern.

According to the 2013 Pew study, the older you are, the more exclusively Jewish your social circle is. Almost half of older Jews have mainly Jewish friends, decreasing to one-quarter for younger Jews.

The three generations of my family are prime examples of this trend. My mother's social connections have always been exclusively Jewish. This was evident when she interrupted a conversation I was having with a cousin about her friend Dave.

"Who's Dave?" Mom asked.

"He's not Jewish," my cousin responded—shorthand for "You don't know him."

My daughter's social circle is the opposite of Mom's. When I asked her to gather a few Jewish friends to provide background for this book, she looked like I had uncovered an F on her math test. "Gee, Mom. I don't really have any Jewish friends." She offered up two co-workers with whom she celebrates the Jewish holidays.

My Jewish friendship network lies between both extremes. To paraphrase that hackneyed statement, "Some of my best friends *aren't* Jewish," but most are.

Like real estate, location also matters for Jewish friendships. Almost half of northeastern Jews have all or mostly Jewish friends, as do one-third of midwesterners and southerners. Western-dwelling Jews are more likely to have diverse friendship networks; only about 15 percent of them are religiously exclusive.

Wherever the home may be, the best way to discern whether a Jew lives there is to step inside.

Inside a Jewish Home

As I sat across from one Jewish juror in her living room, discussing the topic of this book, she revealed, "I do feel a closeness to other Jews, even though I'm not Jewish."

"What do you mean?" I asked, panicking that one of my Jewish jurors wasn't even Jewish.

"Well, I don't belong to a synagogue or go to services, so I'm not really Jewish."

Yet her not-Jewish confession was offered directly across from a ceramic candy dish from Israel, next to a stylized sculpture of a *hamsa* (hand of God), and beneath a china cabinet stuffed with enough menorahs, seder plates, and Sabbath candles for a hundred Jewish families.

Despite her "I'm not Jewish enough" protestations, she and many other secular Jewish jurors had established typically Jewish homes—even sacred homes.

According to tradition, a Jew's house is holy (no matter how untidy). Jews affix the aforementioned mezuzah to remind them that God's presence resides within. *Ha-Makom,* "the place," refers both to a name for the Divine and the sacred space where one dwells. As Rabbi Neal Gold reminds us, the Rabbis also referred to one's dwelling as *mikdash m'at,* a mini-sanctuary, because after the Temple was destroyed, the home replaced the Temple as the central sacred place of Jewish ritual.

The Jewish home, claimed one 1880s observer, is like a stage set where the woman of the house takes the leading role. Aided by religious objects as props to perform the rituals, she creates a powerful emotional experience that will influence generations to come.

To this day, ritual objects in our homes reveal our convictions (and aesthetics), beautify our holiday celebrations, help us pray, and connect us through the generations. Psychologist Mihaly Csikszentmihalyi calls such possessions "icons of our identity that tell us things about ourselves that we need to hear." So laden with meaning are these objects, some scholars believe that at least for certain Jews they have become an extension of—or even replacement for—*halakhah* (Jewish law). Professor of modern Judaism Jeffrey Shandler summarized this thesis by subtitling his academic paper about Jewish identity "I Shop, Therefore I Am."

As far back as the 1940s Jewish women were encouraged to employ ritual objects to make their homes "feel Jewish." As historian Jenna Weissman Joselit explains, American Jewish communal leaders hoped that "as soon as one steps across the threshold of a Jewish home, one should see and feel that this is a Jewish house." Diana Forman, a Philadelphia artist and wife of a rabbi, went so far as to scatter no fewer than sixty-five Jewishly inflected objects throughout her house in order to fashion what she saw as "the quintessential Jewish home." Along with a twenty-five-hundred-volume Judaica library, that home included a rug with a Hebrew monogram, Hebrew alphabet curtains, lampshades with Bible scenes, paintings of Jews crossing the Red Sea, and a mirror displaying Talmud quotations. The porch included a model of a synagogue, along with dolls listed as "personifying rabbis, bar mitzvahs, and Hadassah nurses." The bathroom featured Hebrew-monogrammed towels, and the children's room had biblical character paper-mache dolls she had designed herself.

Though few other Jewish homemakers rose to her sixty-five-item challenge, many women did direct their religious inclinations into home interiors. Beginning in the 1950s many suburban synagogues supported this home-based connection by establishing gift shops to sell Jewish ritual objects. "Educate through the Gift Shop," urged one Sisterhood slogan, encouraging women to learn about the observances to be performed at home—aided, naturally, through their purchases.

These days, Jewish "stuff" also helps unite the disparate denominations of Judaism. Ultra-Orthodox, Modern Orthodox, Conservative, Reform, Reconstructionist, and unaffiliated Jews may disagree on what to eat or do, but they can all appreciate a magnificent menorah or a stylish pair of Shabbat candlesticks.

Shabbat Stuff

Only 10 percent of Jews attend Sabbath services weekly, but I would venture a guess that 90 percent, if not more, possess some Sabbath paraphernalia. A 1931 survey revealed that most Jewish homes had a pair of candlesticks—though, like today, the survey authors conjectured that more homes displayed them as "ceremonial objects than used them." According to the 2013 Pew survey, only one-quarter of Jews today report "always or usually" lighting Sabbath candles.

Just like the family Bible for Christians, for many Jewish women (and men), *Shabbos* candlesticks claim pride of place as our most precious keepsakes. Tucked into blankets and ferried across the ocean by our ancestors, they are family heirlooms exemplifying the literal meaning "a device for interweaving generations."

It is not surprising that candles are Jewish foundational artifacts. Many ancient cultures recognized the intimate relationship between family, religion, and fire. In ancient Greek the word for "family," *hestia*, meant "near the hearth" and included not just blood relatives, but all those gathered around the home fire. For both the ancient Greeks and Romans, maintaining a fire in one's house was deemed a sacred obligation. Responsibility for ensuring that a few coals remained lit fell to the master of the house.

The ancient Jews, too, required that home fires be tended constantly but transferred that task to the women of the house. It is unclear if this was an example of ancient women's liberation or exploitation. Regardless, women became the keepers of the flame, and this continues today, as women are expressly obligated to light the Sabbath candles.

Many ritual objects related to Shabbat are quite lovely, fulfilling the commandment to beautify the Sabbath. "Make beautiful objects in the performance of God's commandments," the Talmud recommends—a practice also known as *hiddur mitzvah*: not just doing a mitzvah, but embellishing it. Though the Rabbis forbade creating images of people, Jewish artists and craftspeople were otherwise granted free rein to design Judaica to their hearts' and eyes' content.

For Eastern European Jews having to get by during times of scarcity, owning and enjoying luxurious items on the Sabbath became a "symbol of spiritual wealth," and "the very definition of Jewish identity," historian Andrew Heinze explains.

Fast-forward to Jewish women in the 1940s, who were urged to fuse high style into Jewish religious objects. "Don't be content with the cheap and tawdry," counseled Mathilde Schechter, founder of the Women's League for Conservative Judaism, and writers such as Trude Weiss Rosmarin. As they argued, beauty is an intrinsically Jewish concept, and these home observances required functional ritual items; therefore, a woman should seize the "singular opportunity for beautifying her home."

And as she did, so do we to this day, aided by an amazing array of available products. Online you can find elegant Sabbath candlestick holders, *Kiddush* cups, and silver trays to carry both from cabinet to table. Specialized boards, knives, and challah covers can be purchased to hold, hide, and slice the Sabbath bread. For twenty-five dollars you can buy a *Shabbos* matchbox with a Jerusalem scene on top, and for the memory-challenged, it's only another forty dollars to purchase one engraved with the words of the blessing. There's even a tiny silver matchbook with its own tiny silver tray. (Since when does a matchbook need a carrying tray?)

Want to customize your Sabbath bread plate? A hundred bucks will get your name engraved in both English and Hebrew. A cover for your challah will run you anywhere from $10 to $200. The Talmudic Rabbis recommended blanketing the bread because the wine gets blessed before the bread. By covering the loaf, they reasoned, the bread wouldn't "be shamed." I would be the shamed one if I spent two hundred bucks to spare my bread's feelings, as I would if I paid $1,499 for the elegant, one-of-a-kind filigreed silver *Kiddush* cup designed by a famous artist whose name I do not recognize. At that price I would be afraid to pour in the wine.

Alternatively, Rabbi Neal Gold suggests a different way of beautifying the mitzvah: use your great-grandmother's *Kiddush* cup. If you're really lucky, maybe your family's hand-me-down will be the self-same *Kiddush* cup Jesus used at the Last Supper—the one some sources believe was also the legendary Holy Grail sought by King Arthur's men.

One of the three *Kiddush* cups I own is also noteworthy, albeit in a different way. It was passed down to me after my grandfather died. When I toured the World Erotic Art Museum (founded by the late Naomi Wilzig, an Orthodox Jew) I was astonished to see on display a pewter cup that looked remarkably like Grandpa's *Kiddush* cup. His, however, didn't have any Kama Sutra positions drawn around the outside.

The final Sabbath-related item in many Jewish homes is a *Havdalah* set—though, like Shabbat candlestick holders, more Jews own them than use them. *Havdalah*, meaning "separation," is the ceremony to close out—separate—the holy time of the Sabbath from the secular week. To perform the ritual, three items are needed: a multi-wick intertwined candle, a spice box, and a *Kiddush* cup. And, of course, most *Havdalah* sets come with—you guessed it—a matching tray to carry them, so *Havdalah* brings forth four more ritual items for Jewish homes.

Come On Baby, Light My Menorah

Adam Sandler begins his famous "Chanukah Song," "Put on your yarmulke. Here comes Chanukah. So much funukah. To celebrate Chanukah." Indeed. Along with plopping on a *kippah*, Jews now have a plethora of proven products for a "funukah Chanukah," starting with the iconic Hanukkah menorah.

To be accurate, the candleholder used for the eight-day holiday is called a *hanukkiah*. The word "menorah" technically refers to the seven-branch candelabra used in the ancient Temple, representing the nation of Israel as "a light of nations." When speaking of the eight-candle item (with a ninth, the *shammash*, added to light the others), we are to call it a "Hanukkah menorah."

No similar standardization exists for the spelling of the holiday, but I wish it did. A non-Jewish co-worker told me that she went to pick out a card for me but, as confessed, "I didn't know if you celebrated Hanukkah or Chanukah, so I didn't buy you one." No matter how it's spelled, the *hanukkiah* has become the ultimate holiday symbol. As the mythical legend has it, when rededicating the ancient Temple one vial of oil miraculously lasted eight full days, now the duration of the holiday. That's a good thing, because many of us need several days to dust and peel the wax off all of our *hanukkiah*s.

What is it about Jews and *hanukkiah*s? One of my most secular cousins, who describes herself as a "Jewnitarian," has a collection that currently numbers fifteen; several of the Jewish jurors own multiple menorahs too. Some usher in the holiday by having each family member light his or her own. A friend of mine hosts an annual Hanukkah party at which each guest is invited to bring and light a *hanukkiah*. Every year she offers the same opening prayer before the group's recitation of the candle blessing: "I hope we don't burn down the house."

The range of Hanukkah menorahs available for purchase reveals yet again the incredible creativity, talents, and whimsy of the Jews. Along with elegant, filigreed works of art, *hanukkiah*s are made out of soft drink cans and Pez dispensers. Some feature characters from *Star Wars*, *The Simpsons*, and Hello Kitty. Others display animals, such as giraffes, dinosaurs, and octopi (the last giving you the appropriate leg up on the holiday—groan). For irony lovers, there's a *hanukkiah* that looks like matches. And, catering to interfaith couples, there's even a *hanukkiah* made from Christmas tree branches.

Interfaith families can also jointly observe their December celebrations with a Christmas dreidel: a four-sided top that replaces the standard Hebrew letters—*nun, gimel, heh,* and *shin*—with Santa and Christmas trees. Though the dreidel game has come to symbolize the Jewish holiday, various people have played it in different languages for centuries. In the sixteenth century, for example, the English played a similar spinning game called "totum" or "teetotum," and the Germans later did the same, using a *torrel* or *trundle.* The Yiddish word *dreidel* derived from the German word *drehen,* which means "to spin."

As with *hanukkiah*s, dreidels now come in a vast array of shapes, materials, and designs. Some are made of elegant silver or bronze; others of Lucite, crystal, or glass. Some holiday tops are shaped like pomegranates, acorns, or flowers. And, wouldn't you know it: one comes with its own carrying case.

Other holiday traditions have also made their way into Hanukkah paraphernalia. The German Brothers Grimm–inspired gingerbread house modeled the Manischewitz Company's "Hanukkah House," a blue-and-white cottage you can construct and decorate. Christmas stockings now come in blue and white, and Jews can even participate in Ugly Hanukkah Sweater contests; past "winning" combinations include reindeers with dreidel antlers.

Beyond these ornamental objects, Hanukkah has become the quintessential time to outdo your neighbors with outdoor decorations. One Jewish juror claimed that unlike garish and ostentatious Christmas décor, Hanukkah decorations are tasteful and subtle. She obviously has not seen my home in December. Beginning at the driveway and continuing throughout the living room and dining room, my house is a carnival of blue, white, and silver. A ridiculous two-foot smiling dreidel blow-up, a sheet-sized Happy Hanukkah banner, and a gaudy fake-snow Hanukkah bush are just a few of my tacky but treasured holiday accessories.

When so festooning my house, I feel a deep connection to my father. Never knowing from "tacky," he often lamented the dearth of Jewish decorations during December. So frustrated was he, the man designed and tried (unsuccessfully) to sell a sixteen-inch wooden Jewish star embedded with electric lights. Likewise, another juror recalled her father fashioning a wooden treelike structure that the family decorated with menorahs and dreidels.

Both dads would probably be pleased with today's selection of Hanukkah decorations. Inflatable snowmen come garbed wearing yarmulke and tallit. Some *hanukkiah*s are now designed to hang on trees and doors. Hanukkah menorahs have grown to heights of five, six, and seven feet—and that's not all. You can purchase a twelve-footer, advertised to "Let your neighbors know it's that special time of year . . . and everyone else around the country!" Walmart and Target are among the big-box stores offering a wide array of Hanukkah decorations—and you can even buy them online from Christmas Central.

Passover the Seder Plate

As if the Sabbath and Hanukkah stuff wasn't enough, Passover also spawns sacred paraphernalia. Anthropologists have found that cultures use artifacts to pass on "the memory of the tribe's origins, triumphs, and humiliations," which right there is a pretty good description of the Passover seder. We remember being enslaved in Egypt, then being liberated when God brought us out "with a mighty hand and an outstretched arm." Religion professor Vanessa Ochs believes that our Passover possessions help make ethereal concepts real. Liberation, exile, freedom are lofty constructs difficult to translate into everyday life, but tastes—such as the bitter *maror*, usually horseradish, representing the embittered lives of the Israelites, and the salty water, representing the Israelites' tears, into which we dip herbs such as parsley or chevril—are easily understood.

Three-fourths of Jews participate in a home-based seder, so that means lots of Jewish homes have seder plates, matzah boxes (to store and keep them fresh), *afikoman* (ceremonial matzah) covers, and Haggadahs (technically *Haggadot*, seder books).

Seder plates especially reflect the marriage of ritual and beauty. The result: some stunning—and stunningly expensive— ritual items. One such plate showcases Marc Chagall's renderings of the twelve tribes of Israel (the original works appearing in stained glass windows at the Hadassah–Hebrew University Medical Center). The porcelain plate with its six matching dishes sells for upwards of $1,000.

At the other end of the economic spectrum are melamine plates—the substance of my *bubbe*'s everyday dishes—selling for $8.95. In between are round, square, octagonal, and even three-dimensional seder plates constructed of everything from cardboard to crystal.

I own and treasure two seder plates: a green and gold metallic plate passed down from my grandmother and a hand-painted ceramic plate gifted to me by African American students in my Jewish History and Culture class. Since I only hold one seder each year (many Jews do two) and both plates are very meaningful to me, it's consistently difficult for me to choose which to use. I try to alternate them every year but can never remember which one I used last.

Haggadahs, the books used to teach the Passover story and perform the seder, also reflect Jewish ingenuity. Long gone are the days when everyone used the *Maxwell House Haggadah,* first launched in 1932 and printed continuously since. According to Jewish history professor Carole B. Balin, the perk—buy one can of coffee and get one Hagaddah free—was based on an honor system. Describing the result diplomatically, she said, "Let's just put it this way. I don't think 50 million cans of coffee were sold."

Fast-forward eighty years. Now we have Haggadahs for hip-hop devotees, Harry Potter fans, and baseball enthusiasts. Feminists, vegetarians, and JewBus (Jewish Buddhists) have their own texts. You can access one via Facebook or JDate or create a do-it-yourself version with an online template. For the "when do we eat?" complainers, there's the *UnHaggadah* and *30 Minute Seder: The Haggadah That Blends Brevity with Tradition.*

Or, to guarantee some laughs at your Passover table, try comedians Dave Barry, Alan Zweibel, and Adam Mansbach's parody *For This We Left Egypt?* This Haggadah includes such thought-provoking questions as could God's real name be "Art Thou," was God's "strong hand" a poker reference, and why aren't there more Jews called Bitter Herb? The authors also offer sage guidance to guarantee you do your seder right. It's important to know that the first page is in the back, because "otherwise you'll tell the Exodus story backward." When breaking the middle matzah, service leaders should "try to find a piece that's not already broken," and any gefilte fish served should be "wild and sustainably caught; avoid farmed gefilte fish if possible."

Presenting the appropriate serving dishes for your gefilte fish and the rest of the festive food is also vital. Because of the holiday's strict dietary restrictions, Jews who keep kosher also maintain two separate sets of dishes used exclusively during this holiday period, one for milk and one for meat. Some Jews I know own not just one but several sets of these Pesach dishes, having inherited them from observant elderly relatives. I have three; an acquaintance has six.

Come to think of it, if you counted each one of my dishes, maybe I do have sixty-five Jewish ritual objects in the home.

Pushke for the Poor

The final religiously related item found in many Jewish homes is the *tzedakah* (charity) box. Also called a *pushke*, in Yiddish, this Jewish piggy bank for the family's donations has been part of Jewish households around the world. Most often it took the form of a little blue Jewish National Fund tin that originated in 1901 to collect donations for purchasing land in *Eretz Yisrael (the Land of Israel)*.

Of the three *pushkes* I own, my favorite is an empty Hershey's cocoa box with a slit in the top that my daughter Amanda decorated in the second grade with pictures of children and the Hebrew word *tzedakah* colored in. Our Shabbat ritual was to drop a few coins into the box before lighting the candles.

When guests were present, we always joked that this was their payment for dinner.

For those who don't have a seven-year-old artist at home, *tzedakah* boxes to inspire and collect charitable giving are available for purchase in a variety of styles—one online website offers 123 different selections. As with seder plates, *tzedakah* boxes can be made of anything, from plastic or tin to ceramic, wood, or glass. Some folks recycled their receptacles, turning tissue boxes, mason jars, or baking powder containers into coin holders. In one style, when a donor deposits coins, a Hasidic rabbi's hat comes off. In another, yarmulke-shaped one, the giver lifts the top half, thereby putting the money where the brain would be—maybe implying that the more generous the gift, the more *sekhel* (smarts) on the part of the giver. As with other ritual items, prices vary widely, from $11.99 to $1,000.00. In my humble opinion, if you have an extra thousand bucks, give it to the poor.

Speaking of donation recipients, when our cocoa tin filled up, we would let Amanda decide the charity to receive our donations. To this day, I'm still getting mail from the Humane Society of Broward County, Feeding South Florida, and Fort Lauderdale Children's Theater. Several Jewish jurors also turned the distribution decisions over to their children. One juror, however, remembers shaking the contents directly into the palm of a wizened, bearded old man known affectionately as "Mommy's friend" who periodically appeared at their door.

Handing money over in person is a rarity today, especially with online giving. New virtual apps make real-time giving easier. For instance, the Tzedakah App allows you to give as much as you want to your favorite Jewish charity. The Jewish Communal Fund created Clink! to help teens prioritize causes and streamline giving. Several Jewish (and other) charities accept giving through apps as well as web donations. Possibly in the future these methods will put a dent in *pushke* use. Alternatively, though, that might drive up the boxes' value. Already, if you have an original Jewish National Fund box, hold on to it. Now proclaimed "vintage," the can can bring you up to $300— which, of course, you would donate as *tzedakah*.

Prayer Paraphernalia

Though most Jews do not attend prayer services regularly, many of us are emotionally connected to our ancestors through the religious items they used when *davening* (praying). Most commonly stowed in a closet or dresser drawer are the two *t*'s of Jewish prayer: tallis and tefillin. Tefillin (sometimes translated as "phylacteries" in English) are cube-shaped black leather boxes containing four scriptural passages attached to the head and arm during weekday morning services. In Talmudic times, extremely pious individuals supposedly wore them all day. (*Oy.*) This practice was subsequently outlawed as being an ostentatious display of piety. (Whew.)

One of my non-Jewish husband's more bizarre Jewish experiences concerned seeing both of these ritual items used at an Orthodox cousin's bar mitzvah. Most bar mitzvahs are held on Saturday, when tefillin is not allowed, but this service was on a Thursday. The significance of this different weekday didn't hit me until we walked into the sanctuary and were astonished to see men in business suits who all looked like they had broken their arms. One arm was thrust through the jacket, but the other arm was not, leaving their suit coats hanging awkwardly around their sides. To finish off this unusual ensemble, a tallis (prayer shawl) lay draped around the half-on, half-off jacket. When the men turned around to greet us, we saw across their exposed forearms the crisscrossed leather bindings and little square boxes affixed to their foreheads. As we slithered into a row of seats in the last row, Rod shot me a "what-the-hell?" look I will never forget.

Nor will I ever shake from memory the look of bemusement on my Jewish gynecologist's face when he asked me about my birth control method and I responded, "We use phylacteries." He snickered. "I think you mean prophylactics, unless you guys are doing something kinky with the tefillin."

Which we weren't, but maybe we should have considered it. They are leather, after all.

The other prayer-related apparatus, the tallis, was traditionally worn by men, but now also adorns women in prayer. The garment holds the biblically required tzitzit (fringes) on its corners and, like other Judaica, is often an exquisite work of art. Traditionally, a deceased man was buried in his tallis, but liberal Jews are now passing on prayer shawls as heirlooms. Many bar or bat mitzvah ceremonies begin with the new Jewish adult being enveloped in Zayde's or Uncle Hymie's tallis—a ritual guaranteed to bring me to tears. A woman sitting next to me at High Holiday services even struck up a conversation by asking, "What's the story behind your tallis?"—assuming that every prayer shawl now comes equipped with a personal narrative.

Should your family be lacking a prayer shawl, you can purchase one for as little as $49.99 or as much as $769.99. Wait. Don't answer yet. For that price you also get a matching carrying case and yarmulke.

A stash of yarmulkes (*kippot* in Hebrew) is almost always hidden somewhere in a Jewish house. Though Orthodox Jews wear head coverings all the time, most liberal Jews put one on only at synagogue, grabbing one from the communal yarmulke box, especially during weddings and b'nai mitzvah. Then these head coverings proclaiming "Michael and Beth" or "Joshua

Cohen, January 12, 2004" are invariably brought home and tossed in with the rest of the household yarmulke collection. One Jewish juror reports that her *kippah* drawer in a cabinet provides an unembarrassing means of recalling the names of those who married into the family whom she hasn't seen in decades. Another juror reports she houses her yarmulkes in a kitchen drawer, right next to the coffee filters. Judaica sellers take note: there may be a market for fancy-schmancy yarmulke containers.

Decorative *siddurim* (prayer books) are also found in many Jewish homes, although for most Jews they serve more as exhibit objects than as prayer or reference books. Mine is a silver-cased, five-inch prayer book embellished with golden filigree and ruby stones. When I showed it to a gathering of six Jewish jurors, three of them said they owned this same prayer book. (One owned three.) When the editor of this book reviewed this paragraph, she glanced over at the very same prayer book displayed just two feet away.

The reason so many people possess this model is that it was sold at gift shops in Israeli airports in the 1960s. Those of us possessing one can probably trace its provenance to a procrastinating gift buyer.

Bound to Be Books

Decorative prayer books are far from the only reading material one will find in a Jewish home. Indeed, "books" was the Jewish jurors' number one answer to the question of how to identify a Jewish home. As religion scholar Ochs notes, in Jewish homes you will find books "filling shelves, piled on floors, spilling off of tables, scattered in children's rooms." Naturally, my publisher The Jewish Publication Society and I expect that most Jewish homes will own at least one of the standard JPS Bibles, such as the *JPS Hebrew-English Tanakh* (blue cover) or *The Torah* (red cover). Go look. I'll bet you have one.

Just like yarmulkes, *siddurim* are sometimes inadvertently—or advertently—brought home from shul. Browsing through my own collection, I find that somehow several copies of my Reconstructionist synagogue's 1994 Shabbat prayer book *Kol Haneshamah* and a 1984 copy of a Reform congregation's *Gates of Repentance* prayer book for the Days of Awe made it home with me. I plan to return them very soon.

Jewish home libraries often include books by some of our people's favorite Jewish authors, among them Leon Uris, Chaim Potok, Isaac Bashevis Singer, Philip Roth, Anita Diamant, and Grace Paley. By the way, should you happen to have a first edition, signed copy of *Exodus* or *The Chosen* on your bookshelf, move it to a more secure location. Rare book dealers estimate each is worth $1,500–$1,900.

Notably, even secular volumes in Jewish homes can also serve as what Ochs calls "uniquely Jewish-signifying objects" that often "embody, create, and express *kedushah* [holiness]" that the owner is not even aware of. As far back as the 1940s, home-decorating advice to Jewish women encouraged them to "let literature occupy the place of honor," underscoring the People of the Book's often sacred love of learning.

Religion scholar Jeffrey Shandler agrees that both buying books and giving books as gifts are significant Jewish community practices. According to an estimate published in the *Discover JCC Magazine* in 2013, American Jews buy almost a quarter of all hardcover books, though they compose just 2 percent of the population. American Jewish women over fifty are estimated to be the largest group of book purchasers. Though exact numbers are difficult to locate, Jewish demographics support the hypothesis. According to a 2016 Pew study, college educated, urban-dwelling women earning more than $75,000 a year—an on-point portrayal of American Jewish women—are the nation's most avid book readers. Novelist Brian Morton puts it bluntly when one of his characters claims, "Jewish women are all that stand between us and the death of the publishing industry."

Though once again numbers here are hard to find, anecdotal evidence suggests that Jewish women are also fervent book club devotees. Every library and college book club I have joined has been predominately peopled by Jews. The fact that I landed this book contract was heavily influenced by expectations that Jews—especially Jewish women—would buy this book. If you're a Jewish woman, thanks for proving my point. (If you're not, I thank you as well. I'd much rather have your purchase than be proved right.) And, of course, Jews buy lots of Jewish books. Jewish book fairs sponsored by Jewish Community Centers and synagogues are ubiquitous. Many are held in conjunction with Jewish Book Month, not coincidently scheduled in November, to encourage the buying and giving of books as Hanukkah gifts.

No discussion of a Jewish book collection would be complete without mentioning the quintessential Jewish book for the home: the Jewish cookbook. My mother authored two Jewish cookbooks, *Mom's Best Recipes* and *Grandma's Kosher Recipes* (see chapter 4, "Noshing"), both of which were sold nationally during the 1950s and '60s, and to this day people tell me they still use her books to make brisket or kugel or honey cake.

These days, Jewish cookbooks are vastly different from those of my mother's generation. Expanding beyond the default Ashkenazic cuisine, many feature dishes from all over the globe. Healthy, vegetarian, low-fat, and/or gluten-free Jewish fare is replacing heavy, shmaltzy, meat-laden recipes. Though many consider low-cholesterol Jewish cooking an oxymoron—how can you have healthy *gribenes* (chicken skin fried in shmaltz)?—some cookbooks do attempt nutritious substitutions. I've had mushroom-based, mock chopped liver that's not bad, though nowhere near as good as the real stuff.

What's on Your Wall?

Jewish identity is also on display on our walls. Even though, historically, Jews were forbidden to duplicate the human form ("You shall not make for yourself a sculptured image, or any likeness of what is in the heavens above") or display an image of a person, lest it lead to idolatrous worship, on the walls of many a Jewish home you'll find renderings of an old man enfolded by a tallis and hunched over a Torah or a Tevye-like figure fiddling away. Art depicting Jerusalem scenes also frequently grace Jewish homes, as do stylized greetings of "Shalom" (meaning "hello, goodbye, peace") or other Hebrew words. Sepia photos of stern-looking immigrants from the turn of the century are often hung, as are personal illuminated *ketubot* (wedding contracts). Descending down the family tree, many Jewish homes likewise have walls and walls of photos from bar and bat mitzvahs, weddings, and family gatherings (sometimes with the face of an ex-spouse cut out). In the kitchen one will usually find a Jewish calendar, provided gratis by the local Jewish funeral home.

One custom that few Jews know about but Rabbi Neal Gold assures me is biblically based is leaving a piece of wall unadorned as a sign of remembrance of the destruction of Jerusalem. Now I know the real reason why one wall in my bedroom wall has nothing on it. Turns out it has nothing to do with my having misjudged and given away too many posters and pictures when I downsized.

Jewish Furniture and Furnishings

When my twenty-year-old sofa began shedding its stuffing, I headed to a local furniture store, one of the few remaining individually owned establishments. The short, balding salesman who approached me turned out to be the owner, and through the detection techniques discussed in chapter 6, we identified each other as fellow Jews. I described the type of sofa I was seeking, pointing to several couches, but he quickly waved me away from that section. "No, not those," he insisted. "They're for the goyim. I've got other ones in the back for you."

Jewish versus goyish furniture? Who knew?

Clearly he knew, because he steered me away from the colonial collection usually avoided by Jews, especially those of my mother's generation; perhaps such furniture was tainted by its connection to Daughters of the American Revolution gentility. Instead, when I was growing up, French provincial pieces were big in Jewish homes; these were later replaced with contemporary styles. According to some of the Jewish jurors, Scandinavian modern-style furniture has become popular among Jews, even though it is incredibly uncomfortable to sit on. Evidently my furniture taste is not typically Jewish. I ended up buying an ugly brown overstuffed love seat—hard on the eyes but soft on the tush.

Regardless of the type of furniture Jews had, one juror insisted that Jews of her parents' generation would always encase sitting furniture in plastic covers. This was evidently not an exclusively Jewish technique, however; a Jew by Choice of Italian heritage says her relatives did the same. In Jewish homes, too, the always-plush carpet was protected with waterproof runners. After all, those Depression-era homeowners worked hard to afford "nice things," and they wanted to keep them that way.

It didn't always work out as they had intended, though. Thinking back to her childhood, one juror remembers always being uncomfortable sitting on the heavy plastic-covered couches and love seats in the family living room. Plastic was the antithesis of cozy. When she protested, her parents repeatedly explained that they were protecting the furniture. After her parents died, she decided to donate the living room furniture to Goodwill. When the movers rang the doorbell, she swiftly removed the plastic covers that had sheathed the furniture for a third of a century, only to discover that the lack of circulating air had petrified the couches stiff as wood. "We're not taking this junk," one of the men announced, "unless you want to pay us." It's a good thing her parents weren't still around. They would have *plotzed* (died) seeing her dole out money to the super to haul their treasures away.

Certain types of home furnishings also telegraph the homeowners' religious identity. One rarely sees wall hangings of Elvis or tigers in a Jewish home, but in previous generations you might have spotted a Sandy Koufax poster in a boy's bedroom. Nor will you see a decapitated moose head mounted on the wall. Jewish law prohibits hunting for sport or food. Besides, moose meat isn't kosher.

Guns also tend to be sparse in Jewish homes, though not because of *halakhah* (Jewish law). In Talmudic times wearing a weapon was so common, the ban on a man wearing woman's clothing included the admonition that he/she not include a weapon with the outfit (even if it matched). Today, however, a 2006 American Jewish Committee survey reveals that American Jews are less likely to own a gun than adherents of any other religion in the United States. Fewer than 10 percent of Jews report owning a firearm, compared to one-fourth of all others.

Fundamentalist Protestants are the highest gun owners, with one-third personally packing.

What is more, Jews who do possess a firearm are more likely to favor obtaining a police permit before making the purchase than all other Americans: 92 percent of Jews, compared to 80 percent of non-Jews. In addition, many national Jewish organizations, among them the Jewish Council for Public Affairs, National Council for Jewish Women, and the Religious Action Center of Reform Judaism, have advocated for improving public safety through some form of gun control.

Nor, according to a few of the Jewish jurors, will you typically find wreaths or doilies decorating Jewish homes. A circular laurel, closely associated with Christmas, can represent the eternal rebirth of Christ, with the berries symbolizing his blood. Doilies are also avoided, not for religious reasons but because, as one juror put it, they are "too Irish."

And Jewish homes will sometimes be free of such *goyishe* knickknacks as the Hummel statues my husband inherited from his mother. I've always associated them with the German/lederhosen/*bierhall* culture. Even the word "knickknack" seems non-Jewish; Jews prefer the Yiddish term *tchotchke*, which has been defined as "a form of knickknack, whatchamacalit, gewgaw, doodad or doohickey." As one Jewish juror noted, there is a certain style of stuff you see in country stores that just doesn't feel Jewish. Statues of angels, for example, rarely grace Jewish homes, even though the Hebrew Bible is replete with them. Nor do Jews tend to buy candles embossed with "The Lord Is My Shepherd," even though we do recite the psalm as one of "our" prayers too.

Tapping into sarcastic Jewish humor (see chapter 5, "Laughing"), Jewish *tchotchkes* often convey a sense of irony. Included in the Jewish Museum of Maryland's exhibit "Tchotchkes! Treasures of the Family Museum" were salt and pepper shakers shaped like potato latkes and a yarmulke-wearing troll doll. One set depicted a *mohel* (ritual circumciser) and rabbi about to circumcise a baby (thereby making the infant 10 percent off).

Overboard with Objects

Despite our great sages' permission to purchase to prettify our homes, many rabbis and religious leaders throughout history have denounced the Jewish emphasis on consumption. In 1887, Rabbi Moses Weinberger berated Jews who had immigrated to this country: "Instead of soaring high on the wings of poetry and song . . . they sink up to their necks . . . in material possessions." In 1923 Rabbi Israel Levinthal admonished the "flappers" in his congregation, "[You] should know that there is something else in the world worthwhile," encouraging them to cultivate their intellects with "the same ardor and interest [you] reserve . . . for shopping."

Granted, crass, competitive, keeping-up-with-the-Cohens buying can elicit more emptiness than satisfaction. But at the same time, when earlier generations stocked up on home-based ritual pieces—which scholars call "consumed nostalgia"—later generations have retained the memories while using them. Polishing Great-Grandma's *Shabbos* candlesticks, digging the wax out from Uncle Jake's menorah, dropping a coin into the Keren Ami Fund charity box can all connect us with our heritage and past.

The challenge, of course, in owning so much meaningful "Jewish stuff" comes when we're forced to part with them. As many of us age and downsize our dwellings, our beloved Judaica treasures can end up at Goodwill. Whenever I spot a menorah or *Kiddush* cup nestled next to a 2005 varsity volleyball trophy, Christmas angel plate, or polka-dot coffee mug, it fills me with sadness. I imagine the stories behind that *hanukkiah* and cup, underpriced at two dollars each, and undervalued far beyond any cost.

Even though I don't know one iota of the backstory behind these items, seeing, touching, holding them evokes an instant connection to my Judaism and the Jewish people. I would even define the experience as religious.

8

Joining

When my daughter was a toddler I decided to form a play-group, so she could be around other children and I could spend a day talking to adults instead of watching *Sesame Street* and picking up toys. In those pre-Internet times I tacked a flier on my local library's bulletin board announcing my intent. Six women responded. For our first meeting, at my house, I set out a plate of mandelbread next to the bowl of Teddy Grahams. "I see you're Jewish," said one of the mothers, noting the traditional Jewish cookie. "I am, too."

"Me, too," said another.

"As am I," said the third.

As it turned out, five of the six of us were Jewish.

After retiring from educational administrative positions, my friend Julie and I were infuriated to discover we had been rendered *persona non grata* at our former workplaces. Phone calls were not returned, emails ignored, and requests for meetings rebuffed. To help us deal with the rejection, we reached out to the Transition Network, a secular national organization that helps professional women transition into retirement. A local chapter didn't exist in our area, so we formed one. Fifteen women came to our initial gathering—and as I learned later, eleven of them were Jewish. That's 75 percent in an area where Jews constitute no more than 8 percent of the population.

There is nothing particularly Jewish about a preschool play-group or a women's retirement association. But, I contend, there is something typically Jewish about voluntarily reaching out to others through groups. Jews are joiners.

I'm not the only one who says so. Asked if they thought Jews were more likely than others to join organizations, my Jewish jurors joined in unanimous agreement. One woman enthusiastically shouted, "One hundred percent!"

"Do you mean 100 percent of Jews fit this description or that they participate 100 percent more than non-Jews?"

"Both," she said.

No statistics could possibly confirm her statement, but who can argue with that level of certainty, especially since she's made my point.

Communal Judaism

When Jewish icon Barbra Streisand belts out these lyrics to her signature song, "People who need people are the luckiest people in the world," she is expressing a typically Jewish sentiment: you can't be a Jew alone. "Do not separate yourself from the community," warns the great religious leader Hillel. The Talmud recounts a Rip Van Winkle–like story of a man named Honi the Circle Maker who awakens from a seventy-year sleep to discover that no one knows him. Realizing he must spend the rest of his life alone, he demands, "Either community or death."

Jews value community so highly, they invented the minyan (quorum) of ten to ensure that even individual prayer is a group activity. When a family member dies, Jewish tradition demands that the mourners recite the memorial *Kaddish* prayer in a minyan—in other words, in the presence of a supportive, like-minded community. When bereaved Jews are at their loneliest, our tradition reminds them that they are not alone.

Notably, Judaism can emphasize communal over private prayer because our religion is not founded on a creed. When a religion is faith-based, the individual believer becomes the all-important foundation. Psychologist William James, whose grandfather was a devout Presbyterian, even defined religion as "the feelings, acts, and experiences that emanate from our solitude."

For Jews, though, it is not the person, but people who form our core. This may account for why sociologist Emile Durkheim, whose grandfather was an Orthodox rabbi, came to believe that religion is primarily a way for "social groups to experience themselves as groups"—the very opposite of James's contention.

Judaism's "we over me" emphasis is evident in the old joke about two synagogue-goers, Jake and Murray. Asked why they chose to spend Saturday morning in shul instead of on the golf course, Jake says piously, "I go to talk to God." Murray points to his friend and says, "I go to talk to Jake."

According to some Jewish thinkers, Murray had it right. Rabbi Harold S. Kushner notes that the root word for "religion," *ligare* (to tie), doesn't necessarily connect a person to God, but binds us to each other. Echoing this sentiment, Jewish philosopher Martin Buber explains, "God is not found in churches or synagogues or holy books. God is not found in the hearts of the most fervent believers. God is found between people."

Even the word "synagogue" derives from the Greek verb *synagein*, "to bring together or gather." And the Hebrew word for the institution, *beit knesset,* means "house [or place] of gathering."

Community beyond the Synagogue

The synagogue is far from the only place Jews find Jewish community. We experience it at home—think circumcisions and baby namings, Passover seders and Hanukkah candlelightings, weekly Shabbat dinners. Speaking of the last, I was amazed to hear one rabbi's sermon urging congregants *not* to come to Friday night services. Instead, the spiritual leader counseled, "If you are having a great time laughing, singing, shmoozing at a Shabbat dinner at home, stay there. That is more important than coming here." Shortly thereafter, he was no longer that synagogue's rabbi.

In America another institution, the Jewish Community Center, also lays claim to being a (if not the) Jewish communal bedrock. "The J," as many Jews like me affectionately call the Jewishly flavored community center, offers everything from cultural events to classes to child care. Throughout the years the two institutions often competed for the hearts, minds, and wallets of Jews.

This continuing tension was evident nearly three decades ago when I asked a local rabbi to officiate at my daughter's baby naming. Apologizing to him for not belonging to his congregation, I admitted we simply couldn't afford it at the time.

"I understand perfectly," he said. Then, to my astonishment, he added, "You should join the Jewish Community Center instead. For a young family like yours, that's more important now. You can start thinking about a synagogue when your daughter is ready for Hebrew school." I had never before heard a rabbi say, "Don't join a synagogue." He, too, shortly thereafter was no longer that synagogue's rabbi.

Since I'm retired and have no job to worry about, I can publicly proclaim that for many Jews, participation in a voluntary nonprofit organization is as—if not more—important than affiliating with a synagogue. Sociologist Susan Chambre should back me up on this. According to her, many Jews turn to Jewish nonprofit organizations as "a way to express their Jewish identity and commitment to Jewish continuity." That was the direction two of my friends took upon retirement. Both viewed participating in a voluntary Jewish association as fulfilling a religious obligation. One joined a committee at JAFCO, the local Jewish social service agency. The other attended a board meeting of her local Hadassah chapter, where she was immediately named president. (A cautionary tale, for sure.)

What World War II Generation Jews Join

My friends are continuing a long-established tradition. For my mother and women of her generation, to be a Jew was to be a member of a Jewish woman's organization. Whenever Mom met a Jewish woman, she'd begin their conversation by questioning where the woman volunteered. She never asked, "Do you belong?" Instead, it was always, "Which organization do you belong to?" And inevitably the woman would reel off one or more of a venerable alphabet soup of Jewish service organizations: ORT, NCJW, NFTS, JWI, JCC, NAAMAT, WLCJ, HIAS. Many of these groups date back more than a century. The National Council of Jewish Women (NCJW) was founded in 1893. In 1912 seven Zionist women (including Henrietta Szold, the first editor of JPS, this book's publisher) formed what ultimately became the world-renowned women's Zionist association Hadassah.

Men of my parents' generation also expressed their Jewish identity by volunteering. Because congregational lay leadership positions were then either completely or primarily open to men, many of them became synagogue leaders. Other men volunteered for local Jewish Federations or Jewish Community Centers. Still others joined B'nai B'rith. Founded in 1843 on New York's Lower East Side by twelve German Jewish men, B'nai B'rith at one time was the largest Jewish fraternal organization in America.

Awesome Array of Associations

These Jewish service groups are but one component of a vast Jewish organizational network. Whereas most religious groups have concentrated their resources on building houses of worship, Jews not only built synagogues and Jewish Community Centers, but also created the aforementioned service organizations, along with Federations, social welfare organizations, youth groups, day schools, college campus groups, Jewish professionals organizations, Israeli support organizations, summer camps, museums, archives, libraries, and Torah study organizations. An outsider might view the lot as a merry messy hodgepodge, but sociologist Daniel J. Elazar explains that all the organizations fall into one of five separate spheres—congregational, education/cultural, community relations, communal welfare, and Israel support—all gathering Jews to serve different Jewish communal needs. Moreover, he champions this organizational network as "one of the great successes of the North American Jewish community," being "far more complex than any other group's." Similarly, Rabbi Sidney Schwarz asserts, "There isn't another ethnic sub-community in America that has the range of organizations and services that Jews enjoy."

Jews—The Original Self-Help Group

These Jewish self-help groups have played a vital role in our people's religious, communal, educational, cultural, and political survival. Time and again history has taught us the wisdom of the saying "God helps those who help themselves."

The tradition of Jews helping Jews in need goes all the way back to the Hebrew Bible. The Torah required communal support for the poor, and the Talmud stipulated that Jewish communities provide a *tzedakah* fund "collected by two people and distributed by three."

Religiously, in Talmudic times burial societies (*hevra kadisha*) assumed responsibility to prepare Jewish bodies and watch over the dead (see chapter 3, "Dying"), a tradition that continues to this day. Some burial organizations also filled additional communal needs. For instance, along with burying the dead, in the 1850s an Austrian *hevra kadisha* established and maintained a synagogue, supervised the koshering of meat, and oversaw the ritual bath. In addition to preparing the dead, the *hevra kadisha* of Budapest also opened an "infirmary and home for the aged needy"—a perverse, though efficient, combination of services. In America, Hebrew Benevolent Societies, established in the same period, provided aid to Jews and oversaw Jewish burials and cemeteries; around the turn of the twentieth century, these morphed into the Jewish Federation.

Even the (non-Jewish) novelist Mark Twain recognized the effectiveness of the Jewish self-help system. "When a Jew is incapacitated, his own people take care of him," Twain said. "Whenever a Jew has need to beg, his people save him."

The Jews have also helped themselves under less dire straits. Most Jews of a certain age can recall the country club in town that the Jews opened because the other ones wouldn't allow Jews to join. As with hospitals, the "Jewish one" often turned out to be better than the ones that didn't want us.

Shmoozing among Friends

Along with providing a safety net, these nonprofit organizations also afforded participants the opportunity to forge social bonds. During the middle decades of the twentieth century, friendships between Jews and non-Jews were sometimes awkward, observes sociologist Herbert J. Gans. As one woman told Gans, "If you talk to a Christian . . . you feel you are doing it as a Jew. With Jewish friends you can tell 'em point blank what you feel."

Though both men and women enjoyed the friendships they developed through volunteering, Gans believes that Jewish women especially came to value the close bonds. Men, he believes, often acted as "lone wolves," seeking power and status rather than social support and conviviality. Women, on the other hand, tended to value organizational over personal accomplishments and cherished the friends they made in the process.

These stereotypical but sometimes truly differing styles of interaction were on display in a library-based book club I belonged to years ago. During our first two sessions the all-female participants had been enjoying relaxed, amiable discussions. At our third session a man showed up. Despite efforts by the leader (yours truly) to control him, Mr. Verbostein dominated the conversation, continually "mansplaining" to us aspects of the book we already knew, perhaps in hopes of garnering some of that aforementioned "power and status." Meanwhile, in the parking lot afterward (where the *real* meeting always happens), we women shared our reactions, which deepened our budding friendships.

As far back as biblical times Jews have recognized the benefit of friendship. The book of Ecclesiastes explains, "Two [friends] are better off than one. . . . For should they fall, one can raise the other." Notably, the Hebrew root for the word "friends," *haverim*, means the same as the Latin word for "religion": "to bind together." Underscoring the importance of friendship, the Talmudic sages recommend, "If your friend calls you an ass, put a saddle on your back."

The great Jewish philosopher Maimonides, a physician by trade, remarked about friends, "When one is in good health, he enjoys them. In time of trouble, he needs them." Clearly he was a man before his time in recognizing the health benefits of social bonds. Contemporary research shows that those who maintain close friendships live healthier as well as more joyful lives. Belonging to a house of worship of any religious persuasion can even add years to your life. According to a 2017 Vanderbilt University study, congregants who attend worship services—presumably where they meet up with friends—decrease their chances of early death by more than 50 percent. How come I've never heard a doctor say, "Take two *davens* [prayers] and call me in the morning"? Maybe they should. For those of us who aren't bent on *shvitzing* (sweating) in the gym, we could try shmoozing in the sanctuary.

The Yiddish term *shmoozing* loosely translates as "shooting the breeze," though it can also mean chatting someone up with a purpose, as in shmoozing to make a sale. *Kibitz*, too, is used for this style of conversation. The fact that Yiddish has two words for this activity denotes the importance we ascribe to connecting with one another. *Kibitz*, by the way, should not be confused with the Israeli collective known as a kibbutz. According to a National Public Radio Yiddish radio program, *kibitzing* means "making wisecracks and giving someone advice and commentary when they are trying to work." (It also explains why, as I wrote this sentence, I just let that call go to phone mail. Thank God for caller ID.)

Jews of my mother's generation were born-and-bred kibitzers and shmoozers. As the owner of a Jewish catering company that provided food for many *simchas* (celebrations) in Kansas City's tight-knit Jewish community, this was how my mother connected with clients. Often their conversations strayed far beyond whether to serve chicken or brisket. Mothers of the bride would complain to her about how much they despised the groom. Wives would reveal that their husband's business wasn't doing so good, so Uncle Harry from Cleveland would be paying for the bar mitzvah. As a result, the mere mention of a Jewish last name in the city could elicit from her an entire family history and genealogical chart. For many she could also fill you in about their divorces, business bankruptcies, breast reductions, and colostomies.

Even when my mother retired from catering and moved into an independent living residence, she continued kibitzing and shmoozing. On her first day there the intake administrator asked that she refrain from sitting at the all-Jewish table. "We like everyone to mix and mingle here," is how the woman put it. My mother nodded and said, "Of course, I understand." Later that day, when Mom entered the dining room for her first meal, she headed straight to the table of Jews, plopped down into an empty chair, and said, "Hello, everybody." She has continued to take her meals there ever since.

What Jewish Baby Boomers Join

Boomer-age Jews (those born between 1946 and 1964) continue to get their shmoozing and kibitzing fixes met through volunteering, but generally support different causes. Jews of my parents' generation, for example, have been much more involved in helping Israel through organizations such as Hadassah or the Jewish National Fund. Baby boomer Jews continue to list Israel as a priority, but not as highly as their parents. Like their parents, boomers do feel connected to the Jewish community when serving on a committee or board of a Jewish organization or synagogue, but they are less likely to belong to a national Jewish organization. Almost two-thirds of World War II generation Jews are currently members of a national Jewish organization, compared to just half of boomer Jews.

Boomer Jews have also rallied behind organizations that are attempting to preserve the demographic future of the Jewish people. By supporting efforts such as Taglit-Birthright Israel trips and campus Hillels, they hope Jews will meet and marry Jews and create new little Jewish babies. However, where Jewish matchmaking is concerned, a commercial venture may be more effective than these nonprofits. According to a survey (conducted in 2011 by—who else?—the company itself), 50 percent of current Jewish marriages began on J-DATE, which required nary a foundation grant, but did necessitate the two participants' enduring that excruciating first date. On my one and only J-date, my suitor provided way too much information about his gastric bypass, leading me to bypass J-dating.

Boomers also place a high priority on improving Jewish-Muslim relations, perhaps because of the religious discrimination historically—and currently—experienced by both populations. This area has been of particular interest to me ever since I became a member of the Interfaith Committee at the Catholic college where I worked. I will never forget the presentation we sponsored exploring our religious death rituals. As the first panel speaker, I stood and briefly outlined many of the Jewish death rituals detailed in chapter 3. Next the Muslim speaker rose, paused for dramatic effect, then said, "Everything Nancy just said about Jews goes for Muslims, too," and sat down.

Differences between the two cultures were more evident at another Jewish-Muslim women's event I attended, where participants were invited to informally ask each other questions about the other's religion. The Muslim women asked the Jewish women about their belief in God. The Jewish women wanted to know about the Muslim women's head coverings. Obviously, for the Jews present, culture trumped religion.

Here's perhaps the biggest difference between Jews who came of age during the Holocaust years and boomers: boomers don't limit their volunteering to Jewish organizations. As Rose Matzkin, Hadassah's national president from 1972 to 1976, explained, for Jews of her generation, "the opportunity to do something for Jews outweighed almost everything else." However, Jews in the following generations felt secure enough to look beyond the confines of the Jewish world for volunteer opportunities. A 2009 Research Center for Leadership in Action study found that only one-third of Jewish baby boomers prefer to work exclusively for a Jewish organization; two-thirds don't care if the cause is Jewish or secular. In general, the Research Center finds that "boomers affiliate, believe, and behave less religiously than their parents." Similarly, sociologist Chaim I. Waxman discovered in 2001 that 10 percent of pre–World War II generation Jews belonged to three or more Jewish organizations, while under 5 percent of Jewish boomers were so involved.

As a member of four Jewish organizations, I'm definitely in the minority for Jews my age. On the other hand, I belong to four non-Jewish organizations, so I also exemplify the opposite. How typically Jewish.

What Gen X–Yers Join

Remember the song "Kids!" (written by Lee Adams: Jewish) that asks, "Why can't they be like we were? Perfect in every way? What's the matter with kids today?" That pretty much sums up the Jewish leadership's reactions when contemplating the younger generation's involvement in Jewish organizations.

To be fair, it's not so much "what's wrong" with them as it is "what's different." Instead of affiliating "in our perfect way," Jews of the X and Y generations (born between 1965 and 1995) are creating their own ways of being Jewish.

These Jews "tend not to join organizations—not just Jewish organizations, but any organizations," writer Anita Diamant says. Like the rest of their generation, they sometimes mistrust institutions. While two-thirds of boomer Jews belong to a

national, non-Jewish organization, only one-third of Generation X and Y Jews do.

But that doesn't mean that younger Jews are not joining anything. Rather, when they see an unmet need, Gen Xers and
Yers often create their own organization to fill it. One example
of this social entrepreneurship is the Center for Earth-Based
Judaism's Wilderness Torah. In 2007 the environmental lawyer Zelig Golden amassed what he called "a not so organized
but well-intentioned little festival" that took thirty-five campers
to the edge of a vegetable field in Northern California to celebrate Sukkot. That little camping trip has developed into a
full-blown organization featuring annual nature-based holiday
celebrations, youth programs, and a training institute connecting Jews "to nature and each other."

Wilderness Torah is just one of many Jewish groups heralding
and protecting the environment—a top concern of Generation
X and Y Jews and less so, or at least rarely mentioned as a priority, of older Jews. For members of the Holocaust generation,
global warming and climate change were not matters of upmost
concern. Even some members of my own generation sometimes
react to predicted environmental catastrophes by saying, "Oh
well. I won't be around when that happens."

Poverty, hunger, and poor health care, unfortunately, are
pressing and ever-present concerns. In 2009 UCLA student
Rachel Sumekh began encouraging her fellow college students
to donate their unredeemed meals to students in need. Her idea
became the nonprofit organization Swipe Out Hunger, which to
date has provided more than 1.3 million complimentary meals.
Following a 2009 backpacking trip to Uganda with her father,
twenty-three-year-old Brooke Stern founded SOUL, Supporting
Opportunities for Ugandans to Learn, an organization providing
immunizations, HIV testing, and maternal health services. To

empower local women, SOUL has also taught tailoring, farming, and computer skills to thousands. More than three hundred have also learned to sew, and many have since bought their own sewing machines—notably, the first step toward economic self-sufficiency for many of our grandmothers, too.

Because many of these initiatives are not directed at Jews or at solving Jewish problems, they frequently fall under the radar of mainstream Jewish leaders. And yet the accomplishments are paradigms of *tikkun olam*, the Jewish imperative to "heal and repair the world"—even when the Jewish pioneers themselves are unaware of the Jewish impetus behind their actions.

What Generation Z Jews Join

When I went to college in 1970 I was seeking my MRS degree, which is how we referred to females on the lookout for potential spouses. (Yes, I'm actually *that* old.) Since my potential husband needed to be Jewish, I'd hang out at Hillel or ride my bike veeeerrrrrry sloooowllllly in front of the AEPi fraternity house, the only two places to find Jewish men.

How things have changed. Almost no one in Generation Z (born after 1995)—Jewish or not—is exclusively seeking a mate at college, and if Jews want to socialize or do "something Jewish" with fellow Jews, those two places are just two gefilte fishes in the sea of campus Jewish opportunities. Everything from politics to social action to LGBTQ concerns are being addressed through new groups.

For instance, at Harvard (just on the not-so-off chance you might be interested in telling your kids or grandkids), Jewish campus groups include the Progressive Jewish Alliance, the immigrant rights group Sanctuary at Hillel, the klezmer band RecKlez, and the nature-going Jewish Outing Club. For another kind of outing, there's BAGELS for Jewish gay, lesbian, bisexual, and transgender students. (Even if you don't fit that description, you gotta love their motto: "There's one in every minyan.") Speaking of minyanim, Harvard has four: Reform, Conservative, Orthodox, and a Worship and Study Minyan for "those of a wide variety of backgrounds." (Sounds like the joke about the synagogue no one sets foot in.) There's more: the Jewish Women's Group, and also the "completely egalitarian Men's Club" sponsoring Shabbat get-togethers and a *cholent* (casserole) cooking contest. The Arts and Sciences, Business, Design, Divinity, and Medical/Dental Schools (of course) each have a Jewish Student Association. To connect business students with Israeli investors and philanthropists, there's the Tamid Israel Investment Group. To provide students with a safe place to discuss the Middle East and organize rallies on behalf of Israel, there's the Harvard Israel Initiative. Should things get too heated, there's the Crimson Krav Maga club, where Jewish students learn Israeli mixed-martial arts self-defense fighting and de-escalating techniques.

Harvard's plethora of Jewish groups is not that unusual. Across America, Jewish college students are continuing the tradition of their grandparents and great-grandparents by coming together for community, comfort, and care of the world. Many new groups have been initiated through Hillel's Campus Entrepreneurs Initiative (CEI) program, which as of this writing has trained upwards of fourteen hundred student interns on forty-eight campuses to launch student-run Jewish campus initiatives. At UCLA, CEI entrepreneurs Alisa Malki and Caryn Roth, for example, pioneered the highly successful Challah for Hunger program. Volunteers in the UCLA Hillel kitchen make, braid, bake, and sell challahs; the proceeds are donated to charities such as Jewish World Watch, which helps genocide victims in the Democratic Republic of Congo and Darfur.

If you're a student who's feeling somewhat unique in this world, CEI can also be a place to connect people a lot like you. Through the CEI program at the University of California, San Diego, Arya Marvazy recognized such a need, so he founded JOPA, Jewish Organization for Persians and Americans. Is it too late for me to matriculate and form Widowed Jewish Librarians Writing Books?

"Jewniversity" students who like to pretend they're someone else can follow the lead of CEI entrepreneur Andrew Coonin. He raised $10,000 to found the University of North Carolina at Chapel Hill's Jewish Theatre Company, which produces works either written by Jewish authors or presenting positive Jewish characters or themes.

Maybe one day the company will put on a musical partnering with one of the fifty—yes, fifty—Jewish choral groups now on college campuses, boosted by the popularity of TV shows such as *Glee* and *The Sing Off.* These groups "are singing a lot more than just '*Adon Olam,*'" according to the *Forward*'s Gary Shapiro, offering repertoires that include Yiddish, hip-hop, and Israeli rock tunes.

The group names are part of the fun. As MIT singer Mauro Braunstein wryly notes, Jewish *a cappella* groups must "have puns in their names. It's the law." Indeed, the following names are right on key: Chai Notes (Cornell University), Meshuga Notes (Ohio State University), Maccabeats (Yeshiva University), Rhythm and Jews (University of Chicago). For the more Jewishly knowledgeable, there is MIT's Techiya (the High Holiday shofar call) and variations on the Hebrew word *shir* (sing): Hooshir (Indiana University), Shircago (University of Chicago), and Shir Appeal (Tufts University).

The proliferation of these groups gives me hope for the future. Okay, so maybe young people are not clamoring for positions on the Federation Board of Directors (who is?). And perhaps they'll never set foot in a Jewish Community Center, because their gym has better elliptical machines. But younger Jews are coming together to sing, agitate, pursue justice, donate, bake challahs and casseroles, and—of course—eat. In short, they too are joining organizations that, just as sociologist Elazar noted, fall into all of the five separate spheres serving different Jewish communal needs: congregational, education/cultural, community relations, communal welfare, and Israel support.

And so, to all of us Jewish worriers out there: it may be time to chill. Generation Z is abiding Hillel's advice, "Do not separate yourself from the community."

Naturally, bagels are available at most of their meetings, though not necessarily at Harvard's gay and lesbian's BAGELS group. When asked what the name stands for, they explain, "We're not entirely certain, but we're sure it's some sort of queer acronym." How comforting to know that the alphabet soup of organizational names continues with the next generation of Jews as well.

Conclusion

What It Means to Be Typically Jewish

Even though it was ninety degrees out and dots of *shvitz* (sweat) were dripping down my bra, I decided to make a pot of chicken soup. I needed to take something to the shivah that evening and would freeze the rest to break my Yom Kippur fast, a tradition I inherited from my mother. As I plopped the bird into the stockpot, an ad came on the radio announcing the upcoming production of *Sunday in the Park with George,* Stephen Sondheim's musical about the life of painter George Seurat.

That's when it hit me. My Jewish identity is like a pointillist painting consisting of thousands of miniature dots. No individual speck is meaningful until you step back and see the exquisite image created by all of those tiny pixels together.

I had set out to see if how I laughed, ate, thought, kvetched, or kvelled made me "typically Jewish." Yet my quest for *the* typically Jewish behavior was largely a fool's errand, because by examining each individual dot, I'd missed the point. No one action or attitude encapsulates what is Jewish—they all do.

Just look at the ostensibly mundane act of my making soup. An infinite number of emotional, historical, and religious ingredients had swirled into that typically Jewish moment. I had chosen to make chicken soup, that iconic Jewish dish joked about by a thousand Jewish comics. I was using a recipe handed down *l'dor vador,* "from generation to generation"—from a kosher cookbook my mother had written after being chastised for writing an earlier nonkosher Jewish cookbook. This soup would comfort a mourner as part of an ancient Jewish system of communal caring, as well as being part of a home-based creative Jewish ritual my mother and I had invented. What a wallop of meaning that soup was laden with, and it didn't even have any matzah balls.

"There are many ways to be Jewish: attitude, family, food, ritual, humor, culture," the *Forward* ad proclaims. Those of us questing for a straightforward solution to our Jewish identity dilemma ought to remember the wisdom of this saying, too: "For every complex problem there is an answer that is clear, simple, and wrong."

Unique Jewish Landscapes

Imagining Jewish identity as a portrait made up of a million dots allows each of us to combine our dots in unique proportions and places. Some Jews concentrate the dots over in this corner, reinterpreting eco-kosher laws. Others spend Tuesday mornings with Talmud instead of tennis. Some flit from the Democratic platform meeting to the J-Street Israel rally to the kabbalist Shabbat service. In cartoonist Amy Kurzweil's comic, Jewish college students grapple with these identity choices: ardent pro-Israel Jew, radical anti-Zionist Jew, politically and culturally apathetic Jew, expert educated Jew.

In unique ways, each Jew is forming what philosopher Bernard-Henri Levy calls Judaism's "vaporous outline." And, like the blind man feeling the elephant, certain Jews will believe that theirs is the correct interpretation. Now I think Tevye in *Fiddler on the Roof* had it right. Two men were arguing in his presence. "You're right," he announced to the first. Then he declared, "You're right," to the other. When an onlooker demanded, "They both can't be right," Tevye nodded and said, "You're right, too."

What's Not in the Jewish Picture

Claiming that there are different ways to be typically Jewish does not mean anything goes. Some splotches have no place in the Jewish panorama. But just like determining what goes into the Jewish picture, each of us will uniquely define what can't appear. Here are my top two thoughts/actions/beliefs that are incompatible with being Jewish:

1. DOGMATIC THINKING

"Why does a Jew answer every question with another question?" asks the gentile. "Why shouldn't a Jew answer every question with another question?" answers the Jew. Along with being a good joke, this exchange encapsulates Jewish philosophy. In Judaism, everything from the existence of God to the molecular constitution of kosher gelatin is open to interpretation, discussion, and debate.

2. DIVINE JESUS CHRIST

Jews are so open-minded, one-third of them told the Pew pollsters that believing Jesus is the Messiah is compatible with being Jewish. I'm still stunned by that one, because for me that's the line in the desert sand. Of course, by *halakhah* (Jewish law), if your mother is Jewish, you are Jewish, regardless of who you believe in. Perhaps those who responded affirmatively to this question had that in mind. But two-thirds evidently agree with Rabbi Neal Gold, who insisted on noting in the margins of this manuscript whenever I mentioned Jews for Jesus, "They're not Jews."

In short, to be Jewish is to refuse to accept any pronouncement on faith alone. As Levy reminds us, "Jews have come into the world less to believe than to study, not to adore but to understand."

What's Essential to the Jewish Picture

How do we Jews go about that understanding? While Jews have argued through the centuries about what's essential to being Jewish, a couple of formulations, more than others, have stood the test of Jewish time: (1) God, Torah, and the People of Israel; and (2) Torah, *avodah* (service or prayer), and *gemilut hasadim* (acts of lovingkindness). You might call both of these versions a Jewish trinity, but, in typically Jewish fashion, without agreement on the three essential elements.

In keeping with this typically Jewish disagreement, I share with you a third trinity that speaks to what makes *me* Jewish: I remember, I feel, I do.

1. REMEMBER

Remembering is an important part of my Judaism, but I forget why.

Just kidding. I agree with Yiddish writer Isaac Bashevis Singer, who said, "Jews suffer from every disease except amnesia." To be Jewish is to remember our collective history. Judaism has been likened to the mythical god Janus, whose two faces are positioned to look both forward and backward simultaneously.

Our history is bred into every fiber of our being. We proclaim "never again" out of recognition that it could, easily, happen again. Lest we try to forget, our rituals force us to remember. At joyous weddings we break a glass to remember the Temple's destruction (at least that's one explanation). At Passover seders we eat *maror* (bitter herbs, usually horseradish) to remember how the Egyptian taskmasters embittered the lives of our Israelite ancestors, and we spill wine from our cups to remember the Egyptians' suffering too. At Purim we noisily grind out the name of Haman, who tried to eradicate the Jewish people. On Yom ha-Shoah we recite special prayers and light memorial candles to remind us of the horrors of the Holocaust and our responsibility to prevent genocides from ever happening again. Many of our homes are laden with seder plates, *hanukkiah*s, and Shabbat candlesticks, reminding us of the Jewish heritage bequeathed to us. The Jewish Publication Society volumes on our bookshelves are testimony to our dedication to the written word. Our framed, illustrated *ketubah* (wedding contract) reminds us of our joyous wedding day—or the *get* (divorce decree) in the drawer shows that you should have listened to your mother. These various rituals and ritual objects have helped us to survive by whatever means necessary, demonstrating what Professor Michael Krasny has called the Jewish "dogged resilience in the face of adversity."

Our first names also help us remember our history. The Ashkenazic practice of naming a child after a deceased relative links us with those who came before us. Honorees called to the *bimah* (pulpit) for an *aliyah* (honor) are announced by their Hebrew name and the Hebrew name of their mothers and/or fathers. Every gathering of the Rosh Hodesh (new moon) women's group at my synagogue begins with introducing us by our own Hebrew name, along our mother's. Converts to Judaism often take biblical names so they can feel included in this history.

Our last names, too, link us to the historical chain of our people. The black students in my Jewish History and Culture class were amazed to learn that Jewish names such as Cohen and Levy can be traced to biblical times. My own last name, Kalikow, was derived from the word *kalika*, which I have been told means either "a little crazy" or "a bit lame." Knowing my family, it's definitely the former.

2. FEEL

Writer Lisa Schiffman tells the story of her non-Jewish husband's confusion about her Jewish identity. "You don't observe the Sabbath," he commented. "You don't go to a Passover seder. You don't even celebrate the major holidays. But your writing makes it sound as though Judaism is a focus of your everyday life."

"It is," she responded.

He could only shrug.

That exchange could have just as easily been between my husband and me. Everything that I am feels Jewish, but I can't explain it. Three of my Jewish jurors said the same thing:

> "I don't know. I just feel Jewish."
> "It's just what I am, not what I believe."
> "It's who I am, but I can't explain it further."

One part of this "it" I do recognize is the crazy cornucopia of emotions. We Jews are champion worriers (see chapter 1). We cringe at the mention of Bernie Madoff. Aptly named the "ever-dying people," we're always afraid we're on the verge of disappearing. (Religion professor Vanessa L. Ochs claims this fear manifests itself as a near obsession with Jewish population counts. Jews argue about whether we're growing or shrinking in part because of the near impossibility of deciding who gets included. Jewish demographer Barry A. Kosmin observes, "Counting Jews is like holding jello.") We also worry that the anti-immigrant and anti-Muslim rhetoric spewing from certain segments of the population sounds ominously familiar. With the slightest provocation, all that venom could be directed at us.

On a more positive note, feeling Jewish means regaling in the fullness of life. Despite our history of persecution—or perhaps because of it—Jews are basically optimistic. To be a Jew is to agree with God, who looked back at Creation and declared it "good."

Many of us experience something I can best identify as "breathing right," imbibing an instantaneous comfort, upon discovering that someone we meet is Jewish. Kvelling also fills out much of my emotional Jewish picture (see chapter 2). The overachievements of fellow Jews infuses me with deep satisfaction and pride.

In this regard I was delighted to read in Lisa Alcalay Klug's *Cool Jew* that "it's never been hipper to be Jewish." Klug is part of a young people's social movement reclaiming the formerly antisemitic word "Heeb." They call themselves Heebsters, which Klug defines as "someone who loves being Jewish, who is not afraid to be a total dork, but has a certain Jewish *savoir faire*." Heebsters display their ethnic pride with T-shirts emblazoned "He'Brew: The Chosen Beer," "Yo Semite," and "Jew.Lo." They dub the Israeli bobsled team (yes, there really is one) "the Frozen Chosen." Klug's book also provides great advice on how to "super Jew your own lovely Heeb self" no matter what your religious upbringing, employing the Heebster motto, "I'm good enough, Jew enough, and *gevalt*, do I like me!"

I also feel proud of other young Jews who unabashedly coined the term "Jewrotica" and proceeded to erect the site jewrotica.org, which strives to "bring sex to Judaism but also Judaism to sex." Among the group's erotic enterprises: a contest to find the sexiest rabbis and recognize them "for their raw awesomeness." In 2013 Rabbi Susan Silverman, sister of comedian Sarah Silverman, won the award in recognition of her work with Women of the Wall, an organization that advocates for women's right to pray at the Western Wall. In accepting the award, Silverman quipped, "I am happy to be called a Torah-loving-hot-ticket."

And I'm proud that Jews find someone boldly taking action to be sexy.

3. DO

In his book *Nine Essential Things I've Learned about Life*, Rabbi Harold S. Kushner titled chapter 6 "Religion Is What You Do, Not What You Believe." Judaism is a religion of action. To be Jewish is to do Jewish.

But what to do—or not to do—is up for grabs. In earlier centuries, there was little question about what a Jew did or refrained from doing. Observing the Sabbath, keeping kosher, marrying a Jew, and being buried in Jewish cemetery were part and parcel of what you did and therefore who you were. Today, American Jews have largely dispensed with most of these activities and crafted new Jewish behaviors.

"Wayfinding" is what anthropologists call the process by which groups create their own ethnic/religious identity rather than having it ascribed. Though all cultures do this, Jews have a tougher time of it because we have no pope or dogma we all accept. Jews must constantly reinvent, reimagine, and reconstruct (as one denomination puts it) religious practices. That's a good thing, because the process lends itself to creativity and innovation, but it also leaves us open to confusion, conflict, and ambivalence. Come to think of it, that pretty much sums up where Jews are today.

One of my most surprising revelations from writing this book is the extent to which we secular Jews "do Judaism." In our homes we dip our pinky fingers into wine glasses, wrap December presents in blue paper, light the candles and kiss the kids on Friday nights, sip from Grandpa Sam's *Kiddush* cup before digging into our traditional Friday night pizza dinners. We write checks to the Jewish Federation, Hadassah, and MAZON: A Jewish Response to Hunger to ensure the health and well-being of Jews and others here and in Israel. Yet we also send funds to Planned Parenthood to protect the right to choose, to the Sierra Club to protect the earth, and to the local chapter of Indivisible.org to protect us from all the divisive political *mishegoss*.

Outside the home we order pastrami on rye at the deli, bring a bundt cake to shivah, and discuss Naomi Ragen's latest novel at the Jewish Community Center's book club. At the same time our Jewishness also inspires us to volunteer for the Friends of the Library book sale, thrust a poster overhead at the ACLU anti-immigration protest, and knock on doors to support a school board candidate.

We're also "doing Jewish" by learning, enrolling in classes at community centers, congregations, and college campuses. Notably, too, Jewish learning is popular among not only the *alter-kacker* set (which literally means "old pooper" or "old fart"; see chapter 4). A 2014 Jewish Federation study found that almost half (44 percent) of adults under thirty-five are taking classes or learning about Jewish topics through the Internet, on their own, and/or with friends.

Finally, we're "doing Jewish" by participating in Jewish cultural events. Socio-psychologist Bethamie Horowitz notes the explosion of American Jewish culture, including "Jewish literature, filmmaking, investigation of Jewish history, social justice practices, giving circles, and klezmerfests."

Typically Jewish Future

So where does all of this Jewish remembering, feeling, and doing end up? While I expect that a great many of you readers will take exception to what I write—Jewish studies professor Chaim I. Waxman warns that it's "almost impossible to say anything about America's Jews without evoking the wrath of one faction or another"—I am nonetheless willing to unleash a bit of Jewish ire and issue a pronouncement: even though marriage to non-Jews is rampant, few of us keep kosher, and almost none of us attend services, I declare Jewish identity alive and well.

How, you may wonder, can I be optimistic with such bleak measurements? Simple. First, I'm Jewish. Second, I change the question.

I'm not the first to point out that survey questions often fail to capture much of the vibrancy of Jewish life. Jewish studies professor Ari Y. Kelman suggests that instead of questioning whether or not people light Shabbat candles, researchers should ask if people feel connected to the Jewish community. Or, I propose, how about asking if people are moved by chanting *Kaddish*, comforted by chicken soup, or proud of Jewish Nobel Prize winners? Better yet, let's ask, "Do you consider yourself part of the funny, maddening, frustrating, wonderful people known as Jews?" I predict the overwhelming response to this question would be positive.

Another challenge with the current incarnation of surveys is their failure to acknowledge the intricacies of intermarried life. A Christmas tree may deck the halls in many homes, but latkes are fried in the kitchen. Remarkably few people in intermarriages take Jesus as their personal savior. And "it's easier for Christians to accept Judaism than it is for a Jew to accept Christianity," notes interfaith counselor Dawn Kepler, who after decades of working with such couples, offers the optimistic assessment, "I don't think Judaism is ever going to come to an end."

Many Jews worry about the Jewish future because fewer young people are joining synagogues. However, writer Anita Diamant contends that relying on membership numbers as a primary indicator of Jewish involvement fails to yield a true picture, because young Jews tend not to join establishment organizations. Demographers Arnold Dashefsky and Ira Sheskin explain that "young Jews are not 'distancing' themselves from Judaism, but 'differencing' themselves. Young Jews are simply being Jewish in different ways than they were fifty years ago." For example, they may not belong to a synagogue, but they are turning out in record numbers for Jewish book fairs, Jewish film festivals, and Jewish musical festivals. In my own Broward County, tens of thousands of people showed up to celebrate Israel Independence Day.

Jewish cultural life is also booming. Dashefsky and Sheskin remind us, "Fifty years ago there were a handful of Jewish museums. There are now 156 Holocaust museums," along with the impressive Jewish infrastructure including 200 Jewish Community Centers, 145 Jewish Federations, 155 Jewish overnight camps, 139 national Jewish publications, and 3,500 synagogues.

Jewish studies professor Leonard Saxe agrees with this positive assessment. "In the future," he says, "we'll see many more people who identify as Jews . . . and appreciate the richness of Jewish cultural and religious life."

Also, the "Gen Next's" will not be recognizable as Jewish by "looking Jewish," whatever that means. "Like the rest of the American population," Diamant says, "we will be more racially and ethnically diverse, thanks to conversion, interracial marriage and interracial adoption, and the immigration of non-white, non-Western Jews." In other words, someone like Rabbi Angela Warnick Buchdahl, who has a Jewish father and Korean mother, will "look Jewish."

Your Turn

Besides all this, what else will the Jewish future hold? Let's discuss it. Or, more precisely, let's talk, debate, discuss, and deliberate what it means to be typically Jewish today and tomorrow. You're creative. Find a few Jews. Get more copies of the book (yes, we can talk group discount). Put on a pot of coffee, set out some bagels, and while you're munching, talk about who sells the best bagels in town. Or better yet, who makes the worst ones?

Once your conversation turns to more substantive subjects, be prepared for meaningful, serious, thought-provoking exchanges. Jews are naturals at this. Playwright Daniel Goldfarb explained the phenomenon this way: "If you are in the process of trying to figure out what it means that you're Jewish, then you're Jewish." Sure enough, the Jewish Jury sessions I conducted revealed that discussing one's Jewish identity touches a nerve buried deep in our *kishkas* (guts) many of us don't even realize exists. Discussing whether there is such a thing as a *Yiddishe kop*, if Jews are different, and how you can tell if someone is Jewish elicited animated, lengthy, and at times contentious conversations among my fellow Jewish jurors. The next morning I'd often find an email or text message that began, "Last night I was thinking about our meeting and . . ." followed by additional insights and anecdotes.

So, shall we begin with your own sense of identity? Turn to the book's Typically Jewish, Atypically Fun Discussion Guide and start with the first question. Do you agree with Goldfarb's statement? All in favor, say "*Oy.*"

Typically Jewish, Atypically Fun
Discussion Guide

Mazel tov. You have decided to hold a *Typically Jewish, Atypically Fun* Discussion Series. We promise you a ton of fun as you learn and discuss how participants live, love, work, eat, and even plan to die as Jews. To start, you'll need books and food, two essential elements for Jews. Let's start with the first.

Bulk Book Purchasing

You're going to like this: if you're a nonprofit organization (who isn't these days?) my publisher will give you a multiple-copy discount. Purchasing even ten copies (anywhere from ten to forty-nine, to be exact) will land you a substantial discount. The discounts increase for larger purchases. Such a deal. Call Longleaf Services at 800-848-6224 to place your order, then get ready to kibitz.

Series Structure

Either clergy or laypersons can lead your group discussions. And of course, you can hold them anywhere from your nearby Jewish organization to your living room to your favorite delicatessen restaurant.

Content is provided for ten approximately one-hour sessions, each discussing a book chapter—Introduction, Worrying, Kvelling, Dying, Noshing, Laughing, Detecting, Dwelling, Joining,

Conclusion—but the segments can be compressed into fewer sessions, or you can omit any not of interest to your participants (though obviously they are all fascinating to everyone).

Each session begins with Shmooze Qs (questions) to get the group talking (though since they are Jews, they probably won't need much prompting). The *Chutzpadik* Comments section segregates the more contentious topics. (Have a shoe ready to bang on the table if things get out of hand. Birkenstocks work well, but that company's founder was not Jewish; the Steve Madden and Michael Kors company originators, however, were members of the tribe.) Once everyone settles down, Silly Spiels will get the group moving around, sharing, and laughing again. Home *Kop*-Work (*kop* meaning "head") suggests ways participants can continue contemplating the topics. To make the rabbis happy, Classic Quotes offers biblical, Talmudic, classical, and contemporary quotations to contemplate. Last, we've furnished Read More, the continue-your-Jewish-education section for librarians, teachers, and future Jewish mavens.

Announcing the Discussion Series

Once you've decided upon the series dates and times, the following sample announcement could be inserted into your newsletter or bulletin announcement.

Typically Jewish, Atypically Fun Discussion Series to Begin

Are you "typically Jewish"? What does that mean?

Is there such a thing as a *Yiddishe kop* (Jewish head)? Do you have one?

Do Jews worry, kvell (burst with pride), work, love, or die differently from non-Jews?

To talk about these and other questions about what it means to be Jewish today, sign up for the *Typically Jewish, Atypically Fun* Discussion Series. Based on Nancy Kalikow Maxwell's paperback *Typically Jewish* (The Jewish Publication Society), the series will include fun, lively, thought-provoking conversations and activities to help you discover what it means to be "typically Jewish."

REFRESHMENTS WILL BE SERVED

Make sure those vital last words appear in your announcement, in all caps. The members of my Jewish Jury assure me that food—bagels and cream cheese (morning), mandelbread and strudel (afternoon), wine and cheese (evening)—is 51 percent of getting people to show up, and 51 percent of the group's success too, so you can rest assured that you already have it made.

Typically Jewish, Atypically Fun
Discussion Guide

Syllabus

Session 1. Introduction and Overview

SESSION GOALS

To provide an overview of the *Typically Jewish, Atypically Fun* Discussion Series, outline the program structure, and have participants get to know each other as they begin discussing what it means to be "typically Jewish." Note: Since personal information may be shared, a confidentiality policy should be explained, along with any ground rules for discussing controversial or contentious issues.

TO BEGIN

Request self-introductions with a brief statement about why each person signed up. The Silly Spiels activities that follow can be used as icebreakers.

SHMOOZE QS

1. Playwright Daniel Goldfarb said, "If you are in the process of trying to figure out what it means that you're Jewish, then you're Jewish." Do you agree with this statement?
2. Maxwell writes that this book sets out to investigate if Jews are essentially different from other people. If you were to undertake a similar quest, how would you go about it, and what do you think you would find?
3. "Two Jews, three opinions" is an oft-repeated cliché, but Maxwell states she has never heard "Two Catholics, three opinions." Do you agree with the cliché about Jews? If so, why? Are certain ethnic, racial, or cultural groups more associated with arguing than others?

CHUTZPADIK COMMENTS

1. Many Jews believe that all humans are made in the image of God, yet many also feel that somehow Jews are different.

Discuss this seeming contradiction. Have you ever felt this way? If so, what do you believe are those differences?

2. Is the search for Jewish identity somehow different from the search for identity would be for other ethnic, racial, or cultural groups? How would this series be different if it was "Typically Black," "Typically Hispanic," or "Typically Asian"?

SILLY SPIELS

1. How Jewish Are You?: Before the first class, prepare a list of "How Jewish are you?" questions that would be appropriate for your group. Questions might include: Have you ever attended a bar or bat mitzvah? Did you attend at least one High Holiday service last year? Do you attend Sabbath services regularly? Do you keep kosher?

   In class, have everyone stand up. Read one of the questions, and anyone answering "no" must sit down. Order the questions to begin with those to which most participants will answer "yes" and end with those to which few, if any, will respond affirmatively. The last one standing is proclaimed the winner.

2. Childhood Memory Exercise: Have participants pair off. Ask those born Jewish to exchange a childhood memory about one of the first times they "felt Jewish." Ask participants not born Jewish to recall an early encounter with a Jew or Judaism that made an impression.

3. Single-Word Slam: Divide participants into groups. Ask each group to list the top five words that describe what it means to be Jewish. Compile all the lists and rank the top five words used across all the groups. Congratulate the group that listed the most ranked words.

If time permits, repeat the exercise, describing what it means to be Christian.

HOME *KOP*-WORK

Have each participant ask one Jew and one non-Jew, "Do you think Jews are different from non-Jews? If so, how?" Compare the two answers.

CLASSIC QUOTES

1. *And God created man in His image, in the image of God He created him; male and female He created them.*—Gen. 1:27. This quote emphasizes the notion of universalism (that we are all the same), yet many Jews still harbor feelings that somehow we are different. How can you reconcile these two notions?

2. *I am a Jew. If you prick us, do we not bleed? If you tickle us, do we not laugh? If you poison us, do we not die?*—Shakespeare, *Merchant of Venice*, act 3, scene 1. This is another entryway to a similar conversation. Discuss the notion of universalism (that we are all the same) and the feelings some Jews harbor that we are somehow different. How can you reconcile these two notions?

3. *One who is bashful will never learn.*—Pirkei Avot / Ethics of the Fathers 2:5. By this point it will be obvious that some people have talked a lot and some have remained silent. Discuss the topic of introverts and extroverts. Is one type more typically Jewish?

READ MORE

To see recent opinion survey results about American Jewish attitudes: Pew Research Center's Religion and Public Life Project, *A Portrait of Jewish Americans* (Washington DC: Pew Research Center, 2013).

To compare the search for Jewish identity with other ethnic groups: Baratunde Thurston, *How to Be Black* (New York: Harper, 2012); and Eric Liu, *The Accidental Asian* (New York: Vintage Books, 1998).

To read a funny, decidedly not politically correct book about ethnic stereotypes: Colin Quinn, *The Coloring Book* (New York: Grand Central, 2015).

To read about Nancy Kalikow Maxwell's experience studying Catholic theology: "A Nice Jewish Girl Studying Catholicism?," *National Catholic Reporter* 40, no. 23 (April 9, 2004): 19.

To read memoirs of two women who had Jewish fathers and non-Jewish mothers: Mary Gordon, *Shadow Man* (New York: Random House, 1996); and Gloria Steinem, *My Life on the Road* (New York: Random House, 2015).

Session 2. Worrying

SESSION GOALS

To discuss Jews' relationship to worry and anxiety in the context of personal and group survival.

SHMOOZE QS

1. Do you think Jews worry more than non-Jews? If so, why? Give examples.

2. Are you or anyone you know superstitious about using expressions such as *kine-ahora* or "pooh, pooh, pooh"? Is there something typically Jewish about using words to ward off evil?

3. The *Huffington Post* ran a blog titled "I'm Not a Hypochondriac, I'm Just a Jew." Do you think Jews are more concerned about their health than non-Jews? If so, why?

4. Have you ever felt uncomfortable when you realized you were the only Jew in the room? If so, tell the story and explain why.

5. Comedian Judy Gold jokes about bringing her new non-Jewish friend home. "Ma, I want you to meet my new friend, Beth." Her mother's immediate response: "What? Do you think she would hide you?" Talk about why this is funny.

CHUTZPADIK COMMENTS

1. Maxwell says, "Even Jews who never attended Hebrew school and have zero Jewish education know this history of Jewish persecution on a gut level." Do you agree or disagree? Why or why not? Discuss the implications of your opinion.

2. Maxwell believes that a long history of persecution has taught Jews a valuable lesson: money equals survival. "Jews know that when forced to escape in the middle of the night, cold hard cash paves the way to freedom." Do you agree or disagree

with this statement? Do you think Jews have a different relationship with money than non-Jews?

3. Maxwell claims, "Beyond a belief in the saving power of
chicken soup, I can't say I believe in an underlying Jewish
dogma." Do you think there is a fundamental Jewish creed?
If so, what are its tenets?

SILLY SPIELS

1. Worry Scale: Ask participants to rank themselves on a "worry
scale" from zero (no worries) to ten (constant worrier). Tally
the results and see where most participants fall. The biggest
worrier gets an extra dessert.

2. The Worry Contest: Before the first class, prepare a list of
"Have you ever worried about this?" questions that would
be appropriate for your group. Possible questions might
include: Have you ever worried that a plane you are on will
crash? Do you arrive at the airport more than one and a
half hours early because you're worried you will miss your
plane? Have you ever seen a doctor to examine something
on your skin that turned out to be nothing? Have you ever
called a loved one because he or she was fifteen minutes
late arriving home? Ten minutes late? Five minutes? Order
the questions to begin with those to which most participants
are likely to answer "yes" and end with those to which few,
if any, will say "yes."

Bring a bowl filled with objects that can easily be removed
from it: candy, pennies, toothpicks, mah jongg tiles. In class,
read the first worry question. Instruct everyone anyone
answering "yes" to take an item from the bowl. When all
the questions have been read, the participant who took the
most objects is proclaimed the "Worry Maven." The Worry
Maven too gets an extra dessert.

3. Jewish Worry: In pairs or small groups, exchange stories about a time you felt apprehensive about being Jewish. When the group reconvenes, ask them to retell the one or two best stories to the entire group.

HOME *KOP*-WORK

Think about what you are doing to help ensure that Judaism will not die out. If you don't think you are doing enough, what else could or should you do?

CLASSIC QUOTES

1. *Whatever happens, it was designated long ago and it was known that it would happen; as for man, he cannot contend with what is stronger than he.*—Eccles. 6:10

   Do not worry about tomorrow's trouble, for you do not know what the day may bring.—Babylonian Talmud, *Yevamot* 63b

   Whatever a man fears may happen to him is only a matter of probability—either it will happen or it will not happen.—Maimonides, *The Preservation of Youth*, 1198

   All worrying is forbidden, except to worry that one is worried.—Rabbi Mordechai of Lechovitz, as quoted in Dov Peretz Elkins, *Wisdom of Judaism* (Woodstock VT: Jewish Lights, 2007), 79

What is your reaction to these rabbinical pronouncements about worrying? If you were to issue your own advice about worrying, what would it be?

2. *He who is rich today may not be so tomorrow.*—*Shemot Rabbah* 31:3

   A lover of money never has his fill of money, nor a lover of wealth his fill of income. That too is futile.—Eccles. 5:9

Discuss the relationship of money and worry. Is there something typically Jewish about your opinion?

3. *Be fruitful and increase.*—Gen. 1:28

    American Jews are an ever-dying people.—Marshall Sklare

It has been said that each generation of Jews worries they will be the last Jews on earth. Do you worry about that? What, if anything, do you do about that concern?

READ MORE

To see what Jews and non-Jews should *really* worry about: John Brockman, ed., *What Should We Be Worried About? Real Scenarios That Keep Scientists Up at Night* (New York: Harper Perennial, 2014).

To read essays and funny memoirs about hypochondria: David Bedrick, "I'm Not a Hypochondriac, I'm Just a Jew," *Huffington Post* blog, July 29, 2013, https://www.huffingtonpost .com/david-bedrick/im-not-a-hypochondriac-im_b_3664073 .html; Jennifer Traig, *Well Enough Alone: A Cultural History of My Hypochondria* (New York: Riverhead Books, 2008); Brian Fraser, *Hyper-chondriac: One Man's Quest to Hurry Up and Calm Down* (New York: Atria, 2007); and Gene Weingarten, *The Hypochondriac's Guide to Life and Death* (New York: Simon and Schuster, 1998).

Session 3. Kvelling

To discuss the phenomenon of Jewish kvelling (bursting with pride) and identify kvell- and cringe-worthy aspects of being Jewish.

SHMOOZE QS

1. Historian Susan Glenn reportedly coined the term "Jewhooing": "the social mechanism for both private and public naming and claiming of Jews by other Jews." How do you feel about the practice of Jewhooing? Have you or others you know engaged in it?

2. Religion professor David E. Kaufman contends that the extent to which Jews seek out famous people who are Jews "is more than simple ethnic pride." Do you agree or disagree? Why or why not?

3. Comedian Colin Quinn has joked, "Without the Jews, the whole country would be like Branson, Missouri." Talk about what he means and why this is funny.

CHUTZPADIK COMMENTS

1. Maxwell kvells (bursts with pride) that Judaism is a "commonsense religion" with a "unique emphasis on pragmatic solutions to daily living." Do you agree or disagree? Give examples to support your answer.

2. Some of Maxwell's Catholic colleagues enlightened her about the notion of redemptive suffering: that human suffering on earth will be redeemed in the afterlife. For Jews, she contrasts, "Life is to be enjoyed, not suffered through." Do you agree or disagree? Explain why.

SILLY SPIELS

1. Jewish/Not Jewish Celebrities: Before class, prepare a list of known celebrities whose assumed Jewish/non-Jewish identity

is often incorrect. To get you started, here are examples of celebrities mistakenly thought to be Jewish: Ernest Borgnine, Ethel Merman, Ringo Starr, Martha Stewart, Robin Williams, Mel Gibson (just kidding). And here are examples of celebrities mistakenly thought to be non-Jews: James Franco, Eva Green, Scarlett Johansson, Natalie Portman.

In class, read the names, mixing up the "real" Jews and the non-Jews. In teams or individually, have participants guess the correct identification. The individual or team with the most correct answers is proclaimed the "Jewhooing Champion."

2. Kvell List: Divide the groups into pairs or small groups. Provide each group with a pad of stick-on notes. Have them write on each note something that makes them kvell about the Jewish religion. Reconvene the class and have all the groups post the notes on a blank wall. As a group, try to rearrange the answers by general topics. Discuss the most popular responses and what, if anything, they say about Jews and Judaism.

3. Cringe List: Repeat the exercise above, but this time identifying what, if anything, makes you cringe about the Jewish religion.

HOME *KOP*-WORK

1. See if you can catch yourself or overhear someone kvelling over the accomplishments of Jews or identifying a public person as Jewish. Think about what, if anything, this says about being Jewish.

2. Repeat the above activity, but this time note examples of cringing over Jews' bad behavior.

CLASSIC QUOTES

1. *Pride goes before ruin; arrogance, before failure. Better to be humble and among the lowly than to share spoils with the proud.*—Prov. 16:18–19

Let the mouth of another praise you, not yours. The lips of a stranger, not your own.—Prov. 27:2

These two quotes warn against excessive pride and boasting. Do you agree? Discuss if kvelling over the accomplishments of fellow Jews should be included.

2. *Turn the Torah over and over, for everything is in it. Look into it, grow old and worn over it, and never move away from it, for you will find no better portion than it.*—Pirkei Avot / Ethics of the Fathers 5:22

   [Jews have] a profound trust in the human mind as an instrument to perfect the world.—Barbara Lerner Spectre

Maxwell kvells over what she claims is the Jewish assumption that "with enough thinking and talking, we humans can figure it out—no matter what *it* is." Do you agree that we can figure everything out this way? Do you agree that this thinking is typically Jewish?

   The pursuit of knowledge for its own sake and an almost fanatical love of justice . . . these are the features of the Jewish tradition which make me thank my lucky stars I belong to it.—Albert Einstein

Do you agree with Einstein that pursuit of knowledge and almost fanatical love of justice are essential features of Jewish tradition? What two features of Jewish tradition would top your list?

READ MORE

For discussions of how Jews are different from non-Jews: Pew Research Center's Religion and Public Life Project, *A Portrait of Jewish Americans* (Washington DC: Pew Research Center, 2013); and Tom W. Smith, *Jewish Distinctiveness in America: A Statistical Portrait* (New York: American Jewish Committee, 2005).

To explore "Jewhooing," the naming and claiming of Jews publicly: David E. Kaufman, *Jewhooing the Sixties: American Celebrity and Jewish Identity* (Waltham MA: Brandeis University Press, 2012).

For lists of Jews who "done good": Philip Brooks, *Extraordinary Jewish Americans* (New York: Children's Press, 1998); Paula E. Hyman and Deborah Dash Moore, eds., *Jewish Women in America: An Historical Encyclopedia*, 2 vols. (New York: Routledge, 1998); Jacob Rader Marcus, *Concise Dictionary of American Jewish Biography*, 2 vols. (Brooklyn NY: Carlson Publishing, 1997); Barry L. Schwartz, *Jewish Heroes, Jewish Values* (Springfield NJ: Behrman House, 1996); and Robert Slater, *Great Jews in Sports* (Middle Village NY: Jonathan David, 2003).

Session 4. Dying

SESSION GOALS

To discuss the Jewish approach to life as revealed through Jewish death rituals and customs.

SHMOOZE QS

1. Maxwell mentions that some people use the words "passing on" to refer to dying. What words do you use or avoid when discussing someone's death and why?
2. Food features prominently in Jewish mourning rituals. Discuss why you think this is. In your experience, does this differ in other cultures?
3. Discuss an experience you or someone you know has had with *Kaddish*, the foundational prayer recited by Jewish mourners. What (if any) was the emotional impact of the prayer on you or the mourner?
4. Covering the mirrors and placing a rock on a gravestone are examples of *minhag*s or *minhagim*, customs Jews observe. What death-related *minhag*s have you or someone you know observed? What was the emotional impact on you or the mourner?

CHUTZPADIK COMMENTS

1. Despite the traditional prohibition against it, an increasing number of Jews are choosing cremation. Discuss the reasons behind the prohibition and your opinion of the practice.
2. Maxwell recounts her *bubbe* saying, "You live on through the good deeds you did on earth and in the memories of loved ones." Did you ever hear this from another Jew? Do you agree that this is how Jews live on? Is this how you would wish to live on? What is your opinion about the afterlife?

SILLY SPIELS

1. Light a Candle: Bring a yahrzeit candle and matches to class. Have each participant come up and light (or if open flames are not allowed, pretend to light) the candle and mention someone who has died. Ask participants to share why this person was important to them.

2. Memorable Shivah: In pairs or small groups, exchange stories about a memorable, funny, terrible, or terrific shivah experience. Reconvene the full group and ask participants to share the most remarkable stories.

3. Meaningful Mourning Ritual: Pair off and tell each other the most meaningful Jewish death ritual you have participated in. What made it so significant?

HOME *KOP*-WORK

1. Find one obituary that you would call typically Jewish and another you think is typically goyish. What elements make these so?

2. Think about what Jewish death rituals you would wish to be observed when you die. Why would you prefer these? Would you omit others? If so, explain why.

CLASSIC QUOTES

1. *I have put before you life and death. . . . Choose life.*—Deut. 30:19. Discuss the meaning of this quote and if or how it is relevant to your life.

2. *He must depart just as he came.*—Eccles. 5:14. This quotation is traditionally used to explain the Jewish tradition of washing bodies upon death. Discuss if there are any other possible meanings.

3. *Though He may slay me, yet will I trust in Him.*—Job 13:15. Job and the *Kaddish* prayer expound upon trusting God. Discuss what this means to you and what, if any, relevance it has for you.

READ MORE

For more on Jewish death and dying: Arthur Green, *Judaism's 10 Best Ideas* (Woodstock VT: Jewish Lights, 2014); Hillel Halkin, *After One-Hundred-and-Twenty* (Princeton NJ: Princeton University Press, 2016); Maurice Lamm, *Jewish Way in Death and Mourning* (Middle Village NY: Jonathan David, 2000); and Rifat Sonsino and Daniel B. Syme, eds., *What Happens After I Die?* (Northvale NJ: Jason Aronson, 1994).

On the history of Jewish funerals: Jenna Weissman Joselit, *Wonders of America* (New York: Hill and Wang, 1994).

For personal reflections on Jewish death rituals and the meaning of life: Lee Eisenberg, *The Point Is* (New York: Twelve, 2016); Michael Kinsley, *Old Age: A Beginner's Guide* (New York: Tim Duggan Books, 2016); Nancy Kalikow Maxwell, "The Mourner's Ribbon," *Forward*, August 16, 2013, 28; and Leon Wieseltier, *Kaddish* (New York: Vintage Books, 1998).

Session 5. Noshing

SESSION GOALS

To discuss the Jewish relationship with food.

SHMOOZE QS

1. Do you think Jews have a different relationship with food than do members of other faiths or cultures? Explain.
2. According to the stereotype, Jewish restaurants offer huge portions, and Jewish hosts and hostesses provide way too much food. Do you find this to be true? Cite examples to support your contention.
3. Historian Hasia Diner claims that throughout history everything connected to cooking and eating for Jews "throbs with sanctity." Do you agree? If so, how does this manifest today?
4. Maxwell says that asceticism (attaining transcendence through self-denial) holds no place within traditional Judaism. Do you agree or disagree? Explain.

CHUTZPADIK COMMENTS

1. Some—not all—studies have pointed to Jews having lower rates of alcoholism than other groups (although rates of drug abuse among Jews appear to be similar to other populations across the board). From your own experience, do you believe Jews are less likely to be alcoholics than others? Why or why not?
2. Do you think Jewish mothers have a different relationship with food than other mothers? If so, how and why?
3. Maxwell quotes a deli patron saying, "My parents didn't send me to Hebrew school, but they did send me to the deli every Sunday." Discuss this preference for "eating Jewish over studying Jewish" and what, if any, implications this holds for Judaism's future.

SILLY SPIELS

1. Jewish Foods: In pairs or small groups have participants create two lists: typically Jewish foods and typically goyish (not-Jewish) foods. Compile all of the lists and discuss why certain foods appeared in each category.
2. Shabbat Food Memories: Pair off and take turns exchanging memories of a special Shabbat food you had or heard about.
3. Favorite Holiday Food: Ask the group to call out their favorite food associated with a Jewish holiday, and write down each response on a chalkboard or flip chart. Read the list aloud and have participants vote by hands for their favorite dish. The winning entry is proclaimed the "Chosen's Chosen." Ask if anyone has a great story to go with that holiday food.
4. Kugel Cookoff: If you are ambitious, hold a kugel contest, and name the winner the "Kugel King or Queen." Or, have everyone bring in their favorite recipe and note the differing ingredients.

HOME *KOP*-WORK

1. Sample a frozen bagel you have never tried before and decide if: A—Actually, it's pretty good or B—Nope, It's still terrible. Try to convince another Jew of your opinion.
2. Consult a recent Jewish cookbook and note how Jewish cooking has changed from "your mother's day."

CLASSIC QUOTES

1. *In the future world, a man will have to give an accounting for every good thing his eyes saw, but of which he did not eat.*—Jerusalem Talmud, *Kiddushin* 4:12. Discuss what this means. Compare this advice to that of other cultures or religions as you understand them.
2. *The people would go about and gather it, grind it between millstones or pound it into a mortar, boil it in a pot, and make it*

into cakes. It tasted like rich cream. When the dew fell on the camp at night, the manna would fall upon it.—Num. 11:8–9. Opinions vary about what, exactly, manna was. What do you think and why?

3. *The less faith a Jew has in the Bible, the more meaning pastrami acquires.*—Michael Wex. Do you agree or disagree? Explain why or why not.

READ MORE

On the history of Jewish American eating: Hasia R. Diner, *Hungering for America* (Cambridge MA: Harvard University Press, 2001); Roger Horowitz, *Kosher USA* (New York: Columbia University Press, 2016); Ted Merwin, *Pastrami on Rye: An Overstuffed History of the Jewish Deli* (New York: New York University Press, 2015); and Michael Wex, *Rhapsody in Schmaltz* (New York: St. Martin's Press, 2016).

On eating in other religions: Benjamin E. Zeller et al., eds., *Religion, Food, and Eating in North America* (New York: Columbia University Press, 2014).

Session 6: Laughing

SESSION GOALS

To explore Jewish humor and what it says about being Jewish.

SHMOOZE QS

1. Maxwell claims, "If you want to understand African Americans, listen to their music," and to know Jews, "consider their comedy." Do you agree or disagree? Give examples to support your answer.
2. Discuss the phenomenon of Jewish clergy pursuing careers in comedy. What, if anything, is similar about both professions?
3. Discuss the nuances of the term "chutzpah." Is it typically Jewish to be *chutzpadik*, and is it—as the saying goes—good for the Jews?

CHUTZPADIK COMMENTS

1. Maxwell contends that there is a relationship between God belief (more specifically, the lack thereof) and the prevalence of a Jewish funny bone. According to the 2013 Pew survey, one-third of Jews say they believe in God, as compared to three-fourths of Christians. Discuss this statistic. Do you agree that God belief and Jewish humor are related in some way? Explain.
2. Maxwell discusses an "inherent self-worth, resulting in a sense of entitlement and self-assuredness," which some believe is prevalent among Jews. Do you agree or disagree that these traits are more likely to be possessed by members of the tribe? Why or why not? Discuss what, if any, implications this would have for Jewish comedians and comedy.
3. What is your prediction about the future of Jewish comedy? Do you believe Jews will remain in the forefront of American comedy in generations to come? Why or why not?

SILLY SPIELS

1. Count the Comedians: In small groups, list all the famous Jewish comedians you can think of, past and present. (No fair using your phone to look them up.) The group listing the most Jewish comedians is crowned the "Wizards of Wit."

2. Jewish Jokes: Read each of the following three jokes aloud. Discuss what makes each Jewish and why it is funny. Have the group vote for their favorite.

   a. The comic Rodney Dangerfield told his psychiatrist that everyone hated him. The shrink said, "That's ridiculous. Everyone hasn't met you yet."

   b. An elderly Jewish man is hit by a car and the ambulance driver carefully places him on the stretcher. "Are you comfortable?" he asks. "Thank God, I make a good living," says the old man.

   c. "Oh, God, help me. If you don't, I'll ask my uncle in New York."—Anonymous

3. Stand-Up Time: Are there any comedians among your group? Invite them to stand up and tell a joke. Analyze the joke and decide whether it's a "Jewish joke."

HOME *KOP*-WORK

1. Attend a comedy show or watch a comedian perform on TV or YouTube. Try to decide if the comedian is Jewish and/or if any of the jokes are specifically "Jewish jokes."

2. Even better, arrange for all of the participants to attend a comedy show together. Afterward, discuss whether the jokes were Jewish. Don't forget to charge a little extra for the tickets and make it into a fundraiser.

CLASSIC QUOTES

1. *And they said to Moses, "Was it for want of graves in Egypt that you brought us to die in the wilderness?"*—Exod. 14:11

   Sarah said, "God has brought me laughter; everyone who hears will laugh with me."—Gen. 21:6

Discuss how the Hebrew Bible approaches humor through the lens of these biblical quotes. Can you think of any contemporary comedian who uses this style?

2. *All humorous stories contain God's truth.*—Rabbi Dovidl of Dinov. Do you agree or disagree with this statement? Why or why not?

3. *Spare me from gentile hands and Jewish tongues.*—Yiddish proverb. What is meant by a "Jewish tongue"? Is it typically Jewish to have one?

READ MORE

There are so many great resources on Jewish humor. Here are just a few: Arthur Asa Berger, *The Genius of the Jewish Joke* (New Brunswick NJ: Transaction, 2006); Jeremy Dauber, *Jewish Comedy: A Serious History* (New York: Norton, 2017); Joseph Dorinson, *Kvetching and Shpritzing: Jewish Humor in American Popular Culture* (Jefferson NC: McFarland, 2015); Marjorie Ingall, *Mamelah Knows Best* (New York: Harmony Books, 2016); Arie Kaplan, "How Jews Revolutionized Comedy in America," *Reform Judaism*, Spring 2002, http://www.reformjudaismmag.net/302ak.html; Michael Krasny, *Let There Be Laughter* (New York: William Morrow, 2016); William Novak and Moshe Waldocks, eds., *Big Book of Jewish Humor* (New York: Harper and Row, 1981); and Joseph Telushkin, *Jewish Humor* (New York: William Morrow, 1992).

Session 7. Detecting

SESSION GOALS

To discuss how and why Jews identify each other.

SHMOOZE QS

1. Do you try to discern if someone you meet is Jewish? If so, why do you do this, and what methods do you use?
2. Describe how you feel when you discover someone you meet in a secular context is Jewish. Do you think this feeling is exclusive to Jews or also experienced by members of other groups?
3. Discuss what it historically meant for someone to "look Jewish." Has this changed in recent years?
4. Discuss what it historically meant for someone to "sound Jewish." Has this changed in recent years?
5. Many people are having their DNA tested to learn more about their heritage. Have you done so, or do you know someone who has? If so, discuss how what was learned affected you or that other person.
6. Discuss the relationship between where you live and your Jewish identity. Do you believe your location has influenced your Jewish life?

CHUTZPADIK COMMENTS

1. Jews have been called a religion, a race, a tribe, an ethnic group, a culture, a civilization. What word(s) would you use to describe Jews and why?
2. Upon discovering that a child hit on his bike was Jewish, Maxwell "felt like someone had punched [her] in the stomach." Have you ever experienced something similar? If so, did it involve a fellow Jew and/or someone with whom you felt especially connected? Discuss this reaction.

3. The subtle detection of fellow Jews is called "Jewdar," and such detection of gays is called "Gaydar." Do you believe these actually exist? If so, compare and contrast them.

SILLY SPIELS

1. My Jewish Name: Have participants discuss the origin of their Hebrew name and/or the "Jewishness" of their first or last name. Those not born Jewish can provide anecdotes about their own name.

2. The J Game: Before class, find photos of Jewish and non-Jewish friends, family, or others whom you know but participants don't. In class, show the photos, mixing up the Jews and non-Jews. In teams or individually, have participants guess which ones are Jewish. The one with the most correct answers is proclaimed the "Jewdar Champion."

3. Jewish Jobs: In teams, using magic markers, have participants create two lists: "Typically Jewish Jobs" and "Typically Non-Jewish Jobs." Hang all the lists up front for everyone to see and discuss why certain jobs appeared in each category.

HOME *KOP*-WORK

1. Surreptitiously observe both a group of Jews and a group of non-Jews talking. How do you know one group is (largely) Jewish and the other is not? What differences, if any, can be detected?

2. Try to figure out if someone you meet is Jewish. Take note of the methods you use.

CLASSIC QUOTES

1. *"Are you an Ephraimite?"; if he said "No," they would say to him, "Then say* shibboleth*"; but he would say* "sibboleth," *not being able to pronounce it correctly. Thereupon they would seize him and*

slay him.—Judges 12:5–6. Discuss how language can identify a person's origins. What experiences have you had along the lines of identification via language?

2. *Jews don't play sports; they own the team.*—Anonymous

When a car owned by gentiles breaks down, in two seconds they're under the car, on top of the car. . . . It becomes an airplane and they fly away. When a Jewish-owned car breaks down, the husband says, "It's in the hood." The wife says, "Where's the hood?" and the husband answers, "I don't remember."—Jackie Mason

Discuss the two jokes above. Do you think they are funny? If so, why? If not, why not?

READ MORE

On the history of Jewish clothing: Karen Engel, "Should a Jewish Girl Wear a Dirndl?," *Lilith*, Winter 2013–14; and Jenna Weissman Joselit, *Wonders of America: Reinventing Jewish Culture, 1880–1950* (New York: Henry Holt, 1994).

On Jewdar: "Gaydar? Jewdar? Does It Exist?," Jon Carroll, "The Mystery of Jewdar," SFGate, March 20, 2009, http://www.sfgate.com/entertainment/article/The-mystery-of-Jewdar-3247374.php.

On how Jews talk: Sarah Bunin Benor and Steven M. Cohen, *Survey of American Jewish Language and Identity* (Hebrew Union College–Jewish Institute of Religion, October 2009), http://www.bjpa.org/Publications/details.cfm?Publicationid=3874.

On tribes and genes: Sebastian Junger, *Tribe: On Homecoming and Belonging* (New York: Twelve, 2016); and Harry Ostrer, *Legacy: A Genetic History of the Jewish People* (New York: Oxford University Press, 2012).

Session 8. Dwelling

To identify items commonly found in a Jewish home.

1. When you are inside the home of someone you don't know, do you try to discern if that person is Jewish? If yes, why and what methods do you use?
2. Do you display a mezuzah on the doorpost of your home? Why or why not?
3. What, if any, Hanukkah decorations do you display outside of your home? What underlies your choices?

1. Maxwell notes, "Guns also tend to be sparse in Jewish homes, though not because of *halakhah* (Jewish law)." Discuss Jews' relationship with guns. Do you believe there should be more or fewer guns in Jewish homes today? Would you give the same answer if the question referred to pre-Holocaust Europe? Explain.
2. Some have argued that reliance on the nostalgia of Jewish objects such as Grandma's Sabbath candlesticks or Uncle Morty's seder plate will not sustain Judaism in the future. Do you agree or disagree? Why or why not?
3. A Jewish furniture salesman waved Maxwell away from a sofa, insisting, "No, not those. They're for the goyim." Discuss his comment and whether there is such a thing as "Jewish furniture."
4. Are most of your friends Jewish? Do you believe there is a difference between having Jewish and non-Jewish friends? If yes, how do you understand that difference?

SILLY SPIELS

1. Yarmulke Stash: Have everyone describe where they stash extra yarmulkes from weddings and b'nai mitzvah at home. Vote on the funniest or most unusual location.
2. Essential Jewish Amenities: In pairs or small groups, list the top five amenities a neighborhood should have in order for Jews to want to live there. Note which of the amenities, if any, your area offers.
3. Significant Jewish Object: Have each participant bring in or describe one significant Jewish object kept at home. What makes it precious?
4. Dish-Off: Have each participant tell how many sets of dishes they own. Pronounce the one with the highest number the "Dish Diva" or "China King."

HOME *KOP*-WORK

1. Identify which Jewish-related items in your home are of special significance. Discuss with family members if and how they will be passed from generation to generation.
2. If you live or work in the vicinity of a Jewish neighborhood, go to a local thrift shop and see what Jewish-related items you can find.

CLASSIC QUOTES

1. *Make beautiful objects in the performance of God's commandments.*—Babylonian Talmud, *Shabbat* 133b; *Nazir* 2b; *Bava Kamma* 9a–9b. Discuss the relationship of aesthetics and holiness. Does beauty make something feel more sacred? Tell of a time that an exquisite, elegant, or magnificent object inspired a powerful emotional response in you.
2. *A court, a charity fund, a synagogue, a bath house, an outhouse, a bloodletter [some believe this is a ritual circumciser], a doctor, a*

scribe, a kosher butcher/slaughterer, and a teacher.—Babylonian Talmud, *Sanhedrin* 17b, referring to the amenities required for a Jew to live in a community in Talmudic times. Why do you believe each of these elements was required for Jews living in Talmudic times? Which, if any, do you believe are still necessary for Jews living today?

READ MORE

On the importance of our things: Winifred Gallagher, *House Thinking* (New York: HarperCollins, 2006); Vanessa L. Ochs, "What Makes a Home Jewish?," *Cross Currents* 49, no. 4 (Winter 1999–2000); and Gideon Reuveni and Nils Roemer, *Longing, Belonging, and the Making of Jewish Consumer Culture* (Boston: Brill, 2010).

On the history of the Jewish home: Andrew R. Heinze, *Adapting to Abundance* (New York: Columbia University Press, 1990); and Jenna Weissman Joselit, *Wonders of America: Reinventing Jewish Culture, 1880–1950* (New York: Henry Holt, 1994).

Session 9. Joining

To discuss the communal aspects of being Jewish.

1. Are there any *machers* among you? Discuss the meaning of the term and whether you think being a *macher* is uniquely Jewish.
2. Compare the roles of synagogues and Jewish Community Centers. Suggest ways to improve both institutions.
3. Some Jews believe they have a special responsibility to other Jews, and some extend that obligation to all humanity. Discuss these differing—and at times conflicting—attitudes.

1. Maxwell claims, "There is something typically Jewish about voluntarily reaching out to others through groups. Jews are joiners." Do you agree or disagree? Why or why not?
2. Maxwell comments that the synagogue is far from the only place Jews find Jewish community. Do you believe that belonging to a congregational community is a necessary aspect of one's involvement in the Jewish community? Does Jewish continuity necessitate synagogue membership and participation?

1. Jewish Friends: On a piece of paper, have participants create three columns: "My Parents," "Me," and "My (Future?) Kids." Ask everyone to estimate (or predict) what percentage of each social circle is or is likely to be Jewish. Compare the results and discuss any generational patterns.

2. Where's Your Community? In pairs or small groups, write down the top five places where participants find and feel a sense of community. Are these places more likely to be Jewish or non-Jewish? Discuss the implications of your answer.

HOME *KOP*-WORK

1. Fantasize about winning the lottery. What, if any, institution or social cause would you work for or create? Would it be Jewishly related? Would you want a testimonial dinner in your honor? What would you want served?

2. Ask two or three Jews under thirty what, if any, organizations or clubs they belong to. Does this exchange give you any insight into Jewish organizations today and/or tomorrow?

CLASSIC QUOTES

1. *Acquire for yourself a friend with whom you can eat, drink and study.—Avot de-Rabbi Natan,* chapter 8. Are these your essential needs in a friend? What would you include and why?

2. *All Jews are responsible for each other.*—Babylonian Talmud, *Shevuot* 39

   If there is a needy person among you, one of your kinsmen . . . do not harden your heart. . . . You must open your hand and lend him sufficient for whatever he needs.—Deut. 15:7–8

Discuss the Jews' responsibility to each other and to all of humankind. Do you believe Jews should take care of other Jews as the first priority?

3. *God is not found in churches or synagogues or holy books. God is found between people.*—Martin Buber. What would you say are the implications of Martin Buber's quote for churches, synagogues, and the study of holy books?

READ MORE

On the importance of friends and community: Harold S. Kushner, *Nine Essential Things I've Learned about Life* (New York: Knopf, 2015); and Alexander Nehamas, *On Friendship* (New York: Basic Books, 2016).

For statistics on Jewish friendship and giving: Pew Research Center's Religion and Public Life Project, *A Portrait of Jewish Americans* (Washington DC: Pew Research Center, 2013); and Sidney Schwarz, *Jewish Megatrends* (Woodstock VT: Jewish Lights, 2013).

On the history of Jewish women's organizations: Paula E. Hyman and Deborah Dash Moore, eds., *Jewish Women in America: An Historical Encyclopedia* (New York: Routledge, 1997).

Session 10: Conclusion

SESSION GOALS

To summarize this series, identify conclusions, and discuss next steps to continue the conversation.

SHMOOZE QS

1. Maxwell likens her Judaism to a pointillist paining with millions of minute dots. Do you agree or disagree with this conclusion? Do you personally relate to it? Why or why not?

2. Maxwell further envisions Jewish identity as fitting into three spheres: remembering, feeling, and doing. Do you agree with these conceptions? Why or why not?

3. Maxwell says she feels most Jewish when chanting *Kaddish*, sipping chicken soup, or kvelling over Jewish Nobel Prize winners. When and where do you tend to feel the most Jewish?

4. Has this book and series helped you to reconsider or better understand aspects of your own Jewish identity? What, if any, insights did you glean? Did anything surprise you?

CHUTZPADIK COMMENTS

1. Some have argued that Judaism's cultural aspects are not enough to sustain the religion in the future. Do you agree or disagree? If you agree, what do you believe may need to be done to preserve and strengthen Judaism in the future?

2. An interfaith counselor told Maxwell, "Very few people feel they can stop being Jewish." Do you agree or disagree with the statement? Why or why not?

SILLY SPIELS

1. Typically Jewish: Divide participants into groups and ask each group to name as many things as they can to complete this

sentence: To be "typically Jewish" someone would ____. Compile the lists and see if any themes or patterns emerge.

2. My Jewish Identity: Give everyone three stick-on notes. Have each person write #1 on the first, #2 on the second, #3 on the third. Then, using a magic marker, write the following eight words—Worrying, Kvelling, Dying, Noshing, Laughing, Detecting, Dwelling, Joining—each on its own large piece of paper. Distribute the eight words around the room. Have participants place their #1, #2, and #3 choice under the three words that best describe the top three aspects of their Jewish identity. Discuss the results.

HOME *KOP*-WORK

1. Kvetch to yourself about how you could have made this *Typically Jewish, Atypically Fun* Discussion Series even more fun. Call the person in charge and volunteer to serve on the committee to plan the next one.

2. Have each participant ask one Jew and one non-Jew, "Do you use mayonnaise on your corned beef sandwich?" Compare the answers and prepare to be amazed!

CLASSIC QUOTES

1. *Our eyes are set in the front and not in the back, so one should look ahead.*—Maimonides

   Jews suffer from every disease except amnesia.—Isaac Bashevis Singer

Beginning with these quotes, discuss the role history plays for Jews.

2. *It's never been hipper to be Jewish.*—Lisa Alcalay Klug. Do you agree or disagree? Do you believe younger American Jews are more or less likely to feel secure and proud about their

Jewish identity than previous generations? What do you believe are the implications for Judaism in America in the years to come?

READ MORE

For experts' predictions about the Jewish future: George E. Johnson, "What Will the Jewish World Look Like in 2050?," *Moment* 42, no. 1 (January–February 2017): 44, https://www.momentmag.com/will-jewish-world-look-like-2050/.

For what others think is essential to Judaism: Edgar M. Bronfman, *Why Be Jewish?* (New York: Twelve, 2016); Harold S. Kushner, *Nine Essential Things I've Learned about Life* (New York: Knopf, 2015); Bernard-Henri Levy, *Genius of Judaism* (New York: Random House, 2017); and Lisa Schiffman, *Generation J.* (San Francisco: HarperSanFrancisco, 1999).

For a funny, positive spin on being Jewish: Bryan Fogel and Sam Wolfson, *Jewtopia* (New York: Warner Books, 2006); and Lisa Alcalay Klug, *Cool Jew* (Kansas City MO: Andrews McMeel, 2008).

Notes

INTRODUCTION

xiii **Jewish women over fifty:** "Jewish Book Month Celebrates Love of Reading," *Discover JCC Magazine,* http://magazine.discoverjcc.com /jewish-book-month-celebrates-love-of-reading/, accessed July 13, 2013; and Andrew Perrin, "Book Reading 2016," September 1, 2016, pewinternet.org/2016/09/01/book-reading-2016-appendix-a.

xiii **gathering to discuss books is a time-honored tradition:** For more on Jews and books, see Amos Oz and Fanie Oz-Salzberger, *Jewsand-Words* (New York: Yale University Press, 2012).

xvi **Like the majority of Jews in America, I rarely go to shul:** Pew Research Center's Religion and Public Life Project, *A Portrait of Jewish Americans* (Washington DC: Pew Research Center, October 1, 2013), 76.

xvi **Jews like me have an "unshakable loyalty":** Alena Janet Strauss, "Experiencing Everyday Prejudice of a Concealable Stigma: Jews in a Non-Jewish World" (dissertation, University of Toronto, 2011).

xviii **As I recounted in a *National Catholic Reporter* article:** Nancy Kalikow Maxwell, "A Nice Jewish Girl Studying Catholicism?," *National Catholic Reporter,* April 9, 2004, 19.

xix **I "married out.":** Pew Research Center, *A Portrait of Jewish Americans,* 35.

xxi **"If you are in the process of trying to figure out":** Daniel Goldfarb, quoted in David E. Kaufman, *Jewhooing the Sixties: American Celebrity and Jewish Identity* (Waltham MA: Brandeis University Press, 2012), 28.

xxii **Baratunde Thurston's book:** Baratunde Thurston, *How to Be Black* (New York: HarperCollins, 2012).

1. WORRYING

1 **classic joke book:** Dan Greenburg, *How to Be a Jewish Mother* (Los Angeles: Price Stern Sloan, 1964), 11.

1   **book on the history of the Jewish mother:** Joyce Antler, *You Never Call! You Never Write!* (New York: Oxford University Press, 2007).

1   **Elaine May and Mike Nichols skit:** Michael Krasny, *Let There Be Laughter* (New York: William Morrow, 2016), 20.

1   **his ever-present state of apprehension:** Moshe Schulman, "A Slice of a New Life," *Forward*, May 29, 2015, 42.

2   **The average adult spends 12 percent:** Frank Partnoy, *Wait: The Art and Science of Delay* (New York: Public Affairs, 2012), 123.

2   **in her autobiography:** Gloria Steinem, *My Life on the Road* (New York: Random House, 2015), 28.

2   **"Do not worry about tomorrow's trouble":** Babylonian Talmud, *Yevamot* 63b.

2   **futility of future-angst:** Moses Maimonides, *The Preservation of Youth*, 1198, quoted in Francine Klagsbrun, *Voices of Wisdom* (New York: Pantheon Books, 1980), 24.

2   **"All worrying is forbidden":** Rabbi Mordechai of Lechovitz, quoted in Dov Peretz Elkins, *Wisdom of Judaism* (Woodstock VT: Jewish Lights, 2007), 79.

3   **the song's composer Bobby McFerrin:** Songfacts, accessed September 24, 2016, http://www.songfacts.com,details.php?id=5362.

3   **wrote in his book:** Albert Vorspan, *Start Worrying: Details to Follow* (New York: UAHC Press, 1991).

3   **knew enough to borrow the word:** Clint Eastwood, quoted in George E. Johnson, "Who's Afraid of the Evil Eye?," *Moment*, September–October 2014.

3   **even if things are good:** Howie Mandel, in *When Jews Were Funny* (First Run Features, 2013).

3   **Jewish therapist blogged:** David Bedrick, "I'm Not a Hypochondriac, I'm Just a Jew," *Huffington Post*, July 29, 2013, http://www.huffingtonpost.com/david-bedrick-im-not-a-hypochondriac-im_b_3664073.html.

4   **Author and self-proclaimed Jewish hypochondriac:** Jennifer Traig, quoted in Lana Gersten, "Medical Meltdown: A Memoir," *Forward*, August 20, 2008, http:// forward.com/articles/14025/medical-meltdown-a-memoir-02380/.

4   **Pew Research Center's 2014 Religious Landscape Study:** "Religious Landscape Study" (Washington DC: Pew Research Center, 2014), http://www.pewforum.org/religious-landscape-study/belief-in-god/.

4 **"Your health comes first":** Joseph Telushkin, *Jewish Wisdom* (New York: William Morrow, 1994), 275.

4 **good health as a neutral void:** Brian Dillon, *The Hypochondriacs* (New York: Faber and Faber, 2009), 7.

4 **Israel has produced more start-up companies:** "Israel #1 in Start-Ups Per Capita, #3 Globally in Patents," *Algemeiner*, May 4, 2012, https://www.algemeiner.com/2012/05/04/israel-1-in-startups-per -capita-3-globally-in-patents/.

4 **Nobel Prize winners have been Jewish:** K. M. Heilman, "Jews, Creativity and the Genius of Disobedience," *Journal of Religion Health*, October 16, 2015, abstract, PubMed, https://www.ncbi.nlm.nih.gov /pubmed/26475313.

4 **chapped lips as a possible brain tumor:** Woody Allen, "Hypochondria," *New York Times*, January 12, 2013, https://www.nytimes .com/2013/01/13/opinion/sunday/hypochondria-an-inside -look.html?_r=0&mtrref=www.woodyallenpages.com&gwh= CD193B34D59629189C179B06A0EADD9F&gwt=pay&assetType= opinion.

5 **On the Larry King show he admitted, "I'm a Jew":** Jon Stewart, quoted in Lisa Rogak, *Angry Optimist: Life and Times of Jon Stewart* (New York: St. Martin's Press, 2014), 7.

5 **original Exodus story:** Exod. 1:22.

5 **the royal vizier Haman's edict:** Esther 3:8–9, quoted in Telushkin, *Jewish Wisdom*, 459.

5 **childhood story:** Judy Gold, in *When Jews Were Funny*.

8 **"He who is rich today":** *Shemot Rabbah* 31:3, quoted in Francine Klagsbrun, *Voices of Wisdom*, 322.

8 **"*shanda far di goyim*" translates literally:** Philologos, "Before Madoff, or the Goyim, a Shande," *Forward*, August 19, 2009, http://forward .com/culture/112432/before-madoff-or-the-goyim-a-shande/.

9 **fellow Jew does something REALLY BAD:** Doron Kornbluth, "Shanda fur di Goyim!," *Keeping Our Families Jewish Newsletter*, http://www.doronkornbluth.com/articles.asp?AID=25#.V_9 _9pUzWUk, accessed October 13, 2016.

9 **The association of Jews and money:** Dan Pine, "Jews and Money," *Jweekly.com*, April 11, 2013, https://www.jweekly.com/2013/04/12 /jews-and-money-the-stereotype-the-history-the-reality-jccsf-series -explores/.

9 **Jews "did well disproportionately":** Jerry Muller, quoted in Pine, "Jews and Money."

10 **one in five Jewish households:** Pew Research Center's Religion and Public Life Project, *A Portrait of Jewish Americans* (Washington DC: Pew Research Center, October 1, 2013), 42.

10 **poorest place in the United States:** Sam Roberts, "A Village with the Numbers, Not the Image of the Poorest Place," *New York Times*, April 20, 2011, http://www.nytimes.com/2011/04/21/nyregion /kiryas-joel-a-village-with-the-numbers-not-the-image-of-the-poorest -place.html.

10 **rank religious groups:** *How Americans Feel about Religious Groups* (Washington DC: Pew Research Center, July 16, 2014), http://www.pewforum .org/2014/07/16/how-americans-feel-about-religious-groups/.

11 **he sometimes grows apprehensive:** Mark Breslin, in *When Jews Were Funny*.

11 **"when one Jew saw three gentiles":** Michael Wex, in *When Jews Were Funny*.

11 **"Two Jews are walking down a dark street":** William Novak and Moshe Waldocks, *Big Book of Jewish Humor* (Harper and Row, 1981).

12 **In a 1976 essay:** Marshall Sklare, quoted in Chaim I. Waxman, *Jewish Baby Boomers: A Communal Perspective* (Albany: State University of New York Press, 2001), 7.

12 **"The gentiles have stopped trying":** Joanne Greenberg, quoted in Elaine Bernstein Partnow, *The Quotable Jewish Woman* (Woodstock VT: Jewish Lights, 2004), 15.

12 **American Jewry was sliding:** Waxman, *Jewish Baby Boomers*, 12.

12 **A *Look* magazine:** Waxman, *Jewish Baby Boomers*, 12.

12 **many of these dire predictions:** Waxman, *Jewish Baby Boomers*, 13.

12 **survey of American Jews reveals:** Jack Wertheimer, quoted in Laurie Goodstein, "Poll Shows Major Shift in Identity of U.S. Jews," *New York Times*, October 1, 2013, https://www.nytimes.com/2013 /10/01/us/poll-shows-major-shift-in-identity-of-us-jews.html.

13 **fall into this category:** Goodstein, "Poll Shows Major Shift."

13 **"has been a matter of lively debate":** Pew Research Center, *A Portrait of Jewish Americans*, 23.

13 **a different demographic scenario:** Ira M. Sheskin and Arnold Dashefsky, "United States Jewish Population, 2016," in *The American Jewish Year Book, 2016* (New York: Springer, 2016).

13 **estimated at 6.856 million:** Sheskin and Dashefsky, "United States Jewish Population, 2016."

13 **the intermarriage rate has grown to 58 percent:** Pew Research Center, *A Portrait of Jewish Americans*, 35, 8.

13 **do not belong to a synagogue:** Goodstein, "Poll Shows Major Shift."

14 **captures my internal reprimand:** Ruth Andrew Ellenson, *Modern Jewish Girl's Guide to Guilt* (New York: Dutton, 2014), 1.

14 **intermarriages have been rising steadily:** Pew Research Center, *A Portrait of Jewish Americans*, 8–9.

14 **Second marriages are often:** Barry A. Kosmin, *Intermarriage: Divorce and Remarriage among American Jews 1982–87* (North American Jewish Data Bank Family Research Series, August 1989), 1.

15 **most children inherit their faith:** Keren McGinity, "Jewish Fatherhood Needs a Makeover," *Lilith*, Spring 2017, https://www.lilith.org/articles/jewish-fatherhood-needs-a-makeover/.

15 **includes different statistics:** Naomi Schaefer Riley, *'Til Faith Do Us Part* (New York: Oxford University Press, 2013), 93.

15 **vast differences in the child-rearing practices of Jews:** Pew Research Center, *A Portrait of Jewish Americans*, 67.

17 **"Adult Jewish learning is a flourishing part":** Lisa Grant and Diane Tickton Schuster, *What We Know about Adult Jewish Education* (Virginia Beach: A.R.E. Press, January 2008), 1, https://www.bjpa.org/search-results/publication/4816.

17 **"enrollments remain relatively low":** Grant and Schuster, *What We Know About Adult Jewish Education*, 4.

18 **"has been challenged by someone or another":** Milton Steinberg, *Basic Judaism* (New York: Harvest Book, 1947), 32.

18 **synagogue attendance:** Pew Research Center, *A Portrait of Jewish Americans*, 71.

19 **"Today I'll be Jewish.":** Lisa Schiffman, *Generation J* (San Francisco: HarperSanFrancisco, 1999), 4.

19 **I don't want to end up:** Franz Kafka, "Letter to His Father," quoted in Telushkin, *Jewish Wisdom*, 239.

2. KVELLING

22 **Jews making up 7 percent of history's:** "Religious Affiliation of History's 100 Most Influential People," Adherents.com, accessed February 29, 2016, http://www.adherents.com/adh_influ.html.

22   **"The Jews constitute but one percent":** Mark Twain, "Concerning the Jews," quoted in Marjorie Ingall, *Mameleh Knows Best* (New York: Harmony Books, 2016), 83.

22   **Nobel Prize winners:** K. M. Heilman, "Jews, Creativity and the Genius of Disobedience," *Journal of Religion Health*, October 16, 2015, abstract, PubMed, https://www.ncbi.nlm.nih.gov/pubmed /26475313.

23   **"a unique mix":** Paula Hyman, quoted in Julian Sinclair, "Naches," *Jewish Chronicle*, March 6, 2009, https://www.thejc.com/judaism /jewish-words/naches-1.8111.

24   **a.k.a. Adam Glasser:** Nathan Abrams, "Triple Exthnics: Nathan Abrams on Jews in the American Porno Industry," *Jewish Quarterly* (UK), 2005, 27–30.

24   **implementing a quota system:** Martha Biondi, *To Stand and Fight* (Cambridge, MA: Harvard University Press, 2003), 106.

24   **Many colleges engaged in:** Arthur Hertzberg, "Numerus Clausus," in *Encyclopaedia Judaica*, 2nd ed., ed. Fred Skolnik (New York: Macmillan References USA, 2007), 15:339, 343.

24   **sue Columbia University:** Arthur Hertzberg, *Jews in America* (New York: Columbia University Press, 1997), 299.

25   **The word, reputedly coined by historian:** Susan Glenn, quoted in David E. Kaufman, *Jewhooing the Sixties: American Celebrity and Jewish Identity* (Waltham, MA: Brandeis University Press, 2012), 266.

26   **"It is more than simple ethnic pride":** Kaufman, *Jewhooing the Sixties*, 270.

27   **an entry entitled:** "Lists of Jews," Wikipedia, accessed August 18, 2017, en.wikipedia.org/wiki/category:Lists_of_Jews.

27   **list of one hundred most powerful:** Steve Linde, "World's 50 Most Influential Jews," *Jerusalem Post*, May 21, 2010.

28   **"the greatest Jewish journalist":** George Steiner, with Laure Adler, *A Long Saturday* (Chicago: University of Chicago Press, 2017), 63.

28   **JewBus (Jewish Buddhists) have had an outsized impact:** Rodger Kamenetz, quoted in Lisa Schiffman, *Generation J* (San Francisco: HarperSanFrancisco, 1999), 37.

29   **The joke about an elderly Jewish woman:** David Harris, "15 Ways of Being Jewish Is Meaningful," *David Harris Blog*, AJC, September 29, 2016, http://blogs.timesofisrael.com/15-ways-being-jewish-is -meaningful-2/.

30 **A scene in a Letty Cottin Pogrebin novel:** Letty Cottin Pogrebin, *Single Jewish Male Seeking Soul Mate* (New York: Feminist Press at the City University of New York, 2015), 96.

30 **study by the philanthropic research group:** Emily Alpert, "Jews Connected to Jewish Community Give More to Charity, Study Shows," *Los Angeles Times*, September 2, 2013, http://articles .latimes.com/2013/sep/02/nation/la-na-nn-jewish-philanthropy -donors-20130830; and Shawn Landres, "When You're Connected, You Give," *Reform Judaism Magazine*, Summer 2014, https://issuu .com/reformjudaism/docs/rj_summer2014_reduced/21.

30 **Jews earning under $50,000:** Maria Di Mento, "Jewish Donors Are Generous, Especially to Non-Jewish Causes," *Chronicle of Philanthropy*, September 6, 2013, https://www.philanthropy.com/article /Jewish-Donors-Are-Generous-to/154439.

30 **"Everybody is obliged to give":** Babylonian Talmud, *Gittin* 7a, in "Charity (Tzedakah): Charity Throughout Jewish History," Jewish Virtual Library, accessed October 3, 2017, http://www .jewishvirtuallibrary.org/charity-throughout-jewish-history, from *Encyclopaedia Judaica* (2008).

31 **Jews "held powerful positions":** Ira Forman, "Politics, United States," in *Encyclopaedia Judaica*, 16:338–350.

31 **the British statesman never ceased to proclaim:** "Beaconsfield, Benjamin Disraeli, Earl of," *New Standard Jewish Encyclopedia*, ed. Geoffrey Wigoder, 7th ed. (New York: Facts on File, 1992), 122.

32 **"most highly politicized ethnic/religious group":** Forman, "Politics, United States."

33 **80 percent of comedians:** Steve Allen, quoted in Joseph Telushkin, *Jewish Humor* (New York: William Morrow, 1992), 19; and Paul Offenkrantz, "Woody Allen: Good for the Jews?" (lecture, Florida Atlantic University, Lifelong Learning Society, Boca Raton FL, November 22, 2016).

33 **"country would be like Branson, Missouri":** Colin Quinn, *The Coloring Book* (New York: Grand Central, 2015), 84.

34 **"The Maurice and Florence Rosenthal Center":** Quinn, *The Coloring Book*, 84.

34 **Israeli survey:** Gad Lior, "What Do Israelis Do in Their Free Time?," Ynetnews.com, December 12, 2016, www.ynetnews.com /articles/0,7340,L-4318880,00.html.

34 **being intellectually curious:** Pew Research Center's Religion and Public Life Project, *A Portrait of Jewish Americans* (Washington DC: Pew Research Center, October 1, 2013), 55.

34 **did his own share of kvelling:** Albert Einstein, quoted in Joseph Telushkin, *Jewish Wisdom* (New York: William Morrow, 1994), 616.

35 **"Justice, justice shall you pursue":** Deut. 16:20.

35 **The biblical prophet Amos proclaims:** Amos 5:24.

35 **The prophet Micah insists:** Mic. 6:8.

35 **the pursuit of justice:** Gideon Sylvester, "Social Justice Lies at the Heart of the Jewish People," *Haaretz*, July 1, 2012, http://www .haaretz.com/jewish/rabbis-round-table/social-justice-lies-at-the -heart-of-the-jewish-people-1.447878.

36 **"Nobody loves his alarm clock":** Maurice Samuel, quoted in Telushkin, *Jewish Wisdom*, 461.

36 **"Jews never follow directions":** Schiffman, *Generation J*, 8.

36 **one thousand organizations that supported:** Hody Nemes, "Jewish Groups Warm to Climate Change," *Forward*, September 16, 2014, http://forward.com/news/205617/jewish-groups-warm-to-climate -change-battle/.

37 **"Jews are the only ones who":** Quinn, *The Coloring Book*, 81–82, 79.

37 **number of schooling years:** Caryle Murphy, "Key Findings of How World Religions Differ by Education," Pew Research Center, December 13, 2016, http://www.pewresearch.org/fact-tank/2016 /12/13/key-findings-on-how-world-religions-differ-by-education/.

37 **virtually no educational gender gap:** "Jewish Educational Attainment," Religion and Education Across the World, December 13, 2016, http:// www.pewforum.org/2016/12/13/jewish-educational-attainment/.

37 **educational attainment in the United States:** Tom W. Smith, *Jewish Distinctiveness in America: A Statistical Portrait* (New York: American Jewish Committee, 2005), 5.

37 **Federal Reserve study:** Francine Diep, "Does More Education Make People Wealthier?," *Pacific Standard*, May 6, 2015.

37 **American Hindus:** Caryle Murphy, "The Most and Least Educated U.S. Religious Groups," Pew Research Center, November 4, 2016. http://www.pewresearch.org/fact-tank/2016/11/04/the-most-and -least-educated-u-s-religious-groups/.

38 **"danger of being loved to death":** Jonathan D. Sarna, quoted in Sarah E. Richards, "You Don't Have to Be Jewish to Love JDate,"

New York Times, December 5, 2004, http://www.nytimes.com/2004 /12/05/fashion/you-dont-have-to-be-jewish-to-love-jdate.html?_r=0.

38 **"the nice Jewish boy or girl":** Richards, "You Don't Have to Be Jewish."

39 **"a light to the nations":** Isa. 49:6, 51:4.

39 *Emet Ve-Emunah* **explains:** Robert Gordis, *Emet Ve-Emunah: State-ment of Principles of Conservative Judaism* (New York: United Syna-gogue Book Service, 1988).

39 *Jews: The Essence and Character of a People*: Quoted in Jonathan Woocher, *Sacred Survival: The Civil Religion of American Jews* (Bloom-ington: Indiana University Press, 1986), 140.

39 **'The room needs cleaning':** Alan Lurie, "What Does It Mean That the Jews Are God's Chosen People?," *Huffington Post*, initial post November 1, 2011, updated January 23, 2014, http://www .huffingtonpost.com/rabbi-alan-lurie/jews-gods-chosen-people_b _1079821.html.

40 **"both glory and weight":** Bernard-Henri Levy, *The Genius of Judaism* (New York: Random House, 2017), 135.

40 **God offered the Torah:** *Sifrei Devarim*, 343.

40 **"God, I know we are your chosen people":** Sholem Aleichem, "Tevye the Dairyman," as quoted in Ronn Torrossian, "Shalom Ale-ichem's Tevye to Nahman Lichtenstein," Times of Israel, December 5, 2013, http://blogs.timesofisrael.com/shalom-aleichems-tevye-to -nahman-lichtenstein-jews-tradition-history-quotes/.

40 **"Every people are chosen":** Personal interview with Dawn Kepler, May 15, 2017.

40 **religion professor David Kaufman sees:** Kaufman, *Jewhooing the Sixties*, 273.

41 **Jewish exceptionalism:** Kaufman, *Jewhooing the Sixties*, 273.

41 **Bagels were on the agenda:** Jane Eisner, "Barack Obama and the Ultimate Jewish Schmear Tactic," *Forward*, August 31, 2015, https:// forward.com/food/320124/barack-obama-and-the-ultimate-jewish -schmear-tactic/.

41 **The Hillel sandwich:** Bee Wilson, *Sandwich: A Global History* (Lon-don: Reaktion, 2010), 26.

41 **outsized impact on chocolate**: Deborah Prinz, quoted in Leah Koe-nig, "Walk Down the Jewish Chocolate Trail," *Forward*, January 22, 2013, http://forward.com/articles/169712/walk-down-the-jewish -chocolate-trail/.

41 **eggplant parmesan:** Debra Rubin, "Dishes of Diversity in Jewish Culinary World," *New Jersey Jewish News*, February 28, 2011, http://njjewishnews.com/article/4016/dishes-of-diversity-in-jewish-culinary-world#.Wh6bHJWWyUk.

42 **Jews live an average of:** Allison Gaudet Yarrow, "May You Live Until 120," *Forward*, August 3, 2011, http://forward.com/culture/140894/may-you-live-until-120-dna-uncovers-secrets-to-je/.

43 **shocked an interfaith gathering:** Harold S. Kushner, *Nine Essential Things I've Learned about Life* (New York: Knopf, 2015), 109.

43 **"adultery in his heart":** Jimmy Carter, quoted in Kushner, *Nine Essential Things*, 107.

44 **"Any man whose wife demands":** Maggie Anton, *Fifty Shades of Talmud* (Los Angeles: Banot Press, 2016), 49.

44 **observant married Jewish women:** Michelle Friedman et al., "Observant Married Jewish Women and Sexual Life: An Empirical Study," https://www.jewishideas.org/article/observant-married-jewish-women-and-sexual-life-empirical-study, as quoted in Marc Tracy, "Jews Do It More," *Tablet*, July 23, 2010, http://www.tabletmag.com/scroll/4041/jews-do-it-more.

44 **2015 Israeli study:** Shachar Kidron, "Doing It by the Numbers: A Statistical Look at Israeli's Intimate Details," *Haaretz*, September 15, 2015, http://www.haaretz.com/isreal-news/.premium-1.675480.

44 **Jews are also "doing it":** Tracy, "Jews Do It More."

45 **"Your rounded thighs":** Song of Songs 7:2,4,9.

45 **"Although some individual rabbis":** Telushkin, *Jewish Wisdom*, 230.

45 **"Eat your bread in gladness":** Eccles. 9:7,9.

45 **"a man will have to give":** Jerusalem Talmud, *Kiddushin* 4:12, quoted in Telushkin, *Jewish Wisdom*, 230.

45 **"signed a pact with life":** George Steiner, "George Steiner Addresses the Jewish Question(s)," *Forward*, March 31, 2017, 27.

46 **Despite what Rabbi Telushkin describes:** Telushkin, *Jewish Wisdom*, 277.

46 **less than half of Jews believe it:** Tom W. Smith, *Jewish Distinctiveness in America: A Statistical Portrait* (New York: American Jewish Committee, 2005), 106.

46 **story of Rabbi Yochanan ben Zakkai:** Telushkin, *Jewish Wisdom*, 425.

47 **"The worst thing you can say to a Jew":** Quinn, *The Coloring Book*, 81–82.

47 **Jews have a deep respect for rationality:** Barbara Lerner Spectre, quoted in Alan Wolfe, *At Home in Exile* (Boston: Beacon Press,
2014), 198.

47 **"Judaism can be a headache":** Daniel Herwitz, "Joel and Ethan
Coen," in *Makers of Jewish Modernity*, ed. Jacque Picard et al. (Princeton NJ: Princeton University Press, 2016), 640.

48 **"the Iron Maiden of Jewish Life, the Jewish Mother":** "Jewish Week-
lies Reject Lord Snow's Theory of Jewish Genetic Superiority," *JTA*,
April 15, 1969, https://www.jta.org/1969/04/15/archive/jewish
-weeklies-reject-lord-snows-theory-of-jewish-genetic-superiority.

49 **"several Parliamentarians":** Mark L. Winer, "Winning Friends of
Other Faiths," ReformJudaism.org, https://reformjudaism.org
/winning-friends-other-faiths, accessed August 20, 2017.

49 **bar and bat mitzvah as "a life-affirming rite of passage":** Corinna
Nicolaou, *A None's Story* (New York: Columbia University Press,
2006), 96–97.

49 **an antisemitic slur:** Georg Wilhelm Friedrich Hegel, quoted in
Steiner, "George Steiner Addresses the Jewish Question(s)," 26.

49 **two jokes highlight:** Steiner, "George Steiner Addresses the Jewish
Question(s)," 26; and Michael Krasny, *Let There Be Laughter* (New
York: William Morrow, 2016), 169.

51 **significant social change:** William H. McNeill, quoted in Thomas L.
Friedman, *Thank You for Being Late* (New York: Farrar, Straus and
Giroux, 2016), 147.

51 **"educational tradition":** William W. Brickman, "Education," in
Encyclopaedia Judaica, 15:159.

53 **proud to be Jews:** Pew Research Center, *A Portrait of Jewish Americans*, 52.

53 **"When it's not terrible":** Helen Telushkin, quoted in Telushkin,
Jewish Wisdom, 617.

3. DYING

55 **"At the age of 88":** "Bryan, Joyce Elaine," obituary, *Sun-Sentinel*,
December 13, 2015.

55 **most prevalent causes of death:** Judy Siegel-Itzkovich, "Cancer
Is No. 1 Cause of Death in Israel," *Jerusalem Post*, November 25,
2015, http://www.jpost.com/Business-and-Innovation/Health-and
-Science/Murder-rate-33-times-more-common-among-Arabs-than
-Jews-435356.

55 **making it to eighty:** Allison Gaudet Yarrow, "May You Live until 120," *Forward*, August 3, 2011, http://forward.com/culture/140894 /may-you-live-until-120-dna-uncovers-secrets-to-je/.

56 **website ObituariesHelp.org:** "Jewish Funeral Customs," ObituariesHelp.org, accessed November 29, 2016, http://obituarieshelp .org/jewish_funeral_customs.html.

56 **"Death was never eroticized":** Hillel Halkin, *After One-Hundred-and-Twenty* (Princeton NJ: Princeton University Press, 2016), 213–14.

56 **The Talmud likens such a pain-free death:** Babylonian Talmud, *Mo'ed Katan* 28a.

57 **"gathered to his kin":** Abraham, Gen. 25:8.

57 **"gathered to his people":** Jacob, Gen. 49:33.

57 **"slept with his fathers":** David, 1 Kings 2:10.

57 **fewer than 40 percent of Jews believe:** Pew Forum on Religion and Public Life, *U.S. Religious Landscape Survey, Summary of Key Findings* (Washington DC: Pew Research Center), accessed October 28, 2016, http://www.pewforum.org/files/2008/06/report2religious -landscape-study-key-findings.pdf.

58 **Flowers are "used primarily at Christian funerals":** Maurice Lamm, *Jewish Way in Death and Mourning* (Middle Village NY: Jonathan David, 2000), 21.

58 **purchase funereal flower arrangements:** Jenna Weissman Joselit, *Wonders of America* (New York: Hill and Wang, 1994), 268.

59 **"I have put before you life and death":** Deut. 30:19.

59 **The Torah also demands that bodies be buried:** Deut. 21:23.

59 **the use of flowers is now considered:** Joselit, *Wonders of America*, 268, 272–73.

59 **obituary for Theodore Roosevelt Heller:** "Deadly Chuckles: Funniest Obituaries Ever," *Life: As I See It* (blog), April 15, 2011, http:// www.chicagonow.com/life-as-i-see-it/2011/04/deadly-chuckles -funniest-obituaries-ever/#image/1.

59 **"I'm not afraid of death":** Woody Allen, quoted in Lee Eisenberg, *The Point Is* (New York: Twelve, 2016), 170.

59 **"The putrefaction of human flesh":** Halkin, *After One-Hundred-and-Twenty*, 20.

59 **"Viewing the corpse is objectionable":** Lamm, *Jewish Way in Death and Mourning*, 35.

61 **The biblical basis for washing the body:** Eccles. 5:14.

61 **"The dead shouldn't be left alone":** Roy Rivenburg, "An Ancient Vigil: In Orthodox Judaism, a *Shomer* Keeps Watch Over Souls of the Dead," *Los Angeles Times*, September 14, 1992, http://articles.latimes.com/keyword/orthodox-judaism.

61 **to keep rodents away:** Lamm, *Jewish Way in Death and Mourning*, 5.

61 **participating in the *tahara*:** Nancy Kalikow Maxwell, "Final Touches," *Reform Judaism*, Spring 2001, 53–56.

62 **Kevin O'Leary:** Elizabeth Meyer, "Mr. Wonderful Loves When People Die," accessed November 12, 2017, https://www.everplans.com/articles/shark-tanks-mr-wonderful-loves-when-people-die.

63 **"brief, starkly simple":** Lamm, *Jewish Way in Death and Mourning*, 38, 46.

63 **"Any funeral service lasting more than 15":** Joseph Stolz, quoted in Joselit, *Wonders of America*, 273.

63 **spent less on funeral expenses:** Joselit, *Wonders of America*, 266–68.

63 **"While the Christian's funeral focuses":** "Jewish Funeral Customs," ObituariesHelp.org, accessed May 5, 2018, https://obituarieshelp.org/jewish_funeral_customs.html.

64 **Judaism is "a polydoxy":** Alvin J. Reines, "Death and Afterexistence," in *What Happens after I Die?*, ed. Rifat Sonsino and Daniel B. Syme (New York: Jason Aronson, 1994), 128.

64 **the Hebrew Bible mentions She'ol:** Halkin, *After One-Hundred-and-Twenty*, 13.

64 **Judaism never permitted the afterlife:** Halkin, *After One-Hundred-and-Twenty*, 101.

64 **preferred to talk about something else:** Halkin, *After One-Hundred-and-Twenty*, 201.

64 **the eulogy:** Brian Fraga, "What Every Catholic Needs to Know about Funerals," *Our Sunday Visitor*, September 28, 2011, https://www.osv.com/Article/TabId/493/ArtMID/13569/ArticleID/10323/What-Every-Catholic-needs-to-know-about-funerals.aspx.

65 **Abraham, who eulogized his wife Sarah:** Gen. 23:2.

65 **"grossly exaggerate or invent":** Lamm, *Jewish Way in Death and Mourning*, 49.

65 **The ritual can be traced back to the Bible:** Lamm, *Jewish Way in Death and Mourning*, 40.

66 **the grave be filled:** Alfred J. Kolatch, *Second Jewish Book of Why* (Middle Village NY: Jonathan David, 1985), 188–89.

67 **several theories have been proposed:** "Why Do Jews Put Stones on Graves?," My Jewish Learning, accessed November 12, 2017, http://www.myjewishlearning.com/article/ask-the-expert-stones-on-graves/.

68 **a quarter-page ad:** Cremation Service of the Palm Beaches, "The Best of Jewish Journal," Special Advertising Section, *Sun-Sentinel*, 2016, 8.

69 **cremation is growing in popularity:** Mindy Botbol, quoted in Josh Nathan-Kazis, "More Jews Opt for Cremation," *Forward*, June 27, 2012, https://forward.com/news/158218/more-jews-opt-for-cremation/.

69 **Rabbi Gamliel began using rough burial:** Babylonian Talmud, *Ketubot* 8b.

69 **"After the Shoah":** Nathan-Kazis, "More Jews Opt for Cremation."

70 **"upload their entire minds":** Ray Kurzweil, quoted in Nicholas P. Rougier, "Silicon Soul: The Vain Dream of Electronic Immortality," The Conversation, January 5, 2016, https://theconversation.com/silicon-soul-the-vain-dream-of-electronic-immortality-52368.

71 **Even the Baal Shem Tov:** Yitzhak Buxbaum, *Jewish Tales of Holy Women* (San Francisco: Jossey-Bass, 2002), 119.

73 **"We cater shivahs":** Joselit, *Wonders of America*, 278.

74 **"Safeguarding the souls of the deceased":** Joselit, *Wonders of America*, 283.

74 **an echo of Job:** Job 13:15.

74 **even harried business people:** Joselit, *Wonders of America*, 282.

75 **visited synagogues, churches:** Corinna Nicolaou, *A None's Story* (New York: Columbia University Press, 2016), 137.

75 **to pen an entire book:** Leon Wieseltier, *Kaddish* (Vintage Books, 1998).

76 **at age thirteen Bella Abzug:** Blanche Wiesen Cook, "Bella Abzug 1920–1998," *Jewish Women's Archive "Encyclopedia,"* accessed May 10, 2018, https://jwa.org/encyclopedia/article/abzug-bella.

77 **burial spot of loved ones:** Gen. 35:20.

78 **"perched atop the refrigerator":** Joselit, *Wonders of America*, 289–90.

78 **memorial electric tablets:** Joselit, *Wonders of America*, 286.

79 **"I want to achieve immortality":** "Woody Allen, Quotes, Quotable Quotes, Allen, Woody," in *The Illustrated Woody Allen Reader*, as cited in Goodreads, accessed November 29, 2017, http://www.goodreads.com/quotes/1066-i-don-t-want-to-achieve-immortality-through-my-work-i.

80 **In his book:** Michael Kinsley, *Old Age: A Beginner's Guide* (New York: Tim Duggan Books, 2016), 129.

4. NOSHING

84 **Jewish versus goyish edibles:** Lenny Bruce, "Jewish and Goyish," My Jewish Learning, accessed July 5, 2016, http:www.myjewishlearning .com/article/jewish-and-goyish.

84 **"Protestant food":** Daniel Sack, *Whitebread Protestants* (New York: St. Martin's Press, 2000), quoted in Samira K. Mehta, "I Chose Judaism But Christmas Cookies Chose Me," in *Religion, Food, and Eating in North America*, ed. Benjamin E. Zeller et al. (New York: Columbia University Press, 2014), 165.

84 **poodle as a "Jewdle":** Erica Jong, *Fear of Dying* (New York: St. Martin's Press, 2015), 122.

85 **Jewish children in the 1930s:** Hasia R. Diner, *Hungering for America* (Cambridge MA: Harvard University Press, 2001), 184.

85 **envy of other kids:** Janna Gur, *Jewish Soul Food* (New York: Schocken Books, 2014), xi.

85 **Jews are big eaters, not drinkers:** "Jackie Mason Jokes," Jokes4us.com, accessed May 10, 2018, http://www.jokes4us.com /peoplejokes/comedianjokes/jackiemasonjokes.html.

85 **Since biblical times:** "Ethnic, Cultural, and Religious Issues in Drug Use and Treatment," in *Drugs, Alcohol and Tobacco*, ed. Rosalyn Carson-DeWitt (Detroit: Thomson Gale, 2003), 2:67.

85 **Sigmund Freud was so convinced:** Sheila Blume, "Jews, Drugs, and Alcohol," *Encyclopedia of Drugs, Alcohol and Addictive Behavior*, 2nd ed., ed. Rosalyn Carson-DeWitt (New York: Macmillan Reference USA, 2001), 673.

85 **studies from the 1950s:** Blume, "Jews, Drugs, and Alcohol," 672–73.

85 **lower per capita alcohol consumption:** Blume, "Jews, Drugs, and Alcohol," 672.

85 **And fewer Israelis die:** Blume, "Jews, Drugs, and Alcohol," 672.

86 **One 2015 Canadian study:** Melanie Baruch et al., "Alcohol and Substance Use in the Jewish Community: A Pilot Study," *Journal of Addiction*, 2015, accessed July 11, 2017, https://www.hindawi.com /journals/jad/2015/763930/cta/.

86 **Jews, especially males, are less apt:** Jonathan Katz, personal communication via Vickie Griffiths, July 11, 2017; and Alexandra Lap-

kin, "Jews Not Immune from Opiate Crisis," *Jewish Advocate,* October 16, 2015, 1, 4.

86 **"There is no *simcha*":** Babylonian Talmud, *Pesachim* 109a.

86 **slivovitz, a powerful plum liquor:** Roger Horowitz, *Kosher USA* (New York: Columbia University Press, 2016), 11.

86 **historically disproportionately represented:** Rich Cohen, "People of the Bottle," *Commentary,* June 2012, 73–75, review of Marni Davis, *People of the Bottle Jews and Booze* (New York: New York University Press, 2012).

86 **Other researchers posit genetics:** Amanda Botfeld, "Are Jews Less Likely to Be Alcoholics?," *Forward,* January 9, 2017, http://forward .com/scribe/359475/are-jews-less-likely-to-be-alcoholics/.

87 **drinking patterns of Jewish men:** Blume, "Jews, Drugs, and Alcohol," 673.

87 **"gustatory Jews":** Jenna Weissman Joselit, *Wonders of America* (New York: Hill and Wang, 1994), 171.

88 **In her memoir:** Betsy Lerner, *The Bridge Ladies* (New York: Harper Wave, 2016), 115.

89 **In the savory words:** Diner, *Hungering for America,* 152.

89 **Jews pay "almost compulsive attention":** Michael Wex, *Rhapsody in Schmaltz* (New York: St. Martin's Press, 2016), xiv, 14–15.

89 **God issues menus, ingredients:** Wex, *Rhapsody in Schmaltz,* 4.

89 **in the final judgment:** Jerusalem Talmud, *Kiddushin* 4:12, 66b; Diner, *Hungering for America,* 151.

89 **divorce his wife:** Mishnah *Gittin* 9:10; Diner, *Hungering for America,* 151.

89 **"He who eats matzah on the day before Passover":** Jerusalem Talmud, *Pesachim* 10:1; Wex, *Rhapsody in Schmaltz,* 11.

90 **other holiday foods originated:** Lise Stern, *How to Keep Kosher* (New York: William Morrow, 2004), 143.

90 *Sephardic Holiday Cooking* **book offers:** Gilda Angel, *Sephardic Holiday Cooking* (New York: Decalogue Books, 1986), as quoted in Stern, *How to Keep Kosher,* 143.

90 **"remember the Sabbath day":** Exod. 20:8.

90 **experienced in "devotional terms":** Weissman Joselit, *Wonders of America* (New York: Hill and Wang, 1994), 259.

90 **Joyous eating on that one day:** Diner, *Hungering for America,* 206.

91 **the Torah commands "taking challah":** Num. 15:18–21.

92 **The Talmud mentions five items:** Stern, *How to Keep Kosher,* 143.

92 **The holiday of Sukkot:** Leah Koenig, "A Food-Lover's Guide
to Sukkot," TheKitchn.com, September 16, 2013, http://www
.thekitchn.com/a-foodlovers-guide-to-sukkot-194869; and Marissa
Fox, "Top Foods to Eat on Sukkot," *Moment*, October 19, 2016,
http://www.momentmag.com/top-foods-eat-sukkot/.

93 **Mention the word "seder":** "Jewish Holidays and Food," Jewish Food Experience, accessed August 24, 2017, http://
jewishfoodexperience.com/celebrating-the-jewish-holidays/
#tubshevat.

93 **carob fruits:** "A Brief on Boksar," *Forward*, February 4, 2005,
http://forward.com/articles/2887/a-brief-on-bokser/.

94 **take our holiday foods seriously:** Yair Rosenberg, "Judaism's Epic
Food Fight," *Tablet*, February 21, 2013, http://www.tabletmag.com
/jewish-news-pand-politics/124811/judaisms-epic-food-fight.

95 **The seder ritual traditionally includes:** Stern, *How to Keep Kosher*,
190–93.

95 **added an orange:** "Journey to Freedom: A Women's Seder Experience," The Haggadah Committee (publisher and year unknown), 21.

95 **eating to our people:** Wex, *Rhapsody in Schmaltz*, 4.

96 **there are more kugel recipes:** Riva Ginsburg, "Schmaltz and
Gribenes" (lecture, Florida Atlantic University, Boca Raton FL,
December 14, 2016).

96 **The word "kugel" derives:** Danielle Feinberg, "What Is Kugel?,"
The Nosher, My Jewish Learning, January 27, 2016, http://www
.myjewishlearning.com/the-nosher/what-is-kugel/.

96 **was asked, "What is that?":** Andrew Lustig, "I Am Jewish," January
11, 2012, https://vimeo.com/113288275.

97 **"eat unleavened bread":** Exod. 12:15,17,24.

97 **three-fourths of Jews fulfill this requirement:** Pew Research Center's Religion and Public Life Project, *A Portrait of Jewish Americans*
(Washington DC: Pew Research Center, 2013), 77; and Joselit, *Wonders of America*, 227.

97 **enjoying a full meal:** Stern, *How to Keep Kosher*, 145.

97 **The Torah offers confusing instruction:** Lev. 23:32.

97 **Rashi came down:** Stern, *How to Keep Kosher*, 145.

98 **"held a great feast":** Gen. 21:8.

98 *seudat mitzvah*: "Educational Message of Seudat Mitzvah," *Jewish Chronicle*, accessed August 25, 2017, http://thejewishchronicle

.net/pages/full_story/push?articleThe+Educational+Message+of +Seudat+Mitzvah-+It+is+More+than+Just+Lunch%20&id=13337201.

98 **at circumcisions and weddings:** Molly Lyons Bar-David and Yom-Tov Lewinski, "Food," *Encyclopaedia Judaica*, 2nd ed., ed. Fred Skolnik (New York: Macmillan References USA, 2007), 15:118.

99 **The first recorded dinner party:** Gen. 18:1–8.

99 **the mitzvah of *hachnasat orchim*:** Laurel Snyder, *Baxter the Pig Who Wanted to Be Kosher* (Berkeley CA: Tricycle Press, 2010).

99 **"Let the doors of your home":** Pirkei Avot 1:5.

99 **bring home "strangers, visitors":** Diner, *Hungering for America*, 168.

99 **The sixteenth-century Shulchan Arukh:** Neal Gold, "Let All Who Are Hungry Come and Eat: Food Ethics, Tzedakah, and How We Celebrate," in *The Sacred Table*, ed. Mary L. Zamore (New York: CCAR Press, 2011), 377.

100 **young Jewish mothers:** Joselit, *Wonders of America*, 182–83.

100 **Even in the Holocaust:** Cara De Silva, ed., *In Memory's Kitchen: A Legacy from the Women of Terezin* (New York: Jason Aronson, 1996), xv, xxvi, xxix.

101 **helped define them as a people:** Julie Michaels, "Everything Old Is New Again," *Pakn Treger*, Summer 2013, 15.

101 **"taste of deli before they die":** Ted Merwin, *Pastrami on Rye: An Overstuffed History of the Jewish Deli* (New York: New York University Press, 2015), 4.

101 **The book of Isaiah forecasts:** Isa. 25:6.

101 **the Leviathan:** Babylonian Talmud, *Bava Batra* 74b.

101 **In his book about keeping kosher:** Horowitz, *Kosher USA*.

102 **the Israelites never complain:** Michael Wex, Michael, *Rhapsody in Schmaltz* (New York: St. Martin's Press, 2016), xii.

102 **"the fatness of shmaltz":** Num. 11:8.

102 **"They whine before me":** Num. 11:13.

103 **eliminates what he has eaten":** Wex, *Rhapsody in Schmaltz*, 15.

103 **"Jewish affliction par excellence":** *Jewish Encyclopedia* of 1906, quoted in Wex, *Rhapsody in Schmaltz*, 16; and "Jewish Genetic Diseases," NSW Board of Jewish Education, accessed August 26, 2017, http://bje.org.au/course/jewish-self/family/genetic-diseases/.

103 **in the Torah hemorrhoids:** Deut. 28:27.

103 **One's heart goes out to the Ashdodites:** 1 Sam. 5:6,9.

103 **And pity the poor Philistines:** 1 Sam. 6:5.

104 **"human beings cannot eat raw vegetables":** Quoted in Wex, *Rhapsody in Schmaltz*, 15–16.

104 **one *yeshivah bucher*:** Chaim Potok, *The Promise* (New York: Anchor Books, 1969), 51.

105 **the Jews who immigrated:** Diner, *Hungering for America*, 192.

105 **brought her mother to tears:** Diner, *Hungering for America*, 194.

105 **significantly fussier:** Joselit, *Wonders of America*, 182.

105 **"Why are Jewish homes such hotbeds":** Diner, *Hungering for America*, 215.

106 **categories of foods:** Leviticus 11.

107 **began to harbor doubts:** Joselit, *Wonders of America*, 172.

107 **consumption of kosher meat:** Joselit, *Wonders of America* 176.

107 **still strictly observing kashrut:** Joselit, *Wonders of America*, 176.

107 **"I just can't do it":** Quoted in Diner, *Hungering for America*, 182–83.

108 **"selectively *treif* behavior":** Joselit, *Wonders of America*, 172.

108 **"that singular American invention: 'kosher-style'":** Joselit, *Wonders of America*, 173.

108 **Her 1958 cookbook:** Betty Kalikow, *Mom's Best Recipe: 151 Jewish-American Dishes* (Kansas City MO: BeKay, 1958).

108 **a follow-up cookbook:** Betty Kalikow, *Grandma's Kosher Recipes: 209 Jewish Dishes Modern Style* (Kansas City MO: BeKay, 1961).

109 **do not keep kosher:** Pew Research Center, *A Portrait of Jewish Americans*, 77.

109 **non-kosher-keeping Jews:** "Nearly 1 in 5 Modern Orthodox Jews Don't Keep Kosher," *New York Jewish Week*, September 1, 2015, http://jewishweek.timesofisrael.com/nearly-1-in-5-modern-orthodox-jews-dont-keep-kosher/.

109 **"fit" or "proper":** Sue Fishkoff, *Kosher Nation* (New York: Schocken Books, 2010), 11; and Roger Horowitz, *Kosher USA* (New York: Columbia University Press, 2016), 4.

109 **organic, humanely treated:** Alix Wall, quoted in Stern, *How to Keep Kosher*, 303.

109 **"Is it eco-kosher":** Arthur O. Waskow, "Eco-Kashrut: Standards for What and How We Eat," My Jewish Learning, accessed August 26, 2017, http://www.myjewishlearning.com/article/eco-kashrut-environmental-standards-for-what-and-how-we-eat/.

109 **cruelty to animals:** Zvi Kaplan, "Animals, Cruelty To," *Encyclopaedia Judaica*, 15:165.

109 **Balaam for smiting his ass:** Num. 22:32.

109 **"your ox and your ass":** Deut. 5:14.

110 **"cutting the animal's throat":** Stern, *How to Keep Kosher*, 31.

110 **shackling and hoisting:** Richard H. Schwartz, *Judaism and Vegetarianism* (New York: Lantern Books, 2001), 110.

110 **"unwelcome dichotomy":** Elliot Dorff, *Modern Conservative Judaism* (Philadelphia: Jewish Publication Society, forthcoming 2018).

110 **awards a Shield of Justice:** Dorff, *Modern Conservative Judaism*.

110 **"'humane slaughter'":** Roberta Kalechofsky, *Vegetarian Judaism* (Marblehead MA: Micah Publications, 1998), 4.

110 **Jewish vegetarian proponent:** Schwartz, *Judaism and Vegetarianism*, xii.

110 **"every seed-bearing plant":** Gen. 1:29.

110 **consider foods:** Lawrence Kushner, "Lawrence Kushner's Easy-to-Do List of Going Kosher," 2010, http://gettingthechutzpah.tumblr.com /post/147238204153/lawrence-kushners-easy-to-do-list-of-going.

111 **no *simcha* without meat":** Babylonian Talmud, *Pesachim* 109a.

111 **"turned every home into a sanctuary":** Neal Gold, excerpt from a Rosh Hashanah sermon, Rosh Hashanah 5773/2013.

112 **It is difficult to overestimate:** Merwin, *Pastrami on Rye*, 4.

112 **the metaphorical homeland:** Merwin, *Pastrami on Rye*, 3.

112 **"the Jewish experience":** Joan Nathan, as quoted in Merwin, *Pastrami on Rye*, 4.

112 **"The less faith a Jew":** Wex, *Rhapsody in Schmaltz*, 256.

112 **"My parents didn't send me to Hebrew school":** Merwin, *Pastrami on Rye*, xii.

113 **George McGovern:** Merwin, *Pastrami on Rye*, 10.

113 **New York institutions:** Diner, *Hungering for America*, 200.

114 **managed to stay in business:** Julie Michaels, "Everything Old Is New Again," *Pakn Treger*, Summer 2013, 15–20.

114 **multicultural fusion:** Lucy Cohen Blatter, "Rise of Jewish-Fusion Restaurants," *Forward*, December 24, 2015.

5. LAUGHING

117 **A 2013 Pew survey:** Pew Research Center's Religion and Public Life Project, *A Portrait of Jewish Americans* (Washington DC: Pew Research Center, October 1, 2013), 55.

117 **80 percent of America's leading comedians:** Joseph Telushkin, *Jewish Humor* (New York: William Morrow, 1992), 19; and Paul Offenkrantz,

"Woody Allen: Good for the Jews?" (lecture, Florida Atlantic University, Lifelong Learning Society, Boca Raton FL, November 22, 2016).

118 **"Jewish cottage industry":** Steve Allen, quoted in Telushkin, *Jewish Humor*, 19.

118 **among the top humorists:** Joseph Dorinson, *Kvetching and Shpritzing: Jewish Humor in American Popular Culture* (Jefferson NC: McFarland, 2015), 208.

118 **dissect humor:** E. B. White, quoted in Dorinson, *Kvetching and Shpritzing*, 11.

118 **"foolish talking and jesting":** Eph. 5:3–4, quoted in Dorinson, *Kvetching and Shpritzing*, 7.

118 **the root word "to laugh":** Neal Gold, "Is There Humor in the Bible?" (unpublished paper, 1996), 2–3.

119 **guffaws at God's promise:** Gen. 18:12.

119 **child Isaac, meaning "laughter":** Gen. 21:3,6.

119 **hides under the great master's bed:** Maggie Anton, *Fifty Shades of Talmud* (Los Angeles: Banot Press, 2016), 52.

119 **"'Take your idol'":** Maurice M. Mizrahi, "Humor in Torah and Talmud," July 2, 2010, https://slideblast.com/humor-in-torah-and-talmud-shulcloud_594d48041723dd96e0715383.html.

119 **Wordplay is also sprinkled:** Zvi Ron, "Wordplay in Genesis, 2:25–3:1," accessed September 2, 2017, http://jbqnew.jewishbible.org/assets/Uploads/421/JBQ_421_1_wordplay.pdf; and Jeffrey L. Rubenstein, *Stories of the Babylonian Talmud* (Baltimore: John Hopkins University Press, 2010), https://books.google.com/books/about/Stories_of_the_Babylonian_Talmud.html?id=NbQK3Yz9F2EC. .

119 **"We make sad people laugh":** Babylonian Talmud, *Ta'anit* 22a; *Keter Shem Tov* 272; Tzvi Freeman, "Two Jesters," Chabad.org, accessed September 2, 2017, https://www.chabad.org/library/article_cdo/aid/1407583/jewish/The-Two-Jesters.htm.

119 **"cup, purse, and anger":** Babylonian Talmud, *Eruvin* 65b.

120 **before the days of Toastmasters:** Babylonian Talmud, *Shabbat* 30b, quoted in David Brodsky, "Did the Widow Have a Goat in Her Bed?," in *Jews and Humor*, ed. Leonard J. Greenspoon, Studies in Jewish Civilization 22 (West Lafayette IN: Purdue University Press, 2011), 14.

120 **doing stand-up was the trailblazing:** "Jackie Mason, Biography," IMDB, accessed September 2, 2017, http://www.imdb.com/name

/nm0556750/bio; Ken Gross, "Too Much of a Ham to Remain a Rabbi, Broadway's Jackie Mason Is Now the Toast of the Town," *People*, February 23, 1987, http://people.com/archive/too-much-of -a-ham-to-remain-a-rabbi-broadways-jackie-mason-is-now-the-toast -of-the-town-vol-27-no-8; and Glenn Collins, "Jackie Mason, Top Banana at Last," *New York Times*, July 24, 1988, https://www.nytimes .com/1988/07/24/movies/jackie-mason-top-banana-at-last.html.

120 **a trio of comedic Reform rabbis:** "Three Rabbis Walk into a Bar: Taking Jewish Comedy Seriously," *RIJ Podcast*, accessed January 15, 2017, http://reallyinterestingjews.com/?p=76.

121 **Modi:** Michael Granberry, "Jewish Comedian Modi Thrives as the 'New and Improved Jackie Mason,'" *Dallas News*, January 4, 2012, https://www.dallasnews.com/arts/arts/2012/01/04/jewish -comedian-modi-thrives-as-the-new-and-improved-jackie-mason.

121 **"we both kinda preach":** Sarah Silverman, quoted in Kevin Fallon, "Sarah and Susan Silverman: Comedian and Rabbi Are Perfect Sisters," *Daily Beast*, March 31, 2014, https://www.thedailybeast.com /sarah-and-susan-silverman-comedian-and-rabbi-are-perfect-sisters.

121 **"We Jews love language":** Bob Alper, quoted in Arie Kaplan, "How Jews Revolutionized Comedy in America," *Reform Judaism*, accessed May 10, 2018, http://www.reformjudaismmag.net/302ak.html.

121 **a different theory:** Mel Gordon, "Catastrophe in Ukraine, Comedy Today," *Reform Judaism*, Spring 2011, http://reformjudaismmag.net /2011-Spring/PDFs/RJ_48_Spr11.pdf.

122 **"the insult comic":** Terry Gross, "Remembering Don Rickles, the Insult Comic Who Made Fun of Everything," *Fresh Air*, NPR, April 7, 2017, http://www.npr.org/2017/04/07/522996727/remembering -don-rickles-the-insult-comic-who-made-fun-of-everything.

122 **a fundamental need:** Rachel Druck, "Inside Out and Outside In: Jewish Humor and the Jewish People," Beit Hatfutsot: Museum of the Jewish People, accessed September 8, 2017, https://www.bh.org.il /blog-items/inside-outside-jewish-humor-jewish-people-rachel-druck/.

123 **the mean kids in school:** Simcha Weinstein, *Shtick Shift* (Fort Lee NJ: Barricade, 2008), 11.

123 **"psychic masochism":** Leon M. Abrami, "Psychoanalyzing Jewish Humor," My Jewish Learning, accessed September 8, 2017, http:// www.myjewishlearning.com/article/psychoanalyzing-jewish-humor/.

123 **Jews killed Christ:** Lenny Bruce, quoted in Weinstein, *Shtick Shift*, 22.

124 **"question the existence of God":** Harold S. Kushner, *Nine Essential Things I've Learned about Life* (New York: Knopf, 2015), 120.

124 **believe in God:** Pew Research Center, *A Portrait of Jewish Americans*, 74.

124 **"who has the best pastrami":** Marjorie Ingall, *Mamelah Knows Best* (New York: Harmony Books, 2016), 74.

126 **"chutzpah" has been used 231 times:** Tzvi Freeman, "What Is Chutzpah?," Chabad.org, accessed March 10, 2017, http://www.chabad .org/library/article_cdo/aid/1586271/jewish/Chutzpah.htm.

126 **defined "chutzpah":** Guy Kawasaki, quoted in Freeman, "What Is Chutzpah?"

127 **honor cultures or dignity cultures:** Ryan P. Brown, *Honor Bound* (New York: Oxford University Press, 2016), xiv, 184.

127 **"the arrogance of belonging":** Elizabeth Gilbert, *Big Magic* (New York: Riverhead Books, 2015), 92–93.

127 **her Jewish girlfriends:** Corinna Nicolaou, *A None's Story* (New York: Columbia University Press, 2016), 97.

128 **a core principle of Judaism:** Barbara Lerner Spectre, quoted in Alan Wolfe, *At Home in Exile* (Boston: Beacon Press, 2014), 198.

128 **"Jews have signed a pact with life":** George Steiner, "George Steiner Addresses the Jewish Question(s)." *Forward*, March 31, 2017, 27.

128 **"Judaism begins not in wonder":** Jonathan Sacks, as quoted in Kushner, *Nine Essential Things*, 163.

128 **"theology of the 'not yet'":** Kushner, *Nine Essential Things*, 164.

129 **God gives this very message:** Thomas L. Friedman, *Thank You for Being Late* (New York: Farrar, Straus and Giroux, 2016), 339.

129 **Jon Stewart, for one:** Lisa Rogak, *Angry Optimist* (New York: Thomas Dunne Books, 2014), 8, 105, 107, 109.

130 **the word "kvetch":** Michael Wex, *Born to Kvetch* (New York: St. Martin's Press, 2005), 5.

130 **"Want of graves in Egypt?":** Exod. 14:11.

130 **Our own Sigmund Freud:** Eliezer Diamond, "But Is It Funny? Identifying Humor, Satire and Parody in Rabbinic Literature," in Greenspoon, *Jews and Humor*, 33.

130 **One of his favorite jokes:** Sharon Heller, *Freud A to Z* (New York: John Wiley, 2005), 158–59.

130 **"Jewish humor is laughter through tears":** Stephen Z. Cohen (lecture, Florida Atlantic University, Lifelong Learning Society, Boca Raton, FL, March 8, 2015).

131 **"The goyim [non-Jews] don't know how to laugh":** Paul Mazursky, quoted in Weinstein, *Shtick Shift*, 11.

131 **"Oppressed people tend to be witty":** Saul Bellow, quoted in Michael Krasny, *Let There Be Laughter* (New York: William Morrow, 2016), 131.

131 **asked if Jewish humor is masochistic:** Krasny, *Let There Be Laughter*, 171.

131 **Comedian Lewis Black:** Arie Kaplan, "How Jews Revolutionized Comedy in America," *Reform Judaism*, accessed May 10, 2018, http://www.reformjudaismmag.net/302ak.html.

132 **"Maybe next time":** Sharon Barcan Elswit, *Jewish Story Finder*, 2nd ed. (Jefferson NC: McFarland, 2012), 110.

132 **love of argument:** A. C. Grayling, *Ideas That Matter* (New York: Basic Books, 2010), 197.

132 **Jews can't stop themselves:** Colin Quinn, *The Coloring Book* (New York: Grand Central, 2015), 81.

132 **"Of the 523 chapters":** Wex, *Born to Kvetch*, 10.

132 **"a bunch of dudes":** Ingall, *Mamelah Knows Best*, 72.

133 **In her joke book:** Esther Cohen, *Don't Mind Me and Other Jewish Lies* (New York: Hyperion, 2008).

133 **"Always let your left hand":** Babylonian Talmud, *Sotah* 47a.

134 **both religions and ethnic groups:** Harold Abramson, "Religion," in *Harvard Encyclopedia of American Ethnic Groups*, 869, quoted in James A. Beckford and N. J. Demerath III, *SAGE Handbook of the Sociology of Religions* (Thousand Oaks CA: SAGE Publications, 2007), 493.

134 **"We're leftists, but we're capitalists!":** Ingall, *Mamelah Knows Best*, 187.

134 **offers her own upbringing:** Ingall, *Mamelah Knows Best*, 84.

135 **book suggesting how nonreligious:** Alain de Botton, "Profile: Life in an Ivory Tower?," *Jewish Telegraph*, accessed September 2, 2017, http://www.jewishtelegraph.com/prof_16.html.

135 **joke of a man who returns:** Telushkin, *Jewish Humor*, 25.

6. DETECTING

138 **Jews recognize each other:** George Steiner, "George Steiner Addresses the Jewish Question(s)," *Forward*, March 31, 2017, 27.

138 **On a blog post discussing this radar-like ability:** "Gaydar? Jewdar? Does it Exist?," Cyburbia, February 5, 2006, http://www.cyburbia.org/forums/showthread.php?t=23324.

138 **"is it good for the white, male"**: Stanley Fish, "Is It Good for the Jews?" *New York Times*, March 4, 2007, http://opinionator.blogs .nytimes.com/2007/03/04/is-it-good-for-the-jews/?_r=0.

139 **Jews are viewed more positively**: *How Americans Feel about Religious Groups* (Washington DC: Pew Research Center, July 16, 2014), http://www.pewforum.org/2014/07/16/how-americans-feel-about -religious-groups/.

139 **"All Jews are responsible for"**: Babylonian Talmud, *Shevuot* 39a, quoted in Joseph Telushkin, *Jewish Wisdom* (New York: William Morrow, 1994), 91.

139 **such detection ability**: Jon Carroll, "The Mystery of Jewdar," SFGate, March 20, 2009, http://www.sfgate.com/entertainment/article /The-mystery-of-Jewdar-3247374.php.

140 **engaging in acts of group cooperation**: Sebastian Junger, *Tribe: On Homecoming and Belonging* (New York: Twelve, 2016), 27.

140 **kinship to Franz Kafka**: Joyce Carol Oates, *Widow's Story: A Memoir* (New York: Ecco Press, 2011), 292.

141 **"Using 'blood logic' remains"**: David E. Kaufman, *Jewhooing the Sixties: American Celebrity and Jewish Identity* (Waltham MA: Brandeis University Press, 2012), 270.

141 **"Race is a word so slippery"**: Ari Feldman, "'Human Biodiversity': Scientific Racism for the 21st Century," *Forward*, August 19, 2016, 29.

141 **"Judaism at one point"**: Frederick Greenspahn, quoted in Ira Winderman, "Stoudemire's Spiritual Journey Takes Him Down Judaic Path," *Sun Sentinel*, September 13, 2015, 16a.

141 **one out of three Ashkenazic Jews**: "Jewish Genetic Diseases," Jewish Genetic Disease Consortium, accessed January 30, 2017, http:// www.jewishgeneticdiseases.org/jewish-genetic-diseases/.

142 **being 92 percent European Jewish**: Andrew Jacobs, personal communication, February 8, 2017.

142 **"shared genetic legacy"**: Harry Ostrer, *Legacy: A Genetic History of the Jewish People* (New York: Oxford University Press, 2012), xvii.

142 **defines a tribe as**: Lee Eisenbeg, *The Point Is* (New York: Twelve, 2016), 22.

143 **The word "shibboleth"**: Judg. 12:6.

144 **"race, color, religion"**: Civil Rights Act of 1964.

144 **preferring "our own"**: Stephen T. Asma, *Against Fairness* (Chicago: University of Chicago Press, 2013), 153.

145 **reclaim the word "tribe":** Junger, *Tribe.*

145 **the Talmud requires that Jews give *tzedakah*:** Babylonian Talmud, *Gittin* 61a.

145 **Maimonides grounded this exhortation:** "Maimonides Saw Jewish Obligation to Non-Jews," On1Foot, accessed May 10, 2018, www .on1foot.org; and "Charity (Tzedakah)," in *Encyclopaedia Judaica*, 2nd ed., ed. Fred Skolnik, vol. 16 (New York: Macmillan References USA, 2007).

146 **"own-ethnic bias":** Joshua Ackerman et al., "Research Report: They All Look the Same to Me (Unless They're Angry)," *Psychological Sciences*, October 2006, 836–40; and Thomas Gross, "Own-Ethnic Bias," *Basic and Applied Social Psychology*, April 2009, 128.

146 **one study conducted by Israeli and Chinese:** Lun Zhao and Shlomo Benton, "Own and Other Race Categorization of Faces by Race, Gender," *Psychonomic Bulletin and Review*, December 2008, 1093–99.

147 **10 percent of Jews are something other:** Michael Lipka, "The Most and Least Racially Diverse U.S. Religious Groups," Pew Research Center, July 26, 2015, /http://www.pewresearch.org/fact-tank/2015 /07/27/the-most-and-least-racially-diverse-u-s-religious-groups/.

147 **Institute for Jewish and Community Research estimates:** "A Black Woman's Journey to the Rabbinate in North Carolina," CNN, May 31, 2009, http://www.cnn.com/2009/LIVING/05/21/north .carolina.black.rabbi/index.html. .

147 **blended in undetected:** Corinna Nicolaou, *A None's Story* (New York: Columbia University Press, 2016), 123.

147 **interracial adoptions:** Debra Nussbaum Cohen, "Multiracial Jewish Families," My Jewish Learning, August 20, 2003, http://www .myjewishlearning.com/article/multiracial-jewish-families/.

147 **support Jews of color:** Jewish Multiracial Network, accessed March 2, 2017, http://www.jewishmultiracialnetwork.org/who-we-are/.

147 **Rabbi Alysa Stanton:** "A Black Woman's Journey to the Rabbinate."

148 **Judaism cannot be about race:** Angela Warnick Buchdahl, quoted in Judea Pearl and Ruth Pearl, eds., *I Am Jewish* (Woodstock VT: Jewish Lights, 2004), 20.

148 **"Uniqueness is not the opposite":** Rabbi Dr. Sharon Shalom, as quoted in Gil Troy, *The Zionist Ideas* (Philadelphia: Jewish Publication Society, 2018), https://books.google.com/books?id= 3ltPDwAAQBAJ&pg=PT679&lpg=PT679&dq=sharon+shalom

+uniqueness&source=bl&ots=JMKAnMiWnM&sig=lYQ7xTIZrA
_CmzJ6HmHs6r5FFHo&hl=en&sa=X&ved=0ahUKEwjfmKTz
__jaAhUDuVkKHXiGCwsQ6AEIQjAD#v=onepage&q=sharon
%20shalom%20uniqueness&f=false.

148 **country's well-known Ethiopian Jews:** Gil Troy, *The Zionist Ideas*
(Philadelphia: Jewish Publication Society, April 2018); and "List of
Israeli Ethiopian Jews," accessed September 11, 2017, https://en
.wikipedia.org/wiki/List_of_Israeli_Ethiopian_Jews.

148 **coffee-table book:** Frederic Brenner, *Diaspora: Homelands in Exile*
(New York: HarperCollins, 2003), ix.

148 **"Aryan-looking" children:** Terrence McCoy, "Perfect Aryan Child
Used in Nazi Propaganda Was Actually Jewish," *Washington Post*,
July 7, 2014, https://www.washingtonpost.com/news/morning
-mix/wp/2014/07/07/the-perfect-aryan-child-the-nazis-used-in
-propaganda-was-actually-jewish/?utm_term=.de11c0ab7c5b. .

149 **the *karan* (beams):** Exod. 34:35; Ismar Schorsch, "What Happened to Moses on Mount Sinai," My Jewish Learning, accessed
May 8, 2018, https://www.myjewishlearning.com/article
/transformative-power/.

149 **"Are we people of the book":** Lisa Schiffman, *Generation J* (San
Francisco: HarperSanFrancisco, 1999), 67.

149 **German antisemitic theories:** Paul Fussell, *Uniforms* (New York:
Houghton Mifflin, 2002), 12.

150 **Jews are among the 30 percent of men:** "Circumcision: Who In
the World Gets Circumcised?," www.circinfo.net, accessed September 13, 2017, http://www.circinfo.net/who_in_the_world_gets
_circumcised.html.

150 **along with trephining:** "Headache," in *Human Diseases and Conditions*, 2nd ed., ed. Miranda Herbert Ferrara (Detroit: Gale Cen-
gage, 2010), 2:765.

150 **"crumpl[ing] their penises":** Franklin Foer and Marc Tracy, eds.,
Jewish Jocks (New York: Twelve, 2012), xi.

150 **an epispasm, or "reverse circumcision":** "Circumcision," in *Encyclopaedia Judaica*, 2nd ed., 4:731.

151 **Derogatory depictions of elongated noses:** Sara Lipton, "The
Invention of the Jewish Nose," *New York Review of Books*, November
14, 2014, http://www.nybooks.com/daily/2014/11/14/invention
-jewish-nose/.

151   **A 1996 Jewish Museum exhibit:** Michael Kimmelman, "Art Review: Too Jewish? Jewish Artists Ponder," *New York Times*, March 8, 1996, https://www.nytimes.com/1996/03/08/arts/art-review-too-jewish-jewish-artists-ponder.html.

151   **Other physical stereotypes:** Klaus Hoedl, "Physical Characteristics of the Jews," accessed July 21, 2016, http://web.ceu.hu/jewishstudies/pdf/01_hoedl.pdf.

151   **"The use of body art":** Ron Dicker, "Jews with Tattoos," *Haaretz*, November 10, 2009, http://www.haaretz.com/1.5345120.

152   **the matter has always been more mottled:** Nili S. Fox, "Biblical Body as Canvas," *Reform Judaism*, Summer 2014, 36, https://issuu.com/reformjudaism/docs/rj_summer2014_reduced/30.

152   **make gashes in your flesh:** Lev. 19:28.

152   **"Nothing in Jewish law prohibits a tattooed person":** Chani Benjaminson, quoted in Marshal Klaven, "Rabbi Debunks Taboo against Tattoos," *Reform Judaism*, Summer 2014, 30, https://issuu.com/reformjudaism/docs/rj_summer2014_reduced/30.

152   **humans are made "in God's image":** Gen. 1:27.

152   **had his grandfather's:** Joseph Metz, "Honoring My Grandfather," *Reform Judaism*, Summer 2014, 30, 34, https://issuu.com/reformjudaism/docs/rj_summer2014_reduced/30.

153   **Even one rabbi:** Marshal Klaven, "Jews and Tattoos," *Reform Judaism*, Summer 2014, 30, https://issuu.com/reformjudaism/docs/rj_summer2014_reduced/30; and Klaven, "Rabbi Debunks Taboo against Tattoos." *Jewish Journal*, August 29, 2014, http://boston.forward.com/articles/185241/rabbi-debunks-taboo-against-tattoos/.

153   **the Torah forbids mixing:** Deut. 22:11

154   **The Talmudic Rabbis also disallowed:** Babylonian Talmud, *Megillah* 24a–b.

154   **"I make myself distinguished":** Babylonian Talmud, *Shabbat* 145b.

154   **wearing a nice outfit on the Sabbath:** Babylonian Talmud, *Shabbat* 113a.

154   **"promulgated a dress code":** Gideon Reuveni and Nils Roemer, *Longing, Belonging, and the Making of Jewish Consumer Culture* (Boston: Brill, 2010), 3.

154   **Jews living in the Venice ghetto:** "Virtual Jewish World: Venice, Italy," Jewish Virtual Library, accessed January 30, 2017, http://www.jewishvirtuallibrary.org/venice-italy-jewish-history-tour.

154 **the mandatory yellow star:** Joshua Arsenault, "Holocaust Badges," Holocaust Memorial Center, accessed September 13, 2017, www .holocaustcenter.org/holocaust-badges, from *Encyclopaedia Judaica*, 2nd ed., and *Encyclopedia of the Holocaust*, ed. Israel Gutman (Jerusalem: Yad Vashem, 1990).

155 *Lilith* **magazine ran a 2014 story:** Karen Engel, "Should a Jewish Girl Wear a Dirndl?," *Lilith*, Winter 2013–14.

155 **"Yes, Elvis wore the** *chai*"**:** Rick Cohen, "Object Lesson Unchained Melody," *Tablet* 2, no. 2 (Shavuot 2016/5776): 12.

156 **counted sixteen different Jewish stars:** Vanessa L. Ochs, "What Makes a Home Jewish?," *Cross Currents* 49, no. 4 (Winter 1999–2000): 9.

156 **featuring the** *hamsa* **symbol:** Menachem Wecker, "What Is a Hamsa?," My Jewish Learning, accessed September 16, 2017, http://www.myjewishlearning.com/article/hamsa/; and "What Does the Hamsa Mean?," Evil Eye Store, accessed September 19, 2017, https://www.evileyestore.com/hamsa-meaning.html.

157 **Lion of Judah jewelry ad:** "Lion of Judah," Greater Miami Jewish Federation, accessed September 19, 2017, http://jewishmiami.org /about/departments/womens/lion_of_judah/.

157 **limited themselves to two rings:** Gideon Reuveni and Nils Roemer, *Longing, Belonging, and the Making of Jewish Consumer Culture* (Boston: Brill, 2010), 3.

157 **2009 HUC-JIR study:** Sarah Bunin Benor and Steven M. Cohen, *Survey of American Jewish Language and Identity* (Cincinnati: Hebrew Union College–Jewish Institute of Religion, October 2009), http://www.bjpa.org/Publications/details.cfm?Publicationid=3874.

158 **"If [Jews] could talk with their feet":** Jack Cooper, quoted in Joshua Rolnick, "Gestures Come in Handy," *Moment*, April 1999, 34–35.

159 **One early study:** Korlei Mensah, "Talking with Our Hands: Who Uses Gestures More Frequently?" (final paper, Male-Female Communications, freshman seminar, University of Pennsylvania, December 6, 2000), http://ccat.sas.upenn.edu/plc /communication/korlei.htm.

159 **The Jewish actress Rachel Weisz:** Eliza Berman, "Quick Talk: Rachel Weisz," *Time*, September 26, 2016, 55.

160 **"Chinese one-downsmanship":** Eric Liu, *Chinaman's Chance* (New York: Public Affairs, 2014), 19.

160   **speaking style is "too aggressive":** Benor and Cohen, *Survey of American Jewish Language and Identity.*

160   **tend to talk more quickly:** "Interrupters: Linguists Say It's the Jewish Way," *Jewish News of North Carolina,* May 12, 2000, https://www.jweekly.com/2000/05/12/interrupters-linguist-says-it-s-jewish-way/.

161   **Yiddish maven Leo Rosten:** Leo Rosten, *The New Joys of Yiddish* (New York: Three Rivers Press, 2001), xv–xvi.

161   **Jewish writer Sophia-Maria Unterman:** Sophia-Maria Unterman, "How to Survive as a Jew in Exile," *Forward,* July 1, 2016, 38.

161   **10.5 percent Jewish, it tops the list:** Ira Sheskin, *Current Jewish Population Reports* (New York: Berman Jewish Data Bank, 2016), 10.

162   **didn't even have a rabbi:** Ragina Garcia Cano, "S. Dakota Gets a Rabbi," *Sun Sentinel,* November 30, 2016, 6a; and Julie Zauzmer, "South Dakota Is Getting Its Only Rabbi," *Washington Post,* November 28, 2016, https://www.washingtonpost.com/news/acts-of-faith/wp/2016/11/28/south-dakota-is-getting-its-only-full-time-rabbi-and-becoming-the-50th-state-for-chabad/?utm_term=.ec85310f7795.

162   **"If you live in Butte, Montana":** Lenny Bruce, quoted in Jon Stratton, *Coming Out Jewish* (New York: Routledge, 2000), 299.

163   **felt tense at home:** Thomas L. Friedman, *Thank You for Being Late* (New York: Farrar, Straus and Giroux), 2016, 374.

163   **personality types:** Melody Warnick, *This Is Where You Belong* (New York: Viking, 2016), 188.

164   **"Distinctive Jewish Names":** Barry Chiswick, "Rise and Fall of the American Jewish PhD," *Contemporary Jewry,* April 2009, 67–84.

164   **"five standard suffixes":** "Growing Up in a Jewish Home in the 50s," *Gantseh Megillah,* December 4, 2009, http://www.pass.to/tgmegillah/nThisnThat.asp?id=340.

165   **to take middle names:** Schiffman, *Generation J,* 49.

165   **"His name is Shlomo":** Michael Krasny, *Let There Be Laughter* (New York: William Morrow, 2016), 132.

165   **biblical names:** Julie Andrews, quoted in Anne Cohen, "Biblical Names Are Making a Comeback," *Forward,* January 3, 2014, http://forward.com/schmooze/190287/biblical-baby-names-are-making-a-comeback/.

165   **Gwyneth Paltrow named her second child Moses:** Cohen, "Biblical Names Are Making a Comeback."

165 **"unscientific but weekend-killing":** Lisa Keys, quoted in Marjorie Ingall, "What's in a Baby's Name?," *Forward*, August 1, 2003, http://forward .com/articles/7815/what-s-in-a-baby-s-name-parents-hopes-and/.

166 **the most popular names:** Joanna C. Valente, "The 2017 Most Popular Jewish Baby Names for Girls," Kveller, accessed September 11, 2017, Kveller.com/the_2017_most_popular_Jewish_Baby_names _for_girls; and Joanna C. Valente, "The 2017 Most Popular Jewish Baby Names for Boys," Kveller, accessed May 8, 2018, https://www .kveller.com/the-2017-most-popular-jewish-baby-names-for-boys/.

166 **the resurgence in biblical names:** Stanley Lieberson, quoted in Peggy Orenstein, "Where Have All the Lisa's Gone?," *New York Times Magazine*, July 6, 2003, http://www.nytimes.com/2003/07 /06/magazine/where-have-all-the-lisas-gone.html?mcubz=0.

166 **The doctor is three:** For another version of this joke see Marjorie Ingall, *Mamaleh Knows Best* (New York: Harmony Books, 2016), 12.

166 **viral video poem:** Andrew Lustig, "I Am Jewish," January 11, 2012, https://vimeo.com/113288275.

167 **a 2007 study:** Barry Chiswick, "Occupational Attainment of American Jewry 1990–2000," *Contemporary Jewry* 27 (2007): 95, 97.

168 **Other occupations traditionally pursued by Jews:** Hasia R. Diner, *Roads Taken* (New York: Yale University Press, 2015), 170–80.

168 **"Conan the Distributor":** Michael Krasny, *Let There Be Laughter* (New York: William Morrow, 2016), 162.

168 **"Turn it and turn it":** Pirkei Avot 5:25–26.

168 **The preponderance of Jews in psychotherapy:** Susan Schnur, "Analyze This," *Lilith*, Fall 2016, 21.

168 **Journalism is another attractive vocation:** "Journalism," *Encyclopaedia Judaica*, 2nd ed., 11:466; and Stephen J. Whitfield, *American Jew as Journalist*, accessed March 2, 2017, http://research.policyarchive .org/10113.pdf.

169 **as non-Jewish reporter:** Jorge Ramos, *Take A Stand* (New York: Celebra Books, 2016), 7.

169 **thank "her Jewish agents":** Amy Poehler, *Yes, Please* (Dey St., 2014), 166.

169 **not known as big farmers:** Barry Chiswick, "Occupational Attainment of American Jewry 1990–2000," *Contemporary Jewry* 27 (2007): 95, 97; and Sheskin, *Current Jewish Population Reports*, 46.

170 **"When a car owned":** Jackie Mason, quoted in Joseph Telushkin, *Jewish Humor* (New York: William Morrow, 1992), 21.

170 **Jews were forbidden from participating:** Franklin Foer and Marc
Tracy, eds., *Jewish Jocks* (New York: Twelve, 2012), xi.

170 **success in several sports:** Robert Slater, *Great Jews in Sports* (Middle Village NY: Jonathan David, 2000), 1–2; Bernard Postal, *Encyclopedia of Jews
In Sports* (Bloch, 1965); and Slater, *Great Jews in Sports,* 9, 164, 229, 265.

171 **Chinese tile game:** Deborah Nussbaum Cohen, "A Mahjong Renais-
sance among Jewish American Women," *Haaretz,* August 14, 2013,
https://www.haaretz.com/jewish/features/.premium-1.541529.

171 **a doctoral dissertation on the subject:** Anneliese Heinze, et al.,
Mahjong, American Modernity, and Cultural Transnationalism (2015),
http://purl.stanford,edu/gv940sg20337.

7. DWELLING

173 **inscribed with the *Shema*:** Deut. 6:9, 11:20.

173 **mezuzah "the Ultimate Protection Agency":** "Mezuzah Guide:
How to Put Up a Mezuzah," Chabad.org, accessed August 8, 2016,
http://www.chabad.org/library/article_cdo/aid/278460/jewish
/Guide.htm.

174 **so is how it is hung:** "As the Expert: Slanted Mezuzah," My Jewish
Learning, accessed May 12, 2018, https://www.myjewishlearning
.com/article/ask-the-expert-slanted-mezuzah/.

175 **a mezuzah should be left in place:** Vernon Kurtz, "Removing a Mezuzah," *Responsa of the CJLS 2001–2009,* yd 291, 2.2003, accessed April 1,
2017, https://www.rabbinicalassembly.org/sites/default/files/public
/halakhah/teshuvot/20012004/Kurtz%20Mezuzah.pdf.

175 **several dwellings in my retirement community:** Nancy Kalikow Maxwell, "House-Hunting in Florida Suburbia Turns into Great Mezuzah Trek: How Can You Tell If People Next Door Are Jewish?,"
Forward, May 31, 2013, http://forward.com/articles/177308/house
-hunting-in-florida-suburbia-turns-into-great/.

176 **One-third of Jewish homes now decorate:** Pew Research Cen-
ter's Religion and Public Life Project, *A Portrait of Jewish Americans*
(Washington DC: Pew Research Center, October 1, 2013), 80; and
Sidney Goldstein, *Profile of American Jewry* (North American Jewish
Data Bank, Council of Jewish Federations, Graduate School and
University Center, CUNY, 1993), 136.

176 **descendants of the Loyal Yiddish Sons of Erin:** Ashley Tedesco,
"Emerald Isle Jews," *Baltimore Jewish Times,* March 16, 2012, 29.

177 **sexual behavior of the drivers:** Babylonian Talmud, *Ketubot* 61b, quoted in Maggie Anton, *Fifty Shades of Talmud* (Banot Press, 2016), 41.

177 **Your Volkswagen may have been a sex symbol:** Jean Rosenbaum, *Is Your Volkswagen a Sex Symbol?* (New York: Hawthorne Books, 1972).

177 **"I still can't think of a Jewish friend":** Neal Gabler, "Of Tattoos, Fords, Volkswagens and Arthur Godfrey," *Forward*, November 20, 2015, 25–26.

177 **intriguingly titled article:** Sheldon Drobny, "What Would Moses Drive?," Salon, November 21, 2002, http://www.salon.com/2002 /11/21/suvs_4/.

178 **"When GM recalled 72,000 Cadillacs":** Jack Benny, quoted in Joseph Dorinson, *Kvetching and Shpritzing* (Jefferson NC: McFarland, 2015), 12.

178 **a 2006 Gallup poll:** Frank Newport, "Gallup Poll Analysis: Political Correlates of Car Choice," Gallup, June 7, 2006, http://news.gallup.com /poll/23230/gallup-poll-analysis-political-correlates-car-choice.aspx.

178 **encourages Jews to "purchase with prudence":** "Driven by Values— Clean Car Campaign," Coalition on the Environment and Jewish Life (COEJL), November 2002, http://www.coejl.org/resources /cleancar.

179 **about 70–80 percent of Jews are Democrats:** Tom W. Smith, *Jewish Distinctiveness in America: A Statistical Portrait* (New York: American Jewish Committee, 2005), 15; and Pew Research Center, *A Portrait of Jewish Americans*, 96.

179 **"Top 60 Schools":** "2017 Top 60 Schools by Jewish Population," *Hillel News and Views—Blog*, March 15, 2018, http://www.hillel.org /about/news-views/news-views—blog/news-and-views/2018/03/15 /2017-top-60-schools-by-jewish-population.

180 **"Trailer parks are so goyish":** Lenny Bruce, "Jewish and Goyish," My Jewish Learning, accessed July 5, 2016, http:www .myjewishlearning.com/article/jewish-and-goyish.

181 **God could dwell among:** Exod. 25:8.

181 **Jews should only live:** Babylonian Talmud, *Sanhedrin* 17b.

181 **a variety of fruits:** Babylonian Talmud, *Berachot* 8a; *Sanhedrin* 17b.

182 **the older you are:** Pew Research Center, *A Portrait of Jewish Americans*, 62.

182 **Almost half of northeastern Jews:** Helen Kiyong Kim, *JewAsian* (Lincoln NE: University of Nebraska Press, 2016), 57.

183 **Rabbis also referred to one's dwelling:** Neal Gold, excerpt from a Rosh Hashanah sermon, Rosh Hashanah 5773/2013.

184 **calls such possessions "icons":** Mihaly Csikszentmihalyi, quoted in Winifred Gallagher, *House Thinking* (New York: HarperCollins, 2006), 64.

184 **subtitling his academic paper:** Jeffrey Shandler, "*Di Toyre Fun Skhoyre*, Or, I Shop, Therefore I Am: Consumer Cultures of American Jews," in Gideon Reuveni and Nils Roemer, *Longing, Belongings, and the Making of Jewish Consumer Culture* (Boston: Brill, 2010), 183.

184 **the 1940s Jewish women:** Jenna Weissman Joselit, *Wonders of America* (New York: Henry Holt, 1994), 135.

184 **sixty-five Jewishly inflected objects:** Joselit, *Wonders of America*, 135.

185 **"Educate through the Gift Shop":** Joselit, *Wonders of America*, 161.

185 **Jews attend Sabbath:** Pew Research Center, *A Portrait of Jewish Americans*, 75.

185 **A 1931 survey:** Joselit, *Wonders of America*, 148.

185 **lighting Sabbath candles:** Pew Research Center, *A Portrait of Jewish Americans*, 77

185 **"family," *hestia*, meant "near the hearth":** Larry Siedentop, *Inventing the Individual* (Cambridge MA: Harvard University Press, 2014), 11.

186 **"Make beautiful objects":** Babylonian Talmud, *Shabbat* 133b; *Nazir* 2b; *Bava Kamma* 9a–b.

186 **"symbol of spiritual wealth":** Andrew R. Heinze, *Adapting to Abundance* (New York: Columbia University Press, 1990), 56.

186 **Jewish women in the 1940s:** Joselit, *Wonders of America*, 151.

187 **Rabbis recommended blanketing:** *Tur, Orach Chayyim* 271, quoting the Jerusalem Talmud.

188 **"a light of nations":** Isa. 42:6.

189 **the dreidel game has come:** "The Surprising Origin of the Dreidl," My Jewish Learning, reprinted from *A Different Light* (Shalom Hartman Institute and Devora Publishing), accessed September 22, 2017, http://www.myjewishlearning.com/article/the-origin-of-the-dreidel/.

190 **Manischewitz Company's "Hanukkah House":** Liz Alpern, "How-To Guide to Hanukkah Gingerbread House," *Forward*, December 4, 2012, http://forward.com/culture/167136/how-to-guide-to-hanukkah-gingerbread-house/.

191 **You can purchase a twelve-footer:** Babylonian Talmud, *Pesachim* 100a, accessed September 22, 2017, http://brainjet.com.

191 **"the memory of the tribe's origins":** Gary Cross, *Consumed Nostalgia* (New York: Columbia University Press, 2015), 9.

191 **"with a mighty hand and an outstretched arm":** Deut. 26:8.

191 **possessions help make ethereal concepts:** Vanessa L. Ochs, "What Makes a Home Jewish?," *Cross Currents* 49, no. 4 (Winter 1999–2000): 2.

191 **participate in a home-based seder:** Pew Research Center, *A Portrait of Jewish Americans*, 77.

192 **the *Maxwell House Haggadah*:** Anne Cohen, "101 Years of the *Maxwell House Haggadah*," *Forward*, March 23, 2013, http://forward.com /schmooze/173621/101-years-of-the-maxwell-house-haggadah/.

192 **Now we have Haggadahs:** Hillary Reinsberg, "13 Alternative Haggadahs to Brighten Up Your Passover Seder," *BuzzFeed*, March 20, 2013, https://www.buzzfeed.com/hillaryreinsberg/alternative -haggadahs-passover-seder?utm_term=.iildxx74G5#.poxqxgM3kl.

192 **parody:** Dave Barry, Alan Zweibel, and Adam Mansbach, *For This We Left Egypt?* (New York: Flatiron Books, 2017), 6, 19, 24, 43, 54.

193 **little blue Jewish National Fund tin:** Joselit, *Wonders of America*, 151.

195 **pious individuals:** "Tefillin (Phylacteries)," My Jewish Learning, accessed August 29, 2016, http://www.myjewishlearning.com /article/tefilln-phylacteries/.

197 **you will find books:** Ochs, "What Makes a Home Jewish?," 12.

198 **what Ochs calls "uniquely Jewish-signifying objects":** Ochs, "What Makes a Home Jewish?," 12.

198 **"let literature occupy the place of honor":** Quoted in Joselit, *Wonders of America*, 151.

198 **buying books and giving books as gifts:** Shandler, "*Di Toyre Fun Skhoyre*, Or, I Shop, Therefore I Am," 183.

198 **American Jews buy:** "Jewish Book Month Celebrates Love of Reading," *Discover JCC Magazine*, accessed July 13, 2013, http://magazine .discoverjcc.com/jewish-book-month-celebrates-love-of-reading/; and Perrin, "Book Reading 2016."

198 **According to a 2016 Pew study:** Andrew Perrin, "Book Reading 2016," Pew Research Center, September 1, 2106, www.pewinternet .org/2016/09/01/book-reading-2016/.

199 **"Jewish women are all that stand":** Brian Morton, *Florence Gordon* (New York: Houghton Mifflin, 2014).

199 **My mother authored two Jewish cookbooks:** Betty Kalikow, *Mom's Best Recipes: 151 Jewish-American Dishes* (Kansas City MO: BeKay,

1958); and Betty Kalikow, *Grandma's Kosher Recipes: 209 Jewish Dishes Modern Style* (Kansas City MO: BeKay, 1961).

200 **"You shall not make for yourself":** Exod. 20:4.

200 **remembrance of the destruction of Jerusalem:** Psalm 137.

202 **a man wearing woman's clothing:** Alex Joffe, "Jews and Guns," *Baltimore Jewish Times*, August 31, 2012, 31.

202 **2006 American Jewish Committee survey:** Tom W. Smith, *Jewish Distinctiveness in America: A Statistical Portrait* (New York: American Jewish Committee, 2005), 236, 241, 43.

203 **advocated for improving public safety:** Alex Joffe, "Jews and Guns," *Baltimore Jewish Times*, August 31, 2012, 31; Suzanne Pollak, "Pro-gun Jews," *Washington Jewish Week*, December 27, 2012, 4; and Kenneth Lasson, "Jews and Guns," *Baltimore Jewish Times*, December 7, 2007, 56–57.

203 **Yiddish term** *tchotchke*: Ian Shapira, "Museum Pays Homage to Tchotchkes," *Washington Post*, July 28, 2000, http://articles.sun -sentinel.com/2000-07-28/lifestyle/0007270449_1_american-jewish -museums-tchotchkes-family-museum.

203 **"The Lord Is My Shepherd":** Psalm 23.

204 **berated Jews:** Moses Weinberger, quoted in Shandler, "*Di Toyre Fun Skhoyre*, Or, I Shop, Therefore I Am," 187.

204 **admonished the "flappers":** Israel Levinthal, quoted in Joselit, *Wonders of America*, 144.

204 **home-based ritual pieces:** Cross, *Consumed Nostalgia*, 9, 15.

204 **treasures can end up at Goodwill:** Nancy Kalikow Maxwell, "At the Thrift Shop: The Lifecycle of Jewish Junk," *Lilith*, Fall 2015, 48, http://lilith.org/articles/at-the-thrift-shop/.

8. JOINING

208 **"Do not separate yourself":** Pirkei Avot 2:4.

208 **a Rip Van Winkle–like story:** Babylonian Talmud, *Ta'anit* 23a.

209 **defined religion:** William James, quoted in Harold S. Kushner, *Nine Essential Things I've Learned about Life* (New York: Knopf, 2015), 143.

209 **a way "for social groups":** Emile Durkheim, quoted in Kushner, *Nine Essential Things*, 111.

209 **root word for "religion":** Kushner, *Nine Essential Things*, 112.

209 **"God is not found in churches or synagogues":** Martin Buber, quoted in Kushner, *Nine Essential Things*, 104.

209 **word "synagogue" derives:** Samuel Gruber, "Jews' Houses Ain't Castles," *Forward,* September 1, 2010, http://forward.com/culture /130921/jews-houses-ain-t-castles-they-re-shuls/.

210 **Jewish nonprofit organizations:** Susan Chambre, "Philanthropy," in *Jewish Women in America: An Historical Encyclopedia,* ed. Paula E. Hyman and Deborah Dash Moore (New York: Routledge, 1997), 1053; and Deborah Dash Moore, "Hadassah," in Hyman and Moore, *Jewish Women in America,* 571, 579.

211 **others joined B'nai Brith:** "Our History," B'nai Brith International, accessed October 6, 2017, http://www.bnaibrith.org/about-us .html; and Linda Gordon Kuzmack, "B'nai Brith Women," *Jewish Women's Archive,* accessed October 4, 2017, https://jwa.org /encyclopedia/article/bnai-brith-women .

212 **five separate spheres:** Daniel J. Elazar, "Organizational and Philanthropic Behavior of the North American Jewish Community," Jerusalem Center for Public Affairs, accessed June 13, 2017, http://www .jcpa.org/dje/articles2/orgphil-najew.htm.

212 **"There isn't another ethnic sub-community":** Sidney Schwarz, *Jewish Megatrends* (Woodstock VT: Jewish Lights, 2013), 227.

212 **Jewish communities:** Babylonian Talmud, *Sanhedrin* 17b.

213 **Some burial organizations:** Elon Gilad, "The History of Jewish Burial Rites," *Haaretz,* April 21, 2015, http://www.haaretz.com /jewish/features/.premium-1.652857.

213 **Jewish self-help system:** Mark Twain, quoted in Marjorie Ingall, *Mamelah Knows Best* (New York: Harmony Books, 2016), 185.

213 **friendships between Jews and non-Jews:** Herbert J. Gans, quoted in Sylvia Barack Fishman, *Jewish Life and American Culture* (Albany NY: State University of New York Press, 2000), 158.

214 **"lone wolves":** Herbert J. Gans, quoted in Fishman, *Jewish Life and American Culture,* 158.

214 **"better off":** Eccles. 4:9–10.

214 **"If your friend calls you an ass":** Babylonian Talmud, *Bava Kamma* 92b.

214 **remarked about friends:** Maimonides, *Guide for the Perplexed,* book 3, chapter 49, quoted in Edward Hoffman, *Wisdom of Maimonides* (Boston: Trumpeter, 2008), 83.

215 **congregants who attend worship services:** Manuella Lamorena, "Attending Church Increases Life Span, Study Shows," *Christian*

Post, June 4, 2017, http://www.christianpost.com/news/attending
-church-increases-life-span-study-shows-186322/.

215 **radio program:** "Kibbitz," NPR, accessed May 26, 2017, http://www
.npr.org/programs/atc/features/2002/yiddish/words.html.

216 **Boomer-age Jews:** David M. Elcott, *Baby Boomers, Public Service and
Minority Communities* (Berman Jewish Policy Archive, Research Center for Leadership in Action, 2009), 34; and David Elcott and Stuart
Himmelbarb, *Generations and Re-Generation: Engagement and Fidel-
ity in 21st Century Jewish Life"* (B3/The Jewish Boomer Platform,
Research Center for Leadership in Action, September 2014, http://
www.jewishdatabank.org/studies/downloadFile.cfm?Fileid=3172.

217 **Jewish marriages began on J-Date:** "J-Date's Success Building
the Jewish Community," J-Date brochure duplicated at "J-Date is
Responsible for More Jewish Marriages [Infographic]," Cyber-
Dating Expert, accessed May 8, 2018, https://cyberdatingexpert
.com/jdate-is-responsible-for-more-jewish-marriages.

217 **Jews who came of age during the Holocaust:** Deborah Dash Moore,
"Hadassah in the United States," *Jewish Women's Archive,* accessed
October 10, 2017, https://jwa.org/encyclopedia/article/hadassah
-in-united-states.

218 **Research Center for Leadership in Action study:** Elcott, *Baby Boomers, Public Service and Minority Communities,* 34.

218 **10 percent of pre–World War II:** Chaim I. Waxman, *Jewish Baby
Boomers* (Albany NY: State University of New York Press, 2001), 86.

218 **These Jews "tend not to join":** Anita Diamant, quoted in George E.
Johnson, "What Will the Jewish World Look Like in 2050?," *Moment*
42, no. 1 (January–February 2017), 4, https://www.momentmag
.com/will-jewish-world-look-like-2050/.

218 **belong to a national:** Elcott and Himmelbarb, *Generations and Re-
Generation,* 108.

219 **social entrepreneurship:** Merissa Nathan Gerson, "In the Desert,
Wilderness Torah Takes Judaism Back to Nature, *Tablet,* December
3, 2013, http://www.tabletmag.com/jewish-life-and-religion/154095
/wilderness-torah.

219 **a top concern of Generation X and Y Jews:** Elcott and Himmelbarb, *Generations and Re-Generation,* 40.

219 **Poverty, hunger, and poor health care:** Amy Oringel, "Meet Five
Jewish Millennials Working to Fight the Trump Agenda," *Forward,*

July 14, 2017, http://forward.com/culture/376897/meet-five-jewish
-millennials-working-to-fight-the-trump-agenda/; and Fern Chertok
et al., "Volunteering Plus Values," in *Repair the World*, 2011, http://
www.brandeis.edu/cmjs/pdfs/VolunteeringValuesReport.Final.pdf.

220 **from politics to social action:** Gary Berger, "What Makes a Campus Jewishly Vibrant?," *Reform Judaism*, accessed October 4, 2017,
https://reformjudaism.org/what-makes-campus-jewishly-vibrant.

221 **new groups have been initiated:** "Leadership and Engagement,"
Hillel, accessed May 8, 2018, http://www.hillel.org/jewish
/leadership-engagement; "Students Create Change; Meaningful Jewish Experiences on Campus," *Hillel News and Views—Blog*,
November 7, 2006, http://www.hillel.org/about/news-views
/news-views—blog/news-and-views/2006/11/07/students-create
-change-meaningful-jewish-experiences-on-campus; and "Mon-
gelli Award, Spring '12—Challah for Hunger," UCLA Volunteer
Center, May 22, 2012, http://volunteer.ucla.edu/mongelli-award
-challah-for-hunger/.

222 **entrepreneur Andrew Coonin: "Students Create Change."**

222 **Jewish choral groups:** Gary Shapiro, "Shir Enjoyment of Vocal
Music," *Forward*, February 16, 2011, http://forward.com/culture
/art/153458/shir-enjoyment-of-vocal-music/.

CONCLUSION

226 **"There are many ways to be Jewish":** *Forward*, October 9, 2015.

226 **Jewish college students grapple:** Amy Kurzweil, "First Week at College," *Lilith*, Fall 2016, 38–39.

226 **Judaism's "vaporous outline":** Bernard-Henri Levy, *The Genius of
Judaism* (New York: Random House, 2017), 136.

227 **believing Jesus is the Messiah:** Pew Research Center's Religion and
Public Life Project, *A Portrait of Jewish Americans* (Washington DC:
Pew Research Center, October 1, 2013), 58.

227 **"Jews have come into the world":** Levy, *The Genius of Judaism*, 217.

228 **"Jews suffer from every":** Isaac Bashevis Singer, quoted in Michael
Krasny, *Let There Be Laughter* (New York: William Morrow, 2016), 209.

229 **"dogged resilience":** Michael Krasny, *Let There Be Laughter* (New
York: William Morrow, 2016), 168.

230 **non-Jewish husband's confusion:** Lisa Schiffman, *Generation J* (San
Francisco: HarperSanFrancisco, 1999), 54.

230   **fear manifests itself:** Vanessa L. Ochs, *Inventing Jewish Ritual* (Philadelphia: Jewish Publication Society, 2007), 155.

230   **"Counting Jews is like holding jello":** Barry A. Kosmin, quoted in George E. Johnson, "What Will the Jewish World Look Like in 2050?," *Moment* 42, no. 1 (January–February 2017), 44, https://www.momentmag.com/will-jewish-world-look-like-2050/.

231   **"it's never been hipper to be Jewish":** Lisa Alcalay Klug, *Cool Jew* (Kansas City MO: Andrews McMeel, 2008); and Sandra Pedicini, "Jewish Is Cool, Products Declare," *Orlando Sentinel*, Knight Ridder Business News, March 4, 2005, https://groups.google.com/forum/#!msg/soc.culture.jewish/UFQwBcSrRhs/T_aKSNkVbNwJ. .

231   **ethnic pride with T-shirts:** For instance, see Modern Tribe, https://moderntribe.com/collections/t-shirts-apparel; JewTee.com, http://jewtee.com/; and Kewlju.com, http://kewlju.blogspot.com/.

231   **the sexiest rabbis:** "'Sexiest Rabbis of 2013' Announced by Jewrotica," *Huffington Post*, January 23, 2014, http://www.huffingtonpost.com/2013/12/30/sexiest-rabbis-of-2013_n_4520115.html.

231   **won the award:** Ashley Ramnarain, "Sarah Silverman's Sister Lands on Sexiest Rabbi List," *Shalom Life*, December 30, 2013, http://jewrotica.org/about-jewrotica/press/sarah-silvermans-sister-lands-on-sexiest-rabbi-list/.

232   **titled chapter 6:** Harold S. Kushner, *Nine Essential Things I've Learned about Life* (New York: Knopf, 2015), 103.

232   **"Wayfinding":** Lisa Schiffman, *Generation J* (San Francisco: HarperSanFrancisco, 1999), 3.

233   **taking classes:** Johnson, "What Will the Jewish World Look Like in 2050?"; and Lisa Grant and Diane Tickton Schuster, *What We Know about Adult Jewish Education* (Virginia Beach: A.R.E. Press, January 2008), 1, 3, 4, http://www.bjpa.org/Publications/details.cfm?Publicationid=4816.

233   **explosion of American Jewish culture:** Bethamie Horowitz, quoted in Johnson, "What Will the Jewish World Look Like in 2050?"

233   **"almost impossible to say anything":** Chaim I. Waxman, *Jewish Baby Boomers: A Communal Perspective* (Albany: State University of New York Press, 2001), 10.

234   **instead of questioning:** Ari Y. Kelman, quoted in Johnson, "What Will the Jewish World Look Like in 2050?"

234 **easier for Christians:** Dawn Kepler, personal interview with Dawn Kepler, May 15, 2017.

234 **relying on membership:** Anita Diamant, quoted in Johnson, "What Will the Jewish World Look Like in 2050?"

235 **"not 'distancing'":** Arnold Dashefsky and Ira Sheskin, quoted in Johnson, "What Will the Jewish World Look Like in 2050?"

235 **Jewish cultural life:** Arnold Dashefsky and Ira Sheskin, quoted in Johnson, "What Will the Jewish World Look Like in 2050?"

235 **people who identify as Jews:** Leonard Saxe, quoted in Johnson, "What Will the Jewish World Look Like in 2050?"

235 **"we will be more racially":** Anita Diamant, quoted in Johnson, "What Will the Jewish World Look Like in 2050?"

235 **Rabbi Angela Warnick Buchdahl:** Judea Pearl and Ruth Pearl, eds., *I Am Jewish* (Woodstock VT: Jewish Lights, 2004), 20.